Cyber Blackout

When the Lights Go Out —
Nation at Risk

John A. Adams, Jr.

FriesenPress

Suite 300 - 990 Fort St
Victoria, BC, Canada, V8V 3K2
www.friesenpress.com

Copyright © 2015 by John A. Adams, Jr.
First Edition — 2015

All rights reserved.

No part of this publication may be reproduced in any form, or by any means, electronic or mechanical, including photocopying, recording, or any information browsing, storage, or retrieval system, without permission in writing from the publisher.

ISBN
978-1-4602-5979-5 (Hardcover)
978-1-4602-5980-1 (Paperback)
978-1-4602-5981-8 (eBook)

1. Computers, Internet, Security

Brazos Bottom Books   = (' ÷ ') =

Distributed to the trade by The Ingram Book Company

Table of Contents

List of Figures
v

Introduction
vii

ONE
Cyber-Space: The Fifth Domain
1

TWO
Dragon and the Bear
25

THREE
Supply Chain Meltdown
67

FOUR
When the Lights go Out: Cyber Threats to Critical Infrastructure
93

FIVE
Communities: Cascading Chaos
119

SIX
Cyber Triage & Trends
147

Cyber Lexicon, Jargon, and Acronyms
165

Selected Bibliography
187

Index
211

About the Author
213

List of Figures

	Figure	Title
Chapter One	1-1	Eleven Hard Problem Areas in Cybersecurity
Chapter Two	2-1	Insider Threat Classification
	2-2	Nation-State Cyber Warfare Capabilities
	2-3	Strategic Measurement of Advanced Disruptive (cyber) Attacks — (SMADA)
	2-4	Suspected Chinese Cyber Attacks
Chapter Three	3-1	Supplier Diversity: Sources and Lead Time
	3-2	Supply Chain Risk Matrix
	3-3	Supply Chain Risk Mitigation
	3-4	Off-Shore Fabrication and Assembly
	3-5	Flow of Supply Chain Information Risk
Chapter Four	4-1	Critical Infrastructure Hierarchy
	4-2	Ten Common SCADA Vulnerabilities
	4-3	Inventory of Critical Infrastructure
	4-4	Robust Cyber Security Program
	4-5	Sector-Specific Agency and CIKR Sectors
	4-6	CFATS Risk-Based Performance Standards
Chapter Five	5-1	Community Cyber Security Maturity Model
	5-2	Stafford Act State Support
	5-3	Community Level Cyber Attack Profile
	5-4	National Domestic Preparedness Consortium
Chapter Six	6-1	Damage of a Cyber Attack
	6-2	Sample List of Cyber Attacks

Introduction

On the cool brisk morning of September 11, 2001, I finished my bowl of cereal and watched the morning business report on CNBC. It was about 7:30 at my Texas home and I delayed going to the office as I awaited a promised interview with Jack Welch, at that time president of GE, and a great barometer on business and the economy. Around 7:40 (8:40 in New York City), the show host, Mark Haynes, interrupted a market update to go to a live shot of the World Trade Center in lower Manhattan. I watched as smoke bellowed from the upper 15 or 20 floors of the South Tower. Mark wondered if the building could have been hit by a plane, and he briefly told the story of a B-25 bomber crashing into the fog-shrouded Empire State Building in 1945 during World War II.

Suddenly, Mark noted a wire report indicting speculation about a twin engine plane hitting the South Tower. Mark paused and wondered if this could be more sinister than just a tragic fire. I put my TV on mute and called my dad, a decorated veteran of three wars, in Atlanta to tell him to turn on his TV. As we watched, a second jet plane appeared out of the right side of the screen and plowed into the upper-floors of the North Tower — emitting a huge fireball and debris. My TV remained on for the rest of the day.

Mark Haynes removed his glasses: "We are under attack."

John A. Adams, Jr.
9:11 EST September 11, 2001

> "America's economic prosperity in the 21st century
> will depend on cyber security."
> The White House

On that September day, as the world watched in shock, few fully appreciated the dramatic shift in world events, or our nation's vulnerability to rogue attacks and terrorist actions. These events happen somewhere else — not here in the US. Did our intelligence fail? Were there warning signs? Who was responsible? Didn't our intelligence services monitor such threats? While not recognized as a pure cyber-attack, the cyber domain played a key part of the preparation, training, communications, and launching of the World Trade Center and Pentagon attacks. Our cyber technology and analysts failed to fully interpret the warning signs that may have curbed the attack.

Cyber-attacks and cyber-intrusions remain greatly underestimated by the American public in general, and government officials at the national, state, and local level in particular. Awareness has increased during the past decade at the national level for cyber threats as agencies, policy makers, and academics wrestled over turf battles. Effective cyber policy continuously gets hung up on one crucial question: at what level does national security depart from conflict with the perceived common good of the public that has come to expect near-total open-access to the Internet? This book is a plain-spoken, non-techy presentation geared for policy makers in government, primarily at the local level, industry, small and large, and most importantly, I hope to reach those who work and protect the vital infrastructure sector of our economy — such as the vast power grid network across the nation. It is vital that these people realize the impending threats. As a nation we have been lulled into a false scene of security. The impact of a full scale cyber intrusion is a thousand times greater than the implied threats espoused during Y2K. It is time to move beyond inactivity and poor awareness. Americans must be aware of the destructive, not just disruptive, magnitude and complexity of a cyber-attack.

The vast 'wired' world brought many breakthroughs and connected the world, at near real time, in ways never before dreamed. The Internet was designed to be open, transparent, and interoperable. Security and identity management were secondary objectives in the system's design. But the same efforts that created the networks spanning the cyberspace domain we all now operate produced new network tools and threats that could, in the wrong hands, cause mass disruption. While concerns of national security remain critical in this new cyber era, the fact remains that there are few fool proof protective systems in place at the local level to detect, stop, or manage a full scale cyber event. Thus, now is the time to address and know our strengths and weaknesses. Cyber threats, ranging from rogue hackers to active nation-state espionage by China, are asymmetric; attacks know no border and may be perpetrated by the few upon the many. Thus, the inherent insecurity of the web has resulted in a scramble to enhance protocols, chain of command clarity (i.e. legitimate authority), firewalls, and recovery triage, before a cyber-attack cascades to the community level.

The ongoing stream of evidence suggests that we as a nation are not fully prepared for the magnitude of what could result from a serious cyber-attack. These actors have the ability to compromise, steal, change, store, transmit, or completely destroy information. The nexus at the national, state, and local levels between the "open source" net and the need for timely, uninterrupted security and vital services has ushered in a totally new and challenging era. The speed at which cyberspace has been linked with the most critical daily functions of our lives and our nation's security is truly spectacular. The very speed of the Internet and our dependence on the interconnectivity of the web, communications, and infrastructure is now the basis of the US economy, public safety, massive infrastructure, and national security. The cyberspace era is ubiquitous, and only just begun.

Lack of preparation to address the security needed to protect the nation is both naïve and short sighted. The benefits from the innovations of the information age are threatened by the dark side of connectivity. Attackers, once known simply as hackers, ranging from rogue individuals to nation-states, have redefined our concerns regarding national security and economic well-being. Cyber-attacks threaten American national security in truly unprecedented ways. Many have issued the call to secure and protect our critical infrastructure — this presentation of cyber concerns is intended to demonstrate the growth, dynamics and vulnerabilities of the new cyber era as an effort to bridge this vital topic.

I have used a cross section of industry, government, and academic materials, interviews, and sources – all after a degree of persistence in the public domain. Care has been taken not to compromise any sources or breach any confidences. A detailed bibliography is included along with a lexicon of terms that grow daily in cyber-space. Foreign nation-states espionage operations and seasoned organized crime groups routinely source and hack every bit of cyber data, financial data, and ID info, and military secrets they can exfiltrate from our systems. Even the movies are not safe!

In December 2014, as this book was going to press, a cyber-attack by what the FBI identified as North Korean hackers on Sony Corporation gained worldwide attention over the release of what was deemed an offensive movie. The Obama administration responded to the incident and industry demanded more safe-security measures. The heightened awareness among both the public sector and private companies that are exposed to such cyber-attacks and compromise of sensitive data may be the tipping point in the struggle to address the seriousness of cyber-attacks and their resulting damage.

The next cyber-attack could be the one that turns out the lights.

ONE
Cyber-Space: The Fifth Domain

> It is only a matter of time before someone employs [cyber] capabilities that cause significant disruption to civilian or government networks and to our critical infrastructure here in the United States.
> General Keith B. Alexander
> United States Cyber Command
> March 22, 2012

The extent of damage and disruption inflicted remotely by a major cyber-attack could exceed the total war-based economic losses sustained during the 20th century in only its first week. Farfetched? No. In an earlier era, supply lines (chains) disruption was purely a physical pursuit of halting rail traffic, blockading ports, cutting communications and power lines, and ultimately taking the war to the advisories manufacturing base. While the United States possesses the capability to deliver massive long range conventional, and nuclear, military strikes, this paradigm of taking the war to the enemy has been shattered in today's high-tech cyber modern era, given the breadth and scope of a potential cyber-attack on all aspects on the nation's economy, survival and security. The cyber threat is real and serious. [1]

---

1 DOD, Defense Science Board, "Task Force Report: Resilient Military Systems and the Advanced Cyber Threat, Washington, D.C.: DOD, January 2013 (public unclassified report released May 27, 2013), pp. 1-2; Phillip J. Bond, "Cybersecurity: Assessing the Immediate Threat to the United States," Subcommittee on National Security, Homeland Defense and Foreign Operations, U. S. House, Washington, D.C., May 25, 2011; Phillip S. Meilinger, "Air Strategy: Targeting for Effect," *Aerospace Power Journal*, Winter 1999; Martin C. Libicki, *Cyberdeterrence and Cyberwar*. Rand: 2009, pp. 11-12; World Economic Forum, "Global Risks 2012," Geneva: 2012, pp. 26-7, 52. See also John Keegan, A *History of Warfare*, New

The scale and spectrum of operations to defend the nation have entered the era of the 'fifth domain', with digital infrastructure and real time connectivity eclipsing war as we have known it on land, sea, air, and space.[2] Cyberspace, a man-made construct, is both a physical and virtual medium. Definitions of words are sometimes tricky, and as cyber intelligence expert Jeffery Carr notes, it is a mistake to simply classify cyberspace as another domain. His argument is compelling, "Cyberspace as a warfighting domain is a very challenging concept. I think that a more accurate analogy can be in the realm of science fiction's parallel universe — mysterious, invisible realms existing in parallel to the physical world, but able to influence it in countless ways… more metaphor than reality." Though it does obviously exist, cyberspace, due to its vast and shifting nature, is difficult to wholly define. Notwithstanding, I will, for simplicity's sake, refer to, and use 'cyber' and 'cyberspace' as a parallel terminology and domain.[3]

> **Cyber-notes:** cyberspace: a global domain within the information environment consisting of the interdependent network of information technology infrastructures, including the Internet, telecommunications networks, computer systems, and embedded processors and controllers.[4]

York: Knopf, 1993; "War in the fifth domain," *The Economist*, July 1, 2010; CSIS, "Securing Cyberspace for the 44th Presidency," Washington, D.C.: December 2008, p. 11; Martin Libicki, "Cyberdeterence and Cyberwar," RAND: 2009, p. 37. Note: Annual cyber-theft and damage has been estimated at over $100 billion in the United States alone in 2012 and the annual gross written premium for cyber risk-related insurance is over $500 million.

2   Note: William Gibson first defined cyberspace in a 1984 science fiction novel *Neuromancer*.

3   Jeffery Carr, *Cyber Warfare*, Sebastopol: O'Reilly, 2012, pp. xiii, 1-2, 39. Note: *Cyber Warfare* (2012) is a must read along with General Michael V. Hayden, "The Future of Things 'Cyber'" *Strategic Studies* Quarterly, Spring 2011, pp. 3-7. These two items are the best overall review of the global scope of cyber threats and vulnerabilities. The December 2006, DOD-JCS release of the National Military Strategy for Cyberspace Operations, defined cyberspace as, "A domain characterized by the use of electronics and the electromagnetic spectrum to store, modify, and exchange data via networked systems and associated physical infrastructure." Mankind added the air domain in 1903 and the space domain in 1957. See also The White House, "Cyberspace Policy Review," May 2011, p. 1. The White House issued guidance curbing public references to cyberspace as fully a military operational domain on par with land, sea, air, and space.

4   *DOD Dictionary of Military Terms*, Washington, D.C.: Joint Staff, Joint Doctrine, J-7, October 17, 2008. See also Sean C. Butler, "Refocusing Cyber Warfare Thought," *Air & Space Power*

Today we have more people, extensive critical infrastructure, and defense resources at imminent risk than at any time in our long history. The United States military is, and will be, the preeminent air, land, space, and sea force worldwide. We dominate all warfighting domains, except cyber. However, the very speed and interconnectivity of all aspects of our daily life, economy, and military capabilities are tied to an extensive cyber backbone that daily grows more vulnerable. In cyberspace, the time between execution and effect can be milliseconds. Not to heed the cyber warnings is folly. To think a full scale cyber-attack can be easily repelled is wishful thinking. And as time and technology progress we will become more vulnerable, the sheer confusion and panic across all sectors of our society, economy, infrastructure, and first responders would be disabling. [5]

The Pentagon, as a doctrinal matter, treats cyberspace as an 'operation domain' — assessing cyber threats as an interwoven-interconnected segment of all future planning and security considerations.[6] Malicious cyber activity has grown exponentially and attacks have been directed at nearly every sector of our critical infrastructure, industry, and government, including attacks on the I.M.F., Citibank, Google, Sony's PlayStation, the White House, NASDAQ, the Pentagon, and multiple energy firms across America. Significant disruptions to any one of these sectors could impact defense operations. With over 140 countries fielding cyber warfare capabilities, it is critical that we are aware of threats and vulnerabilities, with former Secretary of Defense Robert Gates noting that the United States is "under cyber-attack virtually all the time, every day."[7]

Journal, January 2013, pp. 44-57.

5   Stewart Baker et al, "In the Crossfire: Critical Infrastructure in the Age of Cyber War," Center for Strategic and International Studies, July 2010; Sunil Chopra and ManMohan S. Sodhi, "Managing Risk to Avoid: Supply-Chain Breakdown," MIT Sloan Management Review, Fall 2004, pp. 53-61; Scott Dynes et al, "Cost to the U. S. Economy of Information Infrastructure Failure: Estimates from Field Studies and Economic Data," n.d., Cambridge University; AFDD 3-12, *Cyberspace Operations*, pp. 29.

6   For an excellent overview see DOD, Defense Science Board, "Task Force Report: Resilient Military Systems and the Advanced Cyber Threat," Washington, D.C.; DOD, January 2013.

7   William J. Lynn, Deputy Sec. of Defense, "Remarks on the Department of Defense Cyber Strategy," Washington, D.C.: National Defense University, July 14, 2011: David M. Hollis, "USCYBERCOM," *JFQ*, 3rd Qtr, 2010, pp. 48-53; Paul Sonne, "Google's Censorship Juggle," *Wall Street Journal*, June 18, 201. Quote as seen in Carr, *Cyber Warfare*, p. 179;

Project Scope

Thus, the purpose of this presentation is a review of the rapid rise and impact of the cyber arena and cyber's ubiquitous absorption of all facets of the United States' economy, vital support services, and security. The focus is on providing a better understanding of the reach, damage, and recovery from a full scale cyber-attack. This is not a technical book, nor designed to swamp the reader with acronyms, computer hacking tricks, and jargon — but instead is simply an eye-opening read. Some experts will think it simplistic, and most skeptics will think it farfetched, yet it is intended as a timely read for policy makers, first responders, as well as state and regional leaders, who will have to make swift informed decisions if (when) indeed a full scale cyber-attack occurs.[8] What do you do if your community, within minutes of a cyber-event, loses all communication, electricity, and water? The cascading impact would be unimaginable: some hospitals would have backup power, yet many would be in the dark and swamped with patients; the intersections would be blocked as traffic lights would be off-line; 911 would be dead and useless; cell phones, radios, and TV would be cutoff, and local hand held walkie-talkies would be inoperable due to EMP (electromagnetic pulse); pumps, driven by electricity, which limit distribution of both water and fuel, would fail due to transformers outage; the web would go down; within days, food supplies would dwindle; and by week's end, lights on power-packs at emergency shelters would go completely dark. The connectivity of our IT and communication systems developed for speed, real time service, and volume could be interrupted and crashed in a cascading pattern across large sectors of our economy.[9]

Who is in charge, how do you communicate, and how do you triage the response and recovery? The scale and scope of espionage driven cyber hacking

---

"Significant Cyber Incidents Since 2006," seen at http://csis.org/files/publication/110103. Note: While non-critical in nature the PlayStation network attack affected over 100 million customers and cost Sony an estimated $173 million.

8   Bruse Schneier, "It will soon Be Too Late to Stop the Cybers," *Financial Times*, December 2, 2010; Myriam D. Cavelty, "Cyber-Terror — Looming Threat or Phantom Menace? The Framing of the US Cyber-Threat Debate," *Journal of Information Technology and Politics*, 2007, pp. 19-36.

9   Michael McCaul, "Hardening Our Defenses Against Cyberwarfare," *Wall Street Journal*, March 6, 2013.

is staggering. To date, cyber-incidents have cost the United States hundreds of billions of dollars in lost intellectual property, maintenance, defalcation, and increased security, in what General Keith Alexander, director of the National Security Agency and head of the US Cyber Command, calls the "greatest transfer of wealth in history." Vital electric and communication grids are breached daily. Today, the national response plan is at best fragmented. Furthermore, there is no community — small, medium, or metro — across the US aware of the full impact or prepared to react in real time to cyber disruption — meltdown — of vital services. [10]

Terrorist events and natural disasters in the United States have for the most part been localized or regional events. International terrorist attacks since 2000 and the rash of natural disasters ranging from the Asian tsunami to the landfall of four hurricanes that hit the state of Florida in 2004 provide ample evidence of destruction and damage, as well as the resulting psychological distress and challenges to recovery. The true measure of such disruptions is the vulnerability of the impacted area. The lingering impact of the September 11 attacks will be with us for decades. While the 9/11 attacks had little or no warning, in modern times, early warning for weather disturbances has been marginally improved to allow ample notice of impending events. Devastating as they have been to date, the impact of a full scale cyber- attack across the United States, in spite of existing counter measures and robustness of critical infrastructure, would eclipse any other prior terror attack or natural disaster in America.[11]

The multiple attacks of 9/11 forever changed the nations approach to terrorist threats and the means to prevent future events. The "homeland" had been hit and 3,000 Americans killed. In the aftermath, the immediate focus was to find those responsible and to increase security across all sectors of our daily lives, from airport pat-downs, requiring confirmed ID's to open a bank account, and

---

10   Ibid.; Colin S. Gray, *Making Strategic Sense of Cyber Power*, Carlisle barracks, April 2013, pp. 48-52; Senator Sherrod Brown, "Chinese Hacking: Impact on Human Rights and Commercial Rule of Law," Congressional-Executive Commission on China (CECC), Washington, D.C.; June 25, 2013.

11   Kathleen J. Tierney, "Business and Disasters: Vulnerability, Impacts, and Recover," as seen in Handbook of Sociology and Social Research, 2007, pp. 275-296. See also Kenneth J. Knapp, *Cyber Security and Global Information Assurance*, Hershey: Information Science Reference, 2009, pp. xvi-xviii.

the government's monitoring of our daily routines. The Patriot Act (2001) and the establishment of the Department of Homeland Security (2001) were intended to put in motion plans, training, and response action to make Americans safer and stop, or limit, any future attack. Homeland defense in our vast nation has been a daunting task: the US needs to have near perfect systems and intelligence to be right 100 percent of the time, but the terrorists and cyber hackers need only be successful once or twice to inflict vast damage. As the "war-on-terror" intensified, many wondered about the long reach of a cyber-attack on our critical infrastructure and economy.[12]

Given the increasing reliance on the Internet, a massive cyber-attack on the US economy and command and control structure (C4ISR) would be crippling given the cascading effect across critical infrastructure and services. Such an attack by a rogue nation or a group operating in concert would be well targeted. Internet outage and control system failure can spread fast, leaving first responders and governments at all levels helpless to mount a swift, coordinated response. The ability of a cyber-attack to skip or by-pass the traditional "battlefield" and inflict damage and panic on the target's home front is still not fully quantitative, yet the cyber-attacks associated with Estonia, Conficker, and Stuxnet are telling.[13] A cyber-attack, like no other, is in real time. As Richard Clarke has noted, "In cyber war, we may never even know what hit us."[14]

---

12 DOD, "Strategy for Operating in Cyberspace," Washington, D.C.: July 2011; DHS, "National Response Framework," Washington, D.C.: May 1, 2012; DHS, "National preparedness Report," Washington, D.C.: March 2012, pp. 19-29; Jordon, *Hacking*, pp. 84-90; Verton, *Black Ice*, pp. vii-xii, 1-30; Ronald J. Deibert, *Black Code: Inside the Battle for Cyberspace*, Toronto: Signal, 2013, pp. 3-4.

13 Mark Bowen, *Worm: The First Digital World War*. New York: Atlantic Monthly Press, 2011.

14 Richard A. Clarke, *Cyber War*, New York: Harper Collins, 2010, p.68; Eric Schmitt, "Intelligence Report Lists Iran and Cyberattacks as Leading Concerns," *New York Times*, January 31, 2012. See also Martin C. Libicki, "What Constitutes an Act of War in Cyberspace?' in *Cyberdeterrence and* Cyberwar, Rand 2009, pp. 179-181; Brian M. Mazanec, "The Art of (Cyber) War," *Journal of International Security Affairs*, Spring 2009 and Timothy Shimeall et al, "Countering cyber war," *NATO Review*, Winter 2001/2, pp. 16-18; Robert Zager and John Zager, "Combat Identification in Cyberspace," August 25, 2013, http://smallwarsjournal.com/jrnl/art/combat.

> **Cyber-notes:** Information technology standards that support global connectivity do nothing to ensure that the communications they enable will be oriented to achieving understanding and the good of all.[15]

Background

Early alerts on the vulnerabilities of the information and communication infrastructure were often dismissed as scaremongering. Some blamed the concern over cyber-attacks on sensationalism created in the American entertainment industry. To be sure, the cyber threats are no *War of the Worlds* (1898) or *WarGames* (1983) or *Swordfish* (2001) or *Die Hard 4.0* (2007), but in spite of the popularized Hollywood movie hype, there is real danger.[16] As early as 1991, the National Academy of Sciences concluded, "We are at risk. Increasingly, America depends on computers . . . Tomorrow's terrorist may be able to do more damage with a keyboard than with a bomb."[17]

With the growth of personal computers on a worldwide scale in the mid-1980s, incidents involving computer tampering evolved from novice amateur teenage hackers (some inspired by the 1983 movie *WarGames*), to sophisticated hackers gaming the system, to deeper data mining and intrusion by the early 1990s. These novice hackers are exemplified by the Hanover Hackers — led by 15 year old Markus Hess — who masqueraded as a trusted user to hack NASA computers in 1987.[18] The White House, during the administration of George H. W. Bush in 1990, recognized the growing foreign intelligence threats (including terrorist groups and criminal elements) concerning telecommunications and "microelectronics technology" in the IP services, information processing

---

15 Karen Ruhleder and Carolyn, "Globalization and the Tower of Babel," IEEE, 1993, p.464.

16 M. Conway, "Cyberterrorism: Hype and Reality," in L. Armistead (ed.) *Information Warfare: Separating hype from reality*, Washington, D.C: Potomac Books, 2007.

17 National Academy of Sciences (NAS). "Computers at risk: Safe computing in the information age," Washington, D.C.: 1991, p. 7. See also DOD, DSB, "Resilient Military Systems and the Advanced Cyber Threat," pp. 12-15.

18 Katie Hafner and John Markoff, *Cyberpunk*, New York: Touchstone: 1991, pp. 110-115; Rebecca Grant, "Old Lessons, 'New Domain,'" *Air Force Magazine*, September 2013, pp. 86-91.

systems, and security.[19] The "tampering for fun" soon turned to a validated threat in 1991, when Dutch teenagers hacked highly sensitive information systems during US operations in Desert Storm and US Air Force facilities at Rome Research Laboratories using Trojan Horses and networks sniffers to compromise research programs and systems. These activities, and unlimited access to the Internet during the dotcom-1990s, fostered the rapid rise of criminal hacking of financial institutions and communications providers, resulting in the defalcation of millions of dollars and credit card numbers. Both the military and capitalist industry were ill prepared to deal with these threats. In one of the more interesting incidents during this seeming period of 'innocence,' a novice (not rogue) US Air Force captain remotely entered the command and control systems of the US Atlantic Fleet, penetrating deep enough to access both navigational control systems and weapons guidance systems. [20]

The next official act to draw attention to the fact that "certain national infrastructures are as vital that their incapacity or destruction would have a debilitating impact on the defense or economic security" of the nation was an Executive Order issued by the Clinton White House in mid-1996 on the "Critical Infrastructure Protection" (PCCIP) — components that control critical infrastructures –"cyber threats." The awareness was further heightened when the CIA, increasingly aware that the advances of cyberspace challenged the ability of the agency to collect and analyze data in real time, created the Special Projects Staff (SPS), which later morphed into the Clandestine Information Technology Organization (CITO), to expand and enhance the use of the most advanced cyber technology. The dotcom explosion of the 1990s led to the converting of any form of information — text, voice, video, music — to "digital," which accelerated internet growth. Thus, cyber concerns resulted in a presidential cabinet

---

19 The White House, National Security Directive 42, Washington, D.C.: July 5, 1990, unclassified doc. Note: The term 'cyber' was not used in the document, yet the sum total of the directive's intent and objectives were geared toward the emerging 'cyber' threat environment.

20 "Marcus Hess." www.bookrags.com ; Pat Cooper and Frank Oliveri, "Hacker Exposes US Vulnerability," *Defense News*, October 9, 1995, pp. 1, 37; Gray, *Making Strategic Sense of Cyber Power*, pp. 26-30. Note: Hess was later arrested along with eight others and charged with selling secrets to the KGB, the Soviet intelligence agency.

level commission to require the government and private sector to work together to develop and implement strategic protection measures.[21]

Throughout of the 1990s, US policy makers, academics, and the NSA/Pentagon jockeyed at the national level to devise a policy that insured national security while at the same time allowing user demand for open access to the internet. As the White House pushed for a clearer plan to address cyber issues, agencies across Washington expressed little direct interest in lending their support to cyber security, "as it might diminish their independence."[22] The rapidly emerging technology in the IT and communications sector further compounded the challenges presented by increasing cyber-attacks and hackers. In 1996, a GAO report, a public document and testimony to Congress, raised attention at the highest levels to external attacks and data mining attacks on DOD systems by rogue hackers and nation-states, attacks including the installation of "back door" systems in DOD computers that circumvented normal systems protection and allowed hackers unauthorized future access. The attacks were determined to be widespread, including both friends and foe:

> Defense officials and information systems security experts believe that over 120 foreign countries are developing information warfare techniques. The techniques allow our enemies to seize control of or harm sensitive Defense information systems or public networks which Defense relies upon for communications. Terrorists or other adversaries now have the ability to launch untraceable attacks from anywhere in the world.[23]

---

21   White House, Executive Order 13010, July 15, 1996; John Schwartz, "Cyberspace Seen a potential Battleground," *New York Times*, November 21, 2001; Henry A. Crumpton, *The Art of Intelligence*, New York: Penguin Press, 2012, pp. 78-81; John Cassidy, *dotcom: The Greatest Story Ever Sold*, New York: Harper Collins, 2002, pp. 14-24. See also "Internet domain names: .combat," *The Economist*, June 2, 2012, pp. 73-4.

22   James A. Lewis, project Director, "Cybersecurity Two Years Later," Washington, D.C.: CISI, January 2011, p. 4. See also Mark Thompson, "Onward Cyber Soldiers," *Time*, August 21, 1995.

23   GAO, *Information Security: Computer Attacks at Department of Defense Pose Increasing Risk*, Washington, D.C.: May 22, 1996. See also Cavelty, *Cyber-Security*, pp. 24-65 and Kay Hearn

Quite possibly the watershed event with regard to the 'cyber domain' was the international attention given to the autumn 1997 White House sponsored PCCIP and its conclusions and recommendations to security experts and agencies that linked cyber-threats with the importance of critical infrastructure. In a hearing before congress, the Director of the CIA, John Deutch, publicly placed dangers of cyber incidents on equal footing with the concerns over nuclear, biological, and chemical weapons. The resulting presidential executive orders by Bill Clinton launched the first programs to enhance the capabilities of law enforcement to address cyber-crimes, increased surveillance of hackers, and began the first steps of hardening critical infrastructure, while always keeping in mind strategist Colin Gray's admonition, "Cyber power is not about computers and their networks; rather, it is about what networked computers are able to do in passing information and what the consequences might be."[24]

By 1997, it was reported by Defense Information Systems Agency (DISA) that there were an estimated 250,000 cyber-attacks on the Department of Defense per year. Thus, open network access to the internet presented concern about the protection of critical infrastructure and data. The Department of Defense invented the Internet, primarily for enhanced communications and the possibility it could be a tool in future warfare conditions. However, short of 'war,' DOD data and systems were unprotected. In response, by the late 1990s DOD created extensive cyber-network training to provide a cyber means as a part of psychological warfare, or 'psyops.' The era of enhanced electronic espionage was ushered in with the release of the first army IO manual — *Joint Doctrine for Information Operations (3-13)* covering IO network attacks on

---

et al, "international Relations and Cyber Attacks: Official and Unofficial Discourse," Perth: Austrian Information Warfare and Security Conference, December 2010.

24   President's Commission on Critical Infrastructure Protection (PCCIP), "Critical foundations: Protecting America's Infrastructure." Washington, D.C.: 1997; John Deutch, *"Testimony of the Director of US Central Intelligence before the Senate Government Affairs Committee on Intelligence,"* Washington, D.C.: June 25, 1996; The White House, "Fact Sheet. Combating Terrorism: Presidential Decision Directive, 62," and "Protecting America's Critical Infrastructure: Presidential Decision Directive, 63," Washington, D.C.: May 22, 1998; Gray, *Making Strategic Sense of Cyber Power,* p.20; "US and Russian Strategic Nuclear Warheads, 1945-2010," *Air Force Magazine,* January 2011, p.39.

computer network, and attacks on both military and civilian computer systems and infrastructure.[25]

> **Cyber-notes**: cyberspace coming out: Until the mid-1990s, cyberspace was largely "free space," associated with a debate over price, cost, demand, and supply. It was not until the end of the century, 1999, that the full implications of the worldwide commercial explosion became realized.[26]

Failure of Imagination

While GAO reports are generally in the public domain, few Americans were aware of the ongoing serious cyber-attacks against both the Pentagon and industry across the country. Neither government agencies and private industry rarely report and/or confirm publicly that they have been hacked. In spite of numerous warnings from security officials and ongoing hacker attacks to systems, in a follow-up report in late 1999, the GAO "found that significant DOD information security weakness in general persisted for all components evaluated." Open source intelligence (OSINT) is the prime means spies and terrorists employ to collect diplomatic traffic and cables, military intel, trade secrets, and industrial design data — using benign hacking techniques that appear to be commonplace in the public domain. Over a dozen basic procedures and practices were regularly flaunted, which allowed Pentagon computers and systems to be rich hunting grounds for rogue hackers.[27]

The poor controls and passive noncompliance with security procedures included improper user access, confidential files left in open access, poor need-to-know procedures, inadequate password management, security access logs

---

25 Cavelty, *Cyber-Security and Threat Politics*, pp. 68-72; DOD, Joint Chiefs of Staff, *Joint Doctrine for Information Operations*, 3-13, Washington, D.C.: October 9, 1998. Note: In 1987 the Computer Security Act was passed to develop guidelines and standards for protecting unclassified federal computer 'systems'; the only role of the NSA was to provide technical assistance for civilian firms.

26 Nazli Choucri, *Cyberpolitics in International Relations*, Cambridge: MIT Press, 2012, p. 51.

27 GAO, *DOD information Security: Serious Weaknesses Continue to Place Defense Operations at Risk*. Washington, D.C.: August 1999.

not monitored, improperly configured or poorly maintained system software were easily exploited. While the Y2K — Year 2000 bug — created a tremendous amount of hype (and cost millions to mitigate possible disruptions) of the possibility of cascading failed systems, to date there has been no effort to fully sweep all the systems across the US for any malicious code that may have been injected during the remediation period. And the most troubling finding of the report was that critical mission-related applications and the activities they support were at risk because of "inadequate planning for service continuity ... and disaster recovery plans were incomplete."[28] And the risk continued to grow. External hacking attacks on DOD systems, financial institutions, and industry IP became more and more sophisticated.[29]

> **Cyber-notes:** risk — the potential for an unwanted outcome resulting from an incident, event, or occurrence, as determined by its likelihood and the associated consequences.

Thus, by 2000, all sectors of private industry, government, and military began to address what they had long known was the changing landscape of our nation's security, the protection of our vital infrastructure, access to our secrets, designs and data, and warfighting. Communication among intelligence agencies, the military, and the administration was expansive, yet fragmented, and there was no clearing house to review and share intelligence on threat assessments. The reduction of US human intelligence (HUMIT) assets, surveillance, and data collection hampered U. S. intelligence during the late 1990s and allowed terrorists to exploit and attack a dozen western and US targets abroad, as well as make attempts on the homeland, which included: — February 1993, World Trade Center; June 1995, Khobar Towers; August 1998, US embassies in Kenya and Tanzania; and the October 2000 attack on the destroyer *USS COLE* in Aden, Yemen. Long before the establishment of the DHS, protection of critical

---

28 25. Ibid. Note: In 1999, it was estimated DOD wide there were over 2.1 million computers, over 10,000 local area networks, and over 100 long-distance networks. See also Verton, *Black Ice*, p. 37.

29 "Hacking of Pentagon Persists," *Washington Post*, August 9, 2000; Jordon, *Hacking*, pp. 43-52; GAO, "CYBER CRIME: Public and Private Entities Face Challenges in Addressing Cyber Threats," Washington, D.C., June 2007.

Cyber Blackout

infrastructure was a priority. And then, on September 11, 2001, in the most devastating attack on the US homeland since Pearl Harbor, 2,992 people were killed by hijackers on four hijacked commercial airplanes. Two planes hit the Twin Towers of the World Trade Center in New York City, the third struck the Pentagon in Arlington, and finally the fourth, likely targeted to hit the US Capital or White House, went down in Pennsylvania. "The success of the 9/11 conspiracy," according to an early assessment of events, "has been attributed in part to a 'failure of imagination' on the part of US defense and intelligence community."[30]

The backdrop to these events, and other terrorist attacks that would follow, was the increased use of the cyber domain as a component of either a rogue terror attack or the possibility that a foreign nation-state could mount a well-organized cyber warfare program. What followed after 9/11 was a number of cyber-events that coincided with actual physical conflicts. Cyber-attacks and disruption were used a number of times in limited war events — hackers and NATO traded attacks during Kosovo, again during the Palestinian-Israeli conflict of 2002, and between Chechen and Russian hackers. While many assumed these cyber-attacks were benign, the scope and sophistication quickly expanded.

The public was not totally removed from an awareness of cyber threats or incidents, as books such as the fictional *Cyber Invasion* (2002) by Dale Tibbils, in which the protagonist tracked down a sophisticated Trojan Horse virus and the non-fictional, *Black Ice* (2003) by Dan Verton, which chronicled in detail efforts of US security and policy officials to come to grips with national vulnerabilities of a cyber-attack. An example of an early disruptive cyber intrusion that wasn't fiction was the Slammer Worm virus in January 2003, which exploited a vulnerable Microsoft database and resulted in cascading effects on the electronic infrastructure in the major international airline-booking systems and bank ATM machines, as well as reports of degraded computer control networks at an Ohio nuclear power plant.[31]

---

30 Jonathan B. Tucker, "Asymmetric Warfare," *Forum for Applied Research*, 1999, http://forum.ra.utk.edu/1999; Charles Billo and Welton Chang, "Cyber Warfare: An Analysis of the Means and Motivations of selected Nation States," Hanover: ISTS Dartmouth College, December 2004, p. 11; Verton, *Black Ice*, p. xxii; Deibert, *Black Code*, pp. 3-25.

31 Bruce Berkowitz, "Warfare in the Information Age," *Issues in Science and Technology*, Fall 1995, pp. 59-66; Rand Research Brief, "Strategic War in Cyber Space," January 1996; Patrick

By the mid-1990s, the Chinese had a pivotal role in exercising soft power globally, and had positioned both their military and industry to build extensive cyber networks, telecommunications, and IT procedures. US Congressional attention slowly developed to address cyber concerns. In July 2004, the "Security Protect Yourself Against Cyber Trespass Act" or the "Spy Act" was passed to raise the level of awareness against spyware, malware and telecommunication interference. Enforcement was placed with the Federal Trade Commission.[32] The bulk of cyber threats over the past decade stem from China.

Restless Dragon

What most Americans fail to understand is that the People's Republic of China (PRC) is in a geopolitical and economic grasp for power and critical natural resources, primarily oil and gas, for the long-term. With a history, culture, and psyche dating back over 3,000 years, the Chinese dream and strategy for the 21st Century is to be back in the lead on the world stage. With the fall of the old Soviet Union, China has seen a dramatic global economic rise, what Beijing has termed 'going out' or defining a strategy to capture what is seen as their right to step out onto the world stage. The Chinese leadership views the Middle Kingdom as both a rival and equal to the United States. Along with threats from North Korea and Iran to develop nuclear weapons, as well as unresolved tension in the Middle East, the world is a much more complex global security environment than the one that existed during the Cold War.[33]

China's use of all means to achieve their perceived rightful status in the world includes espionage, diplomatic outreach of soft power, and the development

---

D. Allen and Chris C. Demchak, "The Palestinian-Israel Cyber war," *Military Review*, March 2003; CNN, "Computer Worm Grounds Flights, Blocks ATMs, January 25, 2003.

32 U S House, "Security Protect Yourself Against Cyber Trespass Act," 108th Cong, 2nd sess, report 108-619, July 20, 2004; Gray, *Making Strategic Sense of Cyber Power*, pp. 11-54. See also Richard Bernstein and Ross H. Munro, *The Coming Conflict with China*, New York, Vintage Books, 1998; Charles Wolf, "The Strategy Behind China's Aid Expansion," *Wall Street Journal*, October 9, 2013.

33 Robert Kennedy, "Security Sector Reform: Security Challenges of the 21st Century," in Volker Franke and Robert Dorff, eds, *Conflict Management and "Whole of Government:" useful Tools for US National Security Strategy?*, Carlisle Barracks: SSI, April 2012, p. 57.

of a credible show of force.[34] China has repeatedly targeted the United States. Chinese espionage is one of the most robust nation-state programs, and their cyber-attacks are labeled by the intelligence community as robust advanced persistent threats, or APTs. The hallmark of the information collection has been an aggressive electronic campaign that has cost the US billions of dollars, compromised scores of our military secrets, and threatened our technological edge. In a special report by the Defense Science Board dated January 2013, and the declassified version released in late May, it was confirmed that more than two dozen major US weapons systems had been compromised by aggressive Chinese hackers. [35]

We received numerous warnings that to deal with the more complex global intrigue would require enhanced security and extraordinary efforts from all levels of our intelligence community. The dynamics of the cyberspace realm is that it is essentially modern warfare at the operational level, yet we struggle to define boundaries and find a strategic balance of power. As former Director of the CIA, James Woolsey, concluded "... it is as if we were struggling with a large dragon ['bear' in the case of the USSR] for 45 years, killed it, and then found ourselves in a jungle full of poisonous snakes — and the snakes are harder to keep track of than the dragon [bear] ever was."[36]

Experts both in and out of government believe the US continues to be hacked intensely by both China and Russia and their hacker surrogates. Attacks during the late 90s and early 2000s, when our economy was booming and our cyber

---

34 Avery Goldstein, "China's Real and Present Danger," *Foreign Affairs*, September 2013, pp. 136-141.

35 Office of the Director of National Counter Intelligence , "Foreign Spies Stealing US Economic Secrets in Cyberspace: Report to Congress," Washington, D.C.: October 2011; Magnus Hjortdal, "China's Use of Cyber Warfare: Espionage Meets Strategic Deterrence," *Journal of Strategic Security*, Vol. IV, 2011, pp. 1-24; Adam Piore, "Digital Spies: The Alarming Rise of Electronic Espionage," www.popularmechanics.com ; US-China Economic and Security Review Commission, " 2011 Report to Congress," 112th Cong., 1st sess., November 2011, pp. 96-103; DOD DSB, "Resilient Military Systems and the Advanced Cyber Threat," January 2013.

36 "Testimony of R. James Woolsey, "US House of Representatives, Committee on National Security, February 12, 1998. See also Mark A. Stokes, "China's Strategic Modernization: Implications for the United States," Carlisle Barracks: SSI, September 1999. See also Grant Gross, "FBI: Several Nations Eyeing US Cyber Targets," *PC World.com*, October 15, 2008.

security lax or ignored, were extensive. The Chinese, with a national emphasis on 'informationization,' employed both cyber and human espionage to penetrate our atomic research labs, industrial facilities, and universities, as well as netted a wealth of irreplaceable data from military computer networks and large civilian contractors who had poorly guarded their computer systems.[37]

> **Cyber-notes:** informationization — *xinxihua* — the ability to use the latest cyber technologies in command, intelligence, training, espionage, and weapon systems to allow efficient Chinese PLA joint-service command and control.

There is no more blaring example than the Chinese development and formal roll-out of the sleek, dark-gray, twin engine Chengdu J-20 *Jian er shi* 'Annihilator Twenty' stealth fighter! Out of pride or spite, the Chinese, in a provocative display of in-your-face airpower muscle, coincidently held the first test flight of the Jian-20 on the arrival of Defense Secretary Robert Gates in China on January 11, 2011, four years to the day when the military-space-intelligence world was surprised in 2007 by a Chinese missile destroying a decommissioned PRC orbiting satellite, another event the Chinese were not supposed to be able to do for at least a decade.[38]

In size, design, and configuration, the Chinese fighter was a near carbon copy of US stealth designs developed during the 1980s and 1990s. The J-20 has the same angled tailfins which are the trademark feature of the F-22 Raptor, whose production was limited to four test models. The F-22, along with the B-2 and F-35, was intended to be a game changer in maintaining US strength in the Taiwan Strait, as China planned to push out its "outer ring" of homeland defense into the Pacific and South China Sea. While development continued on the F-22 to address the future US strategic defense needs, production was

---

37 Jordon, *Hacking*, p.. 38-9. See also J. Thomas, "The moral ambiguity of social control in cyberspace: A retro-assessment of the 'golden age' of hacking," *New Media and Society*, 7 (5), pp. 599-624.

38 Elizabeth Bumiller, "Test of Stealth Fighter Clouds Gates Visit to China," *New York Times*, January 11, 2011; Jeremy Page, "China Shows Its Growing Might," www.online.wsj.com/article January 12, 2011. See also David E. Sanger, *Confront and Conceal*, New York: Crown Publishers, 2012, pp. 370-3. See also Deibert, *Black Code, pp. 69-81.*

scrapped during budget cuts by Gates, on the advice the Chinese would not be able to produce a similar stealth fighter until 2020. The spectacle of the J-20 rollout raises questions if this was only a one-off prototype, a hallmark of Chinese deception. Regardless, intelligence reports indicated that China at the current time did not have the ability or technology to produce a reliable nextgen jet engine powerful enough for a 70-80,000-pound aircraft such as the J-20. The Chinese stole a page from our play book for one of the most top secret projects in US history, and flaunted it publicly before Secretary Gates.[39]

The leap of technology in the aviation-space sector alone will be daunting to protect. The next-next generation of US jet fighters, the F-35, will be delivered through 2037. The old days of 'fly-by-wire', absent little more than navigation aids and weather reports, have been displaced forever by a level of sophistication and complexity that will redefine the strategic approach to air superiority and area defense. Chinese computer network exploitations (CNE) between 2007 and 2009 exfiltrated extensive top secret data from system at Lockheed Martin and its sub-contractors. The greater the complexity, the greater the targets for hackers; the F-35 alone is challenged with integrating 24 million lines of software code into its complex computer systems.[40]

Both private industry and the government are stoically reluctant to reveal the level and intensity of cyber-attacks during the past few years. By mid-2012, the FBI was working over 2,000 active criminal/espionage cyber cases, raising concerns on both the volume of attacks and the growing sophistication on computer

---

39 US-China Economic and Security Review Commission, "Indigenous Weapons Development in China's Military Modernization," Washington, D.C.: April 2012, pp. 6, 29-34; Robert D. Kaplan, *Hog Pilots, Blue Water Grunts*, New York: Random House, 2007, p. 342; Edward Luttwak, *The Rise of China vs. The Logic of Strategy*, Cambridge: Harvard University Press, 2012, pp. 240-1. Note: The Lockheed Martin F-22 Raptor was conceived in 1981, first flight tested in 1990, operational for service in 2004. China further acquired complex modern weapons systems through imports from Russia and Israel. Other weapons systems hacked include missile defense systems, the F/A-18 fighter jet, V-22 Osprey, the Black Hawk helicopter, the Navy's Littoral Combat Ship, and the F-35 Joint strike fighter.

40 "Two Very Troubled Fighter Jets," *New York Times*, July 15, 2012; Jason Fritz, "How China will use cyber warfare to leapfrog in military competitiveness," Cultural *Mandala*, Vol. 8, 2008. Note: A second prototype, the "J-31," is similar — "a ringer" — in design to the F-35 and conducted its first test flight on October 31, 2012. See "Copy Cats or Thieves," *Air Force Magazine*, July 2013, p. 24.

networks systems. Some 107,655 cyber security incidents were reported in fiscal 2011 by the Office of Management and Budget, with little or no public disclosure. Further compounding cyber incidents are the hacks and ongoing breaches of social networks, such as LinkedIn, Facebook, and Twitter. Cyber problems also include the wide distribution of counterfeit computer components to sensitive supplier and military systems. Complicating the detection is the fact that hardware vulnerabilities are very hard to detect, infected devices can be preloaded in spyware or malware, which once installed are themselves hard to detect. To address the threats, the DOD has issued instructions for all departments to pare down the 15,000 separate networks and monitor supplier sources involved in defense matters. This becomes more problematic given the fact that as companies cut security budgets, they opt for off-the-shelf systems that could have already been compromised.[41]

> **Cyber-notes:** The topic of cyber power and its relationship to national security remains a wicked US national security problem.[42]

The Dark Side of Connectivity

To appreciate the rise and magnitude of the cyber age necessitates a look back at the unfolding nature of the networked world. From the time that Tim Berners-Lee coined the World Wide Web in 1989, there has been a wave of innovation and spread of systems that now globally connects over two billion Internet users, with a 400 percent increase from 2000 to 2010. As one observer has noted, "the commercialization of the Internet had a considerable impact on

---

41 "Scores of US firms keep quiet about cyber-attacks," www.cnbc.com , June 13, 2012; "US communication equipment subject to China cyber espionage," www.securityaffairs.co/wordpress/6306 ; Dan Rueckert and Cathy Ransom, "It's Never Too Early to Protect Utility Assets," May 29, 2012, www.uimonline.com/index/webapp . See also Jim O'Neill, *The Growth Map*, New York: Penguin, 2011, pp. 86-8, 150-1 and Bernard R. Horovitz, "Blunting the Cyber Threat to Business," *Wall Street Journal*, January 10, 2013; Sydney Freedberg, "Top Official Admits F-35 Stealth Fighter Secrets Stolen," *Breaking Defense*, June 13, 2013, http://breakingdefense.com/2013/06/20.

42 Dennis M. Murphy, Director of Information Warfare Group, US Army War College, Carlisle Barracks, Pa.

making the network inherently insecure because of significant market-driven obstacles to information technology (IT) security: there is no direct return on investment, time-to-market impedes extensive security measures, and security mechanisms often have a negative impact on usability, so that security was and is often sacrificed for functionality."[43]

Thus, the changes facing the nation's leaders and responders at all levels of government threats are well beyond our physical borders and in the daily routine of our lives. Active players, both nation-state and rogue hackers, have used the open source of the Internet to further their political, economic, criminal, and individual agendas and strategies. The proceeding chapter covers the role of China and Russia, as well as other active participants, who would challenge our way of life by use of the dark side of connectivity. Threats to the United States are both internal and external.[44]

It is the real time nature of cyber threats that causes ample concern about the way we do business across the globe, and the way we are dependent on both the global supply chain and the network of critical domestic infrastructures of electricity, oil and gas, transportation, communications, and water. These prime 'grid' systems are coupled with the massive sea, land, and air transportation (air traffic control), and a broad range of services ranging from agricultural inputs to hospitals.[45] At issue is the fact that these very systems and services we highly depend are vulnerable to terrorist and cyber-attack. A recent trend and risk report by IBM X-Force 2012 issued a sobering study, noting that "the rate of unpatched vulnerabilities (excluding the top ten vendors) for the first half of 2012 were the highest that IBM has seen since 2008, 47% of all vulnerabilities

---

43   Cavelty, *Cyber-Security and Threat Policy*, p. 67.

44   Jasyon M. Spade, *Information as Power: China's Cyber Power and America's national Security*, Carlisle Barracks: US War College, May 2012., pp. 2-3; NIST, "Challenging Security Requirements for the US Government Cloud Computing Adoption," Draft, SP 500-296, May 2012. Note: Berners-Lee defined the first standards for both URLs and HTML and was knighted by Queen Elisabeth II for his pioneering work.

45   Emilio Iasiello, "Getting ahead of the threat: Aviation and cyber security," *Aerospace America*, July 2013, pp. 22-25. Note: Communication between aircraft and air traffic controllers remains unencrypted and unsecured, allowing for a hostile disturbance.

disclosed this year (2012) remain without a remedy." Note the qualifying word — 'disclosed.' How many were either not reported or worse, yet not detected?[46]

Cyberspace is truly an open and wild domain. Unlike the years of threats, stress, and negotiations over the last half of the 20th Century regarding the use and safety of nuclear weapons, largely brokered between the United States and the Soviet Union, there is no common ground or global framework on the international cyber regulation and/or policing of the growing open source Internet.[47] While 'cyber' has been cloaked in mystery and secrecy and shrouded in the "fog of uncertainty", and despite invalid efforts to link cyber to the Cold War, there is no comparison: "nuclear weapons remain in a class all their own."[48] Notwithstanding, the Chinese response to the increased charges of the highly sensitive issue of cyber spying is that cyber attacks could be "as serious as a nuclear bomb." These statements made in April 2013 by General Fang Fenghui, chief of staff of the People's Liberation Army, were further fueled by the shift of US intentions to have a larger military presence in the western Pacific Ocean. Thus, cyber will be at the core of US-China geo-political policy and "strategic distrust" well into the coming decades.[49]

The two features of the nuclear standoff and deterrence during the Cold War were limiting the spread of nuclear weapons, and a strong regimen of verifiable

---

46 "IBM X-Force 2012 – Mid-Year trend and Risk Report," Somers, New York: IBM Corporation, September 2012, p. 10. Note: The top ten vendors with assets and staff to provide enhanced security practices of PSIRT programs, Product Security Incident response Reports, boasted a patch remedy rate of over 94% of all vulnerabilities disclosed.

47 Peter Jones, "The Long Road to Nuclear Zero," *Global Brief*, Summer 2012, pp. 28-33. Note: Currently there is an estimated 20,500 nuclear weapons, the US and Russia have an estimated combined total of 19,500, France 300, and China 240.

48 Gray, *Making Strategic Sense of Cyber Power*, p. 35; Andrew F. Krepinevick, *Cyber Warfare: A "Nuclear Option?"*, Washington, D.C.: Center for Strategic and Budgetary Assessments, p. 79. See also Henry Sokolski and Bruno Tertrais, eds. *Nuclear Weapons Security Crisis: What Does History Teach?*, Carlisle Barracks: Army War College, July 2013. See also Jeremy Page, "China Spins new Lessons From Soviet Fall," *Wall Street Journal*, December 11, 2013.

49 Andrew Browne, "Beijing Equates Cyberattacks with the Use of nuclear Bombs," *Wall Street Journal*, April 23, 2013; Brian Spegele and A. Browne, "US, China to Skip Pomp as Tensions Brew," Ibid, May 22, 2013. See also Office of the Secretary of Defense, "Annual Report to Congress: Military and Security Developments Involving the People's Republic of China 2013, Washington, D,C.: May 2013.

Cyber Blackout

attribution, to limit a misguided first strike or rogue nation inciting a war. While the threat of nuclear or bio terrorist incidents remains plausible, the speed and ubiquity of the cyber domain has prevented any conclusive management or control of cyber-attack systems.[50] As Gray notes, unlike the other domains of land, air, sea and space, cyber is unique:

The absence of meaningful physicality in cyberspace and cyber power amounts to an uncomfortable intangibility ... To state the blindingly obvious, cyber is information and communication of information for all manner of strategic purposes ... [C]yber is technically extraordinary, but so too was the electric telegraph in the 1840s.[51]

> **Cyber-notes:** Technology-facilitated transactions can be designed to be invisible — alternatively, they can be designed to be visible but anonymous.[52]

The era of the Cold War can provide only indicators; the cyber age brings an added layer of complexity and urgency to insure systems are safe and protected. Multiple agencies, both nationally and internationally, have since early 2003 spent countless time and resources to limit and counter the dark side of connectivity. The act of addressing a more active approach to overall systems security was one of "catch-up" and reaction, and only in recent years came to be addressed in real time. The leap to "get out in front" to mitigate threats is both critical and never ending as we address the daily more complex issues of cyberspace.[53]

---

50 Paul Bracken, *The Second Nuclear Age: Strategy, Danger, and the New Power Politics*, New York: Times Books, 2012; Walter R. Mead, "The Return of a Nightmare," *Wall Street Journal*, November 16, 2012; Steve F. Kime, "America Needs a Strategy for the Second Nuclear Age," *Proceedings*, November 2012, p. 10. Note: We no longer live in a bipolar world dominated only by the United Sates and the Soviet Union; today there are nine nuclear powers — US, Russia, China, France, Britain, India, Pakistan, Israel, and North Korea. (Iran)

51 Gray, *Making Strategic Sense of Cyber Power*, p. 16, 19.

52 Christopher Brock et al, "The Dark Side of Cyber Finance," *Survival*, April 2012, p. 130.

53 Eric Schlosser, *Command and Control: Nuclear Weapons, the Damascus Accident, and the Illusion of Safety*, New York: Penguin, 2013, pp. 3-156.

One of the most troubling aspects of the post-Cold War era are the rise of various forms of asymmetric warfare that complicated and redefined a unified approach to security. The asymmetric tactics of today are not unlike the 'insurgency tactics' or guerrilla fighters of old — their intent is to circumvent an opponent's advantages by avoiding their strengths and exploiting weaknesses, thus transforming any adversary's perceived strengths into vulnerabilities. This hit-and–run approach, either by insurgents or unattributed cyber hackers, is often intended to have socio-political ramifications rather than simply a military affect. In the realm of cyber warfare and asymmetric attacks, the United States, as the lone remaining super power, was destined to become the prime target of such rogue attacks.[54]

FIGURE 1-1

The Eleven Hard Problem Areas in Cybersecurity

- Scalable trustworthy systems
- System evaluation life cycle
- Combatting malware and botnets
- Survivability of time-critical systems
- Provenance (systems and hardware)
- Usable security[55]
- Enterprise-level metrics
- Combatting insider threats
- Global-scale identity management
- Situation understanding & attribution
- Privacy-aware security

---

54 Cavalty, *Cyber-Security and Threat politics*, 68; Michael Breen and Joshua A. Geltzer, "Asymmetric Strategies as Strategies of the Strong," *Parameters*, Spring 2011, pp. 41-55; T. J. O'Conner, "The Jester Dynamic: A Lesson in Asymmetric Unmanaged Cyber Warfare," Sans Institute, 2012. See also Rod Thornton, *Asymmetrical Warfare: Today's Challenge to US Military Power*, Washington, D.C.. 2007.

55 DHS, "A Roadmap for Cybersecurity Research," November 2009, p. viii. See also IBM, "IBM X-Force 2012: Mid-Year Trend and Risk Report," IBM, September 2012, pp. 52-57.

Over the past decade, a group of inter-agency representatives, in addition to partner organizations form the UK and Canada, formed the INFSEC Research Council (IRC). In addressing the threats to cybersecurity, the IRC developed the original 'Hard Problem List' or HPL. The first list contained three broad strategic objectives: prevent cyber- attacks against American critical infrastructure, reduce national vulnerability to cyber-attacks, and minimize damage and recovery time from cyber-attacks.[56] This grew to eight critical challenges and threats in 2005, and the most recent list contains eleven topics that require both real time and long term solutions to the vulnerabilities of today's ongoing threats. One paramount aspect of the cyber age is that no one single federal or private group "owns" the issue and response to cybersecurity, yet in fact it is a national and global challenge.[57] As one observer noted, "The global networking community that has evolved emerged from the confluence of technological innovation, the wind of war, business and consumer behavior, and economic and political transformation."[58] See Figure 1-1

Given the national policy debate on who controls and dictates the future course of the cyber domain among government agencies, foreign allies (and enemies), the open market, academics, and private industry, there has been no clear resolution or precedents on how the nation at the state, regional, and community level will protect itself, respond to, and recover from a cyber-attack in a timely manner.[59] The first extensive nationwide attempts to address a cascading terrorist attack or pandemic in general and a cyber-attack in particular have only begun to be implemented. National preparedness, citizen awareness, local leadership training, and a sense of urgency could forestall a crippling cyber event which might otherwise cause "economic and social panic, weakening national

---

[56] The White House, "The National Strategy to Secure Cyberspace," Washington, D.C., February 2003, p. viii.

[57] "Cyber Incident Annex," National Response Plan, December 2004, pp. 1-9. See also GAO, "CYBERCRIME," June 2007.

[58] Carafano, Wiki at War, p. 90.

[59] Peter Sommer and Ian Brown, "Reducing Systemic Cybersecurity Risk," OECD: January 14, 2011, notes that there is a lack of agreement on basic terminology, for example what is the use and measure or scale of an "incident", an "attack", or "cyberwar." See also Choucri, Cyberpolities in International Relations, p. 13.

cohesion and political will."[60] When the lights go out, and the systems supporting electricity, telecommunications, water, gas, food distribution, and health services are disrupted over what could be an extended period of time, who will be in control of the cascading disruptions that could drive communities into chaos?

> "Faster information boosts output only when matched with more astute ways of interpreting and acting on new data."
> *Economist* June 2, 2012, p. 92.

---

60 Spade, *Information as Power*, p. 10.

TWO
Dragon and the Bear

All warfare is based on deception.
Sun Tzu c.500 B.C.

We've been thinking 90% defense, 10% offence.
That's bass-ackwards for us. The offense always has the advantage.
General James "Hoss" Cartwright, Ret. Vice-Chairman of the Joint Staff

For the past two decades, the primary rivals of the United States in the cyber domain have been China and Russia. The rise of the Internet, coupled with geopolitical change, emboldened a new form of cyber espionage and disrupted the norms of security and international commerce. Today, some three dozen nation-states and scores of rogue hackers, daily attack all levels of American networks: commercial, industrial, military, financial, government, and personnel computers. The story begins some two decades ago. Three events signaled the changes that have ushered in concerns on cyber security: first was the rise and rapid growth and dependence on the Internet in all facets of our daily lives; second was the fall of the Berlin Wall and the abrupt dismantling of communism and the Soviet Union; and third was the amazement and awe of both the Chinese and Russians at the overwhelming military and cyber dominance of the battlefield in the 1991 Desert Storm offensive against Iraq. The scale and execution to shut down the enemies command and control (C4ISR), radar systems, air space, communications, and critical infrastructure — and thus, ultimately their will to fight in a matter of hours captured the attention of America's two greatest challengers.[1]

The bipolar era of the Cold War, pitting the United States and Russia in a five decade standoff based on limited regional warfare and nuclear warfare chess game, with the two sides holding each other in a balance of terror, all came to an end in 1991.[2] Pundits and political analysis filled the media with reports of Wilsonian rhetoric that the world was at last a very safe place to live, and the so called 'peace dividend' would allow all nations to grow in perpetual harmony. However, in time, the global expansion of China and the demise and realignments in the former Soviet Union brought new challenges. First, China began an economic recovery and rise as one of the big three players on the world stage; and second, the operatives known as the *Siloviki,* or 'men of power', of the old KGB and St. Petersburg clique led by Vladimir Putin, took over Russia. With the control of a strong hand and manipulation of all aspects of the economy — an authoritarian form of government was gradually re-instilled, absent only the formal label of communism.[3]

---

1   Charles Billo and Welton Wang, "Cyber Warfare: An Analysis of the Means and Motivation of Selected Nation States," Institute for Security Technology Studies, Hanover, December 2004. See also Richard Power, *Tangled Web: Tales of Digital Crime from the Shadows of Cyberspace,* Basingstoke, UK, 2000; Lech J. Janczewski and Andrew Colarik, eds. *Cyber Warfare and Cyber* Terrorism. IGI Global 2008; and Dan Verton, *Black Ice: The Invisible Threat of Cyber Terrorism,* New York: Osborne, 2003; James J. Carafano, *Wiki at War,* College Station: Texas A&M University Press, 2012, pp. 98-111; Lawrence S. Sheets, *6 Pieces of Empire: A 20-Year Journey Through the Soviet Collapse,* New York: Crown, 2011. Note: The term 'Cold War' was coined by George Orwell in 1945. 'Hoss' Cartwright quote: Sydney Freedberg, "Military Debate Who Should Pull the Trigger for a Cyber Attack," May 22, 2012, http://defense.aol.com/2012/05/22

2   Richard J. Barnet, *Roods of* War, New York: Penguin, 1973, p. 47, 65; Thomas C. Reed, *At the Abyss: An Insider's History of the Cold War,* San Francisco: Presidio Press, 2005; Ben R. Rich and Leo Janos, *Skunk Works,* Boston: Little, Brown and Company, 1994, pp. 6-9, 17-19; John L. Gaddis, *The Cold War,* New York: Penguin, 2005, pp. 79-81, 198-202. See also Schlosser, *Command and Control,* pp. 80-100. Note: The Soviets detonated their first atomic test device, RDS-1, on August 29, 1949.

3   Edward Lucas, *The New Cold* War. New York: Palgrave, 2009, pp. 6-12; Peter D. Feaver, "Nuclear Command and Control in Crisis: Old Lesson From New History," Sokolski and Tertrais, eds. *Nuclear Weapons Security Crisis, pp. 205-225;* Masha Gesser, *The Unlikely Rise of Vladmir Putin,* New York: Riverhead Books, 2012, p. 8. See also David E. Hoffman, *The Dead Hand: The Untold Story of the Cold War Arms Race,* New York: Anchor Books, 2009. Edward

FIGURE 2-1
Insider Threat Classification

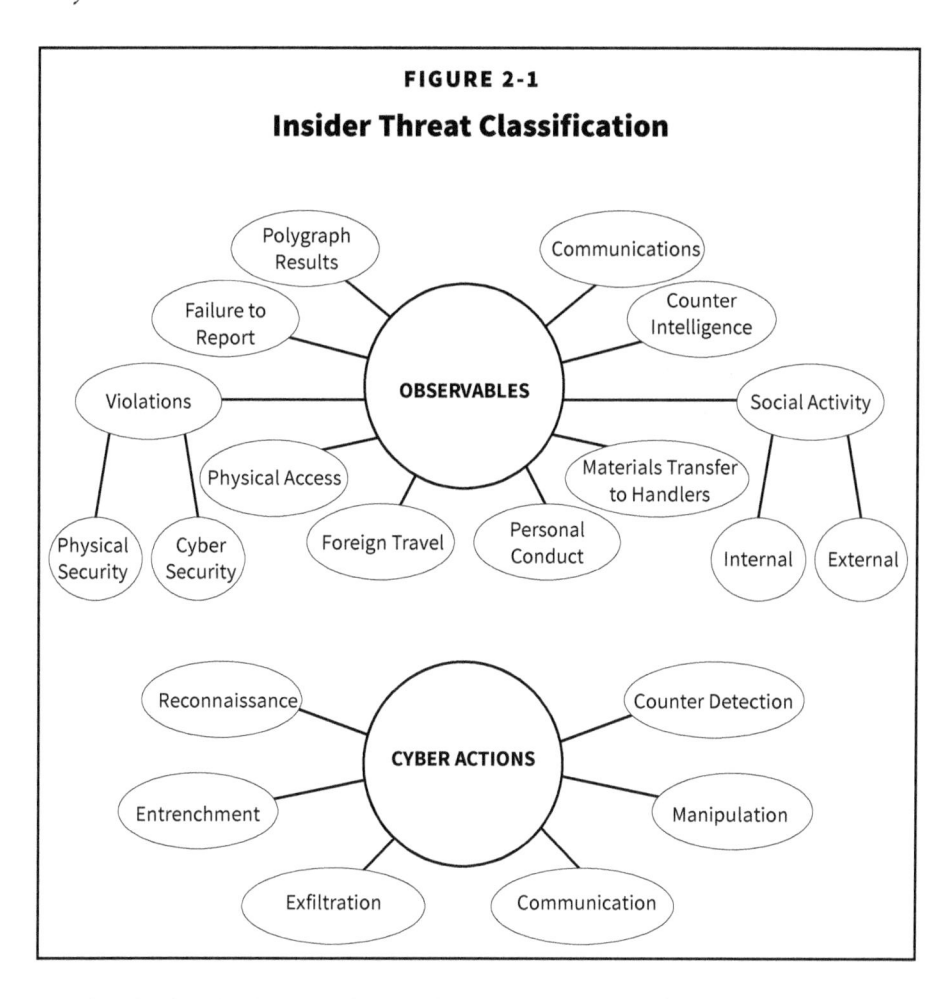

OBSERVABLES
- Polygraph Results
- Communications
- Failure to Report
- Counter Intelligence
- Violations
- Social Activity
- Physical Access
- Materials Transfer to Handlers
- Physical Security
- Cyber Security
- Foreign Travel
- Personal Conduct
- Internal
- External

CYBER ACTIONS
- Reconnaissance
- Counter Detection
- Entrenchment
- Manipulation
- Exfiltration
- Communication

In hindsight, the biggest shock of the altering global landscape and power structure was received by the Chinese — who referred to the Gulf War and the extraordinary one-sided US global military reach as *zhongda biange*, "the great transformation." Live coverage on CNN of precision bomb strikes over Baghdad by F-117 stealth tactical fighters and cruise missiles was an eye opener and a game changer. The new age of warfare enabled by the cyber domain was defined as the 'revolution in military affairs,' or RMA. The changing nature of the 'battlefield' and conduct of warfare by asymmetric means included a wide range of innovations, to include precision targeting systems such as cruise

---

Lucas, *Deception*, New York: Walker and Company, 2012, pp. 6-7; "How Putin Does It," *Wall Street Journal*, June 10, 2013.

missiles, real time computer-based communications, and stealth fighters, armed drones and UAVs. The soldier of the future will be the most wired and technologically advanced warfighter. The enhanced methods for improved battlefield awareness will be the direct result of cyber-connectivity and assurance enabled by the integration of — Command, Control, Communications, Intelligence, Surveillance and Reconnaissance — C41SR. This RMA leap forward in cyber innovation blurs the boundary and the focus on the Internet-cyber-domain "as part of warfare means that a notion of the 'military' clearly and absolutely distinct from civilian realms is almost impossible."[4]

> **Cyber-notes**: the great leap — In 1991, Beijing watched the US military rout Saddam Hussein and recognized the same could happen to the People's Liberation Army. Chinese leaders resolved to study US "network-centric warfare," mimic it in part, and attack it asymmetrically. China would try to get inside US networks, steal their secrets and find vulnerabilities. ... cyber attacks were essential to their great military leap forward.[5]

Following the collapse of the USSR and the Gulf War, the Chinese launched an extensive assessment to determine why and at what speed the Soviet Union had imploded. Could it happen to China? What did they have to do to avoid the fate of the Soviets? Additionally, how could the US travel so far, so fast, and exert such precision fire power in the Persian Gulf? Soon Chinese strategists, realizing just how far behind they were, began to pepper the formulation of their military and political doctrine with terms such as "networkization," "information dominance," "computer network attacks (CAN),"and "asymmetric warfare" — the cyber domain. Given the People's Liberation Army (PLA) lack of combat experience, there seems to be a major effort in China to compensate for

---

[4] Jordan, *Hacking*, p. 84; Richard Bernstein and Ross H. Munro, *The Coming Conflict with China*, New York: Vintage Books, 1998, p. 41; Barry D. Watts, "Maturing Revolution in Military Affairs," Washington, D.C.: CSBA, 2011; Jason Kelly, "A Chinese Revolution in Military Affairs?" *Yale Journal of International Affairs*, Winter 2006, pp. 58-71; Joseph S. Nye, Jr. "Nuclear Lessons for Cyber Security, *Strategic Studies Quarterly*, Winter 2011, pp. 18-21; Spencer Ante, "Military Takes Apps to War," *Wall Street Journal*, September 4, 2012.

[5] "China's Cyber Stonewall," *Wall Street Journal*, editorial, June 11, 2013.

the 'revolution in military affairs' (RMA) and a massive effort to 'leapfrog' into the future. Beyond the tenants of ground, air, and sea warfare, senior Chinese officials reflected on the growing importance and role of the Internet and the 'cyber' realm, incorporating in all future strategic planning a maxim dating from the 500 B.C. teachings of strategist, Sun Tzu, "a superior force that loses information dominance will be beaten, while an inferior one that seizes information dominance will be able to win."[6]

Concerned that the PLA would face its 'next' enemy with incomplete information technology, General Wang Pufeng, the god-father of Chinese cyber-doctrine, noted that "sometimes superior tactics can make up for inferior technology, China will still carry out its traditional warfare methods of 'you fight your way, I'll fight my way,' and use the strengths to attack the enemies weaknesses and adhere to an active role in warfare." By the mid-1990s, the general set the tone for the rise of Chinese cyber warfare and strategy by formulating six basic principals in the emerging cyber era in order to adapt to the needs and implementation of modern information warfare — warfare is no longer the simple conquest of territories or destruction of enemy troops, but the destruction of the enemy's will to resist:

- Fully utilize the advantages of the national homeland and carry out active reconnaissance on the enemy's situation and protect ourselves.

- Develop, improve and utilize China's information weapons in a concentrated way to carry the attack to the enemy.

---

[6] Major General Wang Pufeng, "The Challenge of Information Warfare," *China Military Science,* Spring 1995 seen at www.fas.org/irp/world/china; Daniel Ventre, "Chinese Information and Cyber Warfare," April 13, 2010, http://www.e-ir.info; Douglas Dearth, "Implications, Characteristics, and Impact of Information Warfare," *Military Intelligence,* Jan-Mar 1997; Dean Chen, "Chinese Lessons from the Gulf War," in Andrew Scobell et al eds., *Chinese Lessons from Other Peoples' War,* Carlisle Barracks: SSI, November 2011, pp. 153-200. "Sun Tzu and the art of soft power," *The Economist,* December 17, 2011, 71-4. See also Timothy L. Thomas, "China's Electronic Strategies," *Military Review,* May-June 2001seen at http://fmso.leavenworth.army.mil.documents_china and Clarke, *Cyber War,* pp. 48-52. Note: Global Reach: the ability to move, supply, and position assets — with unrivaled velocity and precision anywhere — to exercise global power — the ability to hold at risk or strike any target, anywhere and project swift, frequently decisive, precise effects, see Jabbour, "The Science and Technology of Cyber Operations," *High Freedom,* May 2009.

- Emphasize mobile warfare in the context of information warfare.

- Conscientiously organize sabotage operations, grasp exploitable opportunities, and make continuous raids to wear down the enemy.

- Organize specialized combined warfare units with information technology weapons to attack the enemy infrastructure.

- Cultivate talent in information science and technology and place talented people in command and control (C2).[7]

The emergence of the Internet and the wired world in the mid- 1990s spurred governments, military, and industry to explore both the strategic and tactical use of information warfare (IW) in crafting strategy for the 21st century. Most active in the application of the new information technology and cyber tactics are Russia and China. Defining the emerging cyber domain soon included information warfare that included both offensive and defensive operations, and could be conducted in times of peace, crisis, or war. The main components of information warfare include command and control (C2), psychological warfare, intelligence and espionage, economic disruptions, and electronic warfare. Decades of research and invention soon merged eight aspects of the scientific-technology revolution, referred to by Toffler as the "Information Wave," — advanced computing, networking and semiconductors, cellular/wireless communications, digital transmission/compression, fiber optics, improved real time human-computer interaction, and satellite technology.[8] The challenge to our national security will be to combine this emerging set of technologies' increased capacity, speed, and flexibility to gather, sort, and transmit data regardless of borders, time zones, weather, culture, or politics. Thus, the era of asymmetric warfare enabled by the cyber domain is born.[9]

---

7 General Wang, "The Challenge of Information Warfare," *China Military Science*, Spring 1995. See also Bill Gertz, *The China Threat: How the People's Republic Targets America*. Washington, D.C.: Regnery Publishing, 2000; and Mark A. Stokes, "China's Strategic Modernization: Implications for the United States," Carlisle Barracks: SSI, September 1999.

8 Myrian D. Cavelty, *Cyber-Security and Threat Politics*, New York: Routledge, 2008, pp. 18-20, 68-9; A. and H. Toffler, *War and Anti-war: Survival at the Dawn of the Twenty-first Century*, Boston. Little Brown, 1993; Brown Commission Report, *Preparing for the 21st Century: An Appraisal of US Intelligence: Roles and Capabilities of the United States Intelligence Community*, Washington, D.C.: GPO, 1996

Cyber Blackout

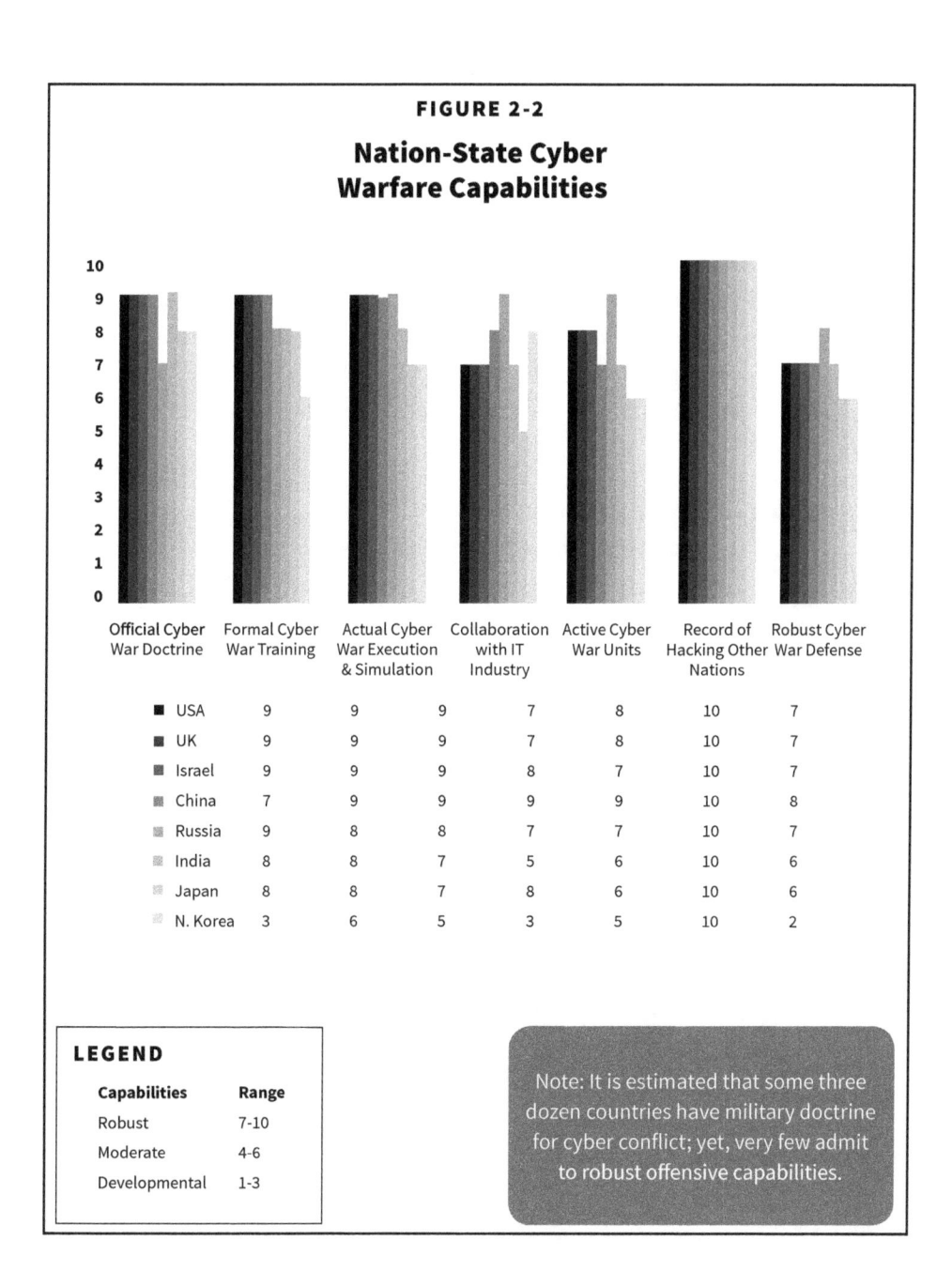

FIGURE 2-2
Nation-State Cyber Warfare Capabilities

	Official Cyber War Doctrine	Formal Cyber War Training	Actual Cyber War Execution & Simulation	Collaboration with IT Industry	Active Cyber War Units	Record of Hacking Other Nations	Robust Cyber War Defense
USA	9	9	9	7	8	10	7
UK	9	9	9	7	8	10	7
Israel	9	9	9	8	7	10	7
China	7	9	9	9	9	10	8
Russia	9	8	8	7	7	10	7
India	8	8	7	5	6	10	6
Japan	8	8	7	8	6	10	6
N. Korea	3	6	5	3	5	10	2

LEGEND

Capabilities	Range
Robust	7-10
Moderate	4-6
Developmental	1-3

Note: It is estimated that some three dozen countries have military doctrine for cyber conflict; yet, very few admit to robust offensive capabilities.

9   Andrew Krepinevich et al, "The Challenges to US National Security: Strategy for the Long Haul," Washington, D.C.: CSBA, 2008, pp. 1-41.

What fully emerged in Washington during the 1990s was a vast behind-the-doors debate and policy-making review as to who should control the internet. The military, NSA, and private sector began to understand the vulnerability of the information infrastructure — the Internet grid. The open source approach by industry, coupled with the rapidly advancing technology, created tension between the military, government agencies, and commercial interests that has turned into a high stakes turf battle. The military and NSA felt they were losing control, and the private industry/academic sector demanded openness and transparency. The irony is that the very country that invented the internet and introduced cyber global connectivity in virtually all aspects of our lives, was now, due to its rapid development, more vulnerable to hacking by less developed countries.[10]

The military and state sponsored cyber-attacks date back over two decades, as nations and their surrogates shaped both their cyber doctrines and technical skills. While the Chinese government was a relative latecomer to the dynamics of the Internet, the teachings of General Pufeng refined a new generation to advance China's awareness of information warfare or 'cyber solutions' in military operations. China has repeatedly targeted the United States. For example, in 1999 two Chinese Air Force Colonels, Qiao Liang and Wang Xiangsui drafted the now somewhat famous "Unrestricted Warfare." Their treatise chronicles the art of full scale inclusion of 'cyber' dominated asymmetric warfare and its impact:

> … technological progress has given us the means to strike at the enemy's nerve center directly without harming other things, giving us numerous new options for achieving victory, and all there make people believe that the best way to achieve victory is to control, not kill….. warfare will be unrestricted….the battlefield is next to you and the enemy is on the network…..[11]

---

10   Ted G. Lewis, *Critical Infrastructure Protection in Homeland Security*, Hoboken: Wiley, 2006, pp. 28-112.

11   Qiao Liang and Wang Xiangsui *Unrestricted Warfare*, Beijing: PLA Literature and Arts Publishing, 1999; Ralph D. Sawyer, *The Tao of Deception*, New York: Basic Books, 2007, pp.55-66. See also Spade, *Information as Power*, pp. 14-6. See also US-China Economic and

This is a straight forward statement of doctrine that has since become the cornerstone of the Chinese military modernization efforts to employ what Sun-Tzu deemed the "orthodox and unorthodox" use of cyber tactics to weaken and destroy the information superiority and operational response, to include limiting command and control, just-in-time logistics, and cripple vital infrastructure services such as the power grid, water, financial networks, and communications.[12] There have been numerous reports of foreign information warfare exercises conducted by the military, yet the full capabilities of China, Russia, and rogue nations such as Iran and North Korea remain unknown. The enemy in a cyber-war has the advantages of stealth, anonymity, and unpredictability, a modern day 'assassin's mace.' Issues further compounding the difficulty in determining our response to such a cyber-attack were made clear in recent Pentagon exercises: first, it is difficult to determine if such a cyber-attack was a low grade hacker vandalism, industrial espionage, or a state-sponsored effort to cripple the nation; and second, if the source was determined, we lacked clear legal authority to respond. Thus, if you are not on the cyber offensive, playing defense and catch-up is very, very difficult.[13]

Security Review Commission, "Indigenous Weapons Development in China's Military Modernization," Washington, D.C.: April 5, 2012.

12 Avery Goldstein, "China's Real and Present Danger," *Foreign Affairs*, September 2013, pp. 136-144; Bryan Krekel, Patton Adams, and George Bakos, *Occupying the Information High Ground: Chinese Capabilities for Computer Network Operations and Cyber Espionage*, Washington, D.C.: US-China Economics and Security review Commission (prepared by Northrop Grumman Corp.), March 7, 2012; Gary M. Jackson, *Predicting Malicious Behavior*, Indianapolis: Wiley, 2012, pp. 51-7.

13 John Markoff, et al "In Digital Combat, US Finds No Easy Deterrent," New York Times, January 26, 2010; Samuel Liles, "Cyber Warfare: As a Form of Low-Intensity Conflict and Insurgency," Conference of Cyber Conflict, Proceedings, 2010, pp. 47-57: Bowden, *Worm*, pp. 224-5: David Hambling, "China Looks to Undermine US Power, with 'Assassin's Mace,'" July 2, 2009, www.wired.com/dangerroom/2009; Victor N. Corpus, "America's Acupuncture Points: The assassin's mace" *Asia Times*, October 20, 2006, www.atimes.com

John A. Adams, Jr.

> **Cyber-notes**: assassin's mace — *shashou jiang* — a term of ancient Chinese strategy to swiftly incapacitate the enemy, suddenly, and totally, by rapid initiative and surprise to take advantage when confronting superior foe[14]

Cold War Clues

In the Cold War, when the nuclear powers went head-to-head in an arms race, they eventually dampened after years of arms limitation talks and a broad understanding of the concept of "mutually assured destruction" (MAD). In the nuclear age, deterrence was an all or nothing proposition. While nuclear, chemical, bio-weapons, and precision weapons (CBRNE) remain a deadly threat in the wrong hands, the next forty years will add the potential hostile use of the Internet and cyber-space as the place for an inevitable "cyber arms race."[15]

Where do you draw the 'line' in the open, uncontrolled cyber-domain? The legal community and policy makers remain engaged in an expanding debate, attempting to quantify cause-and-effect, establishment of attribution, jurisdictions, what constitutes a 'just' war, and the bottom line: does a cyber-attack represent a qualitative change in the meaning and the nature of warfare? And to what degree of external cyber-warfare threat or perceived hostile action merits a counter cyber and/or military response? In short, what are the rules of engagement?[16] Currently, the United States government has no policy that

---

14 For an excellent review of the China's historical approach to warfare, tactical implementation, and strategy see, Ralph D. Sawyer, *The Tao of Deception: Unorthodox Warfare in Historic and Modern China*, New York: Basic Books, 2007.

15 Joseph S. Nye, Jr. "Nuclear Lessons for Cyber Security?" *Strategic Studies* Quarterly, Winter 2011, pp. 18-24; Gaddis, *The Cold War*, pp. 79-81; Goldstein, "China's Real and Present Danger," p. 140; Richard A. Falkenrath, Robert Newman, and Bradley A. Thayer, *America's Achilles' Heel: Nuclear, Biological, and Chemical Terrorism and Covert Attacks*, Cambridge: MIT Press, 1998; Schlosser, *Command and Control*, pp. 5-25. See also Regina E. Dugan and Kaigham J. Gabriel, '"Special Forces" Innovation: How DARPA Attacks problems," *Harvard Business Review*, October 2013, pp. 74-84.

16 Scott J. Shackelford, "From Nuclear War to Net War: Analogizing Cyber Attacks in International Law," at http://works.bepress.com/scott_shackelford/5. See also Jabbour,

articulates the parameters of cyberspace in terms of a hostile intent against the nation and/or its allies. Not knowing where the 'cyber-boundaries' are precludes a unilateral cyber/military response. As noted earlier, clearly defining what cyberspace is remains a difficult task. Not being clearly defined assists those nation-states, and especially rogue hackers, most of which are not held accountable in their native countries, to flourish. Rogue states have leveraged-up the skills of these hackers to serve their own political and espionage ends.[17]

Unlike a narrow range of nuclear players during the Cold War, the range of cyber threats is as numerous as the number of players developing and targeting the cyber domain. The Cold War era's select club of antagonists is, at best, only an indication on how to partly approach control of the cyber domain, but is by no means the full answer to the complex threats on the horizon. The ease of access to the cyber world allows the amateur, both foreign and domestic, to openly hack at will, yet the greater concern is with a cross-section of enemies ranging from well-organized rogue gang assaults to fully funded state-sponsored probes and attacks. China alone rose from fewer than 1 million Internet users in 1997, to 22 million in 2003, and to more than 540 million Internet users today.[18] I have divided the range of disruptive cyber intrusions and/or attacks into six categories: the Strategic Measurement of Advanced Disruptive (cyber) Attacks (SMADA). Certainly other categories could be added and the six noted further sub-divided. The aim is to present an overview of the dynamics and breathe of threats, players, and scope in the growing complexity of the cyber domain. See Figure 2-3

"The Science and Technology of Cyber Operations," *High Frontier*, May 2009, pp. 11-15.

17 Jeffery R. Schilling, "Defining Our National Cyberspace Boundaries," Carlisle Barracks: Army War College, 2010; Melissa Hathaway, "Cyber policy: A National Imperative," Harvard Kennedy School, March 1, 2011; The White House, "Cyberspace Policy Review," Washington, D.C.: May 29, 2009.

18 J. P. London, "Made in China,' *Proceedings*, April 2011, www.usni.org

Figure 2-3
Strategic Measurement of Advanced Disruptive (cyber) Attacks (SMADA)

Nation-state frontal offensive

Nation-state probe: espionage

Rogue state assault

Nation-state defense

Nation-stimulation exercise

Rogue hacker intrusion

Nation-state frontal offensive:

No such full-frontal cyber offensive has been launched to date, yet nation to nation cyber espionage conflicts date from the mid-1990s, thus plans are well underway in a cross section of countries to pull the first punch against a perceived stronger opponent. Animosities, for example, date back to tensions between India and Pakistan over nuclear testing (1998), ongoing incidents between China and Taiwan (1998-2006), and China and US friction following the US spy plane collision over Hunan Island (2001). The focus of this section will be open source data on the actions and intent of Russia and China to expand and enhance their cyber influence.[19]

Cyber-attacks on both public and military systems across America have been active for over two decades. Given the unprotected nature of American computers, as well as a general unawareness of the damages of hacking, the US continues to be a very rich target of opportunity. What was first passed off as rogue 'hacktivist' (such as the so-called "Solar Sunrise" launched against DOD targets in 1998 by three teenagers!) and criminal elements (of which there remain thousands) each with varying political, criminal, or social agendas, has grown into state sponsored and government funded efforts by over a dozen active countries to penetrate the networks of both their friends and enemies. Of the millions of cyber incidents over the past two decades, some have gained fame

---

19 DOD, DSB, "Resilient Military Systems and the Advanced Cyber Threat," p. 2; Scott Borg, "How Cyber Attacks Will be Used In International Conflicts," power point, 2010, www.usccu.us; Desmond Ball, China's Cyber Warfare Capabilities," *Security Challenges*, Winter 2011, pp. 81-103.

in the cyber-intelligence community by being named and where possible the attacked. While attribution remains fuzzy and nation-states invoke 'plausible deniability' —, some hackers have been outed.[20]

What appear to distinguish an incident from the category of a random rogue hacker event from a nation-state attack are the scale, extent, and scope of the invasion. While many have the will or capacity to attack the American system, an orchestrated effort requires expertise, funding, and, if truly expansive, state sponsorship. While an active defense and counter-terrorism IW will always be paramount, nation-states particularly want to know and test their strengths and ability to launch an offensive cyber strike. Thus is the case with Russia and China: such named events as Love Bug – 2000, Honker Union – 2001, Moonlight Maze – 2001, and Titan Rain – 2003. Interestingly, in February 2006, the United States finally went on the active defensive and cyber planning with its own domestic cyber-security exercise: Cyber Storm I.[21]

The pre-planned state-sponsored Russian offensive cyberspace operation (OCO) against Estonia, which began in April 2007 and Georgia in 2008,[22] in conjunction with the limited use of conventional armed forces, was a glimpse into the future, a hint at what a blended cyber-kinetic situations could look like, and what question s it would raise. What are the rules? Has the international community determined what constitutes a cyber-attack? Should NATO respond to obligations to protect an attacked member nation? How do you confirm who and why the attack was launched? And such events are further clouded by who is the 'confirmed aggressor', and if the attack is confirmed, what sanctions should be made and by what authority. Thus, the ability of rogue

---

20   Adam P. Liff, *Cyber War*, pp. 414-7.

21   Elinor Abreu, "Epic cyberattack reveals cracks in US defense," CNN, May 10, 2001; B. Graham, "Hackers Attack Via Chinese Web Sites," Washington Post, August 25, 2005; Clive Thompson, "Open Source Spying," December 3, 2006, www.nytimes.com/2006/12/03/magazine . See also Steven A. Hildreth, "Cyberwarfare," Washington, D.C.: CRS Report to Congress, June 19, 2001; L. Gordon Crovitz, "Cybersecurity 2.0," *Wall Street Journal*, February 27, 2012.

22   Shaun Waterman, "Georgia Hackers Strike Apart from Russian Military," *The Washington Times.com*, August 19, 2008; Noah Shachtman, "Georgia under Online Assault," *Wired*, *August 10, 2008;* Peter Svensson, "Georgian President's Web Site Mover to Atlanta," *AP News*, August 11, 2008, www.usatoday.com/tech/products.

players to be shielded (and sanctioned) by nation–states increasingly impacts timely and accurate attribution. There are few better examples of this cyber threat than the 2007 attack on Estonia.[23]

> **Cyber-notes**: the vetted: the select few of the trusted Internet and the world's largest ISP elite individuals with the power to monitor and removecut off global Internet rogue computers off the network.[24]

The Bronze Statue

The attack on Estonia is a small snapshot on how a cyber-attack cascades and cripples a country, from its capital, Tallinn on the Baltic, to the local level. Estonia, a former pre-Cold War satellite state of the Soviet Union which was "liberated" from Nazi Germany, is the size of New Hampshire with a population of 1.3 million. Taking the place of Estonia's previous occupier, the Soviets took pains to establish reminders of their role in the Great War across Eastern Europe, and one step of that was to install a giant bronze statue of a Russian soldier in downtown Tallinn. In February 2007, the Estonian legislature passed a law to remove any structure or reminders of the hated foreign occupation, which included vocal calls to remove the bronze soldier. Ethnic Russians living in Estonia, fueled by support from Moscow, protested the move and by late April riots erupted. To restore order, the legislation was vetoed by the president and the statue moved to a military cemetery on the outskirts, where it could be better protected. These actions, on the eve of Russia's annual Victory May Day celebrations to commemorate the defeat of Nazi Germany in Red Square, only heightened tensions between Moscow and Tallinn.[25]

---

23   Shaun Waterman, "Who was behind Estonia's cyber attack?" *World Peace Herald*, June 11, 2007; Sean C. Butler, "Refocusing Cyber Warfare Thought," *Air & Space Power Journal*, January 2012, pp. 54, 57. Note: Many have argued that the Estonian and Georgia cyber attacks fall short of open warfare in the cyber domain; yet they do represent "strong examples of cyber war. Did the cyber component have a meaningful impact given the disparity between the two sides?

24   Joshua Davis, "Hackers Take Down the Most Wired Country in Europe," *Wired*, August 12, 2007.

25   Davis, "Hackers Take Down the Most Wired Country in Europe," *Wired*, August 21, 2007.

Then, suddenly Estonia, one of the most wired and internet connected countries in the world, was the target of an escalating cyber-attack from Russia and its surrogates.[26] The DDOS attack, a distributed denial of service, jammed and crashed networks. The attack was in the form of tens of thousands of electronic pings from an estimated one million untraceable computers around the world. Empowered by Moscow's trademark *maskirovka*, script kiddies and rogue hackers assembled computer botnets (robot networks) that surreptitiously inflicted malicious 'zombie' worms into control systems to slow, stop, and damage networks across Estonia. The cyber assault mushroomed to penetrate servers in banks, government ministry offices, the parliament, telephone networks, news agencies, credit card readers, as well as thousands of internet sites. Government and private sector websites that normally received 1,000 visits per day crashed after being pinged at upwards of 2,000 hits per second! Yet, still to this day, many question the magnitude of the two weeks of cyber-attacks.[27]

Cyber-notes: *maskirovka* — Soviet military warfare doctrine of deception, 'trickery,' combining procedures and techniques to confuse, mislead, conceal, and camouflage oneself from the enemy[28]

DDOS attacks are very difficult to defeat precisely because they target otherwise well-protected systems and networks. The first well-known DDOS attacks occurred in early 2000. Over the years, increased sophistication has allowed hackers to link millions of unwitting computers into botnets to launch attacks. The programs that convert third-party computers into bots only need to work against the least well-protected Internet-linked computers in order to compromise the system and take over control. The result is a cascading event that shuts

---

26   Joshua Keating, "Who was behind the Estonia cyber-attack?" cable, June 6, 2007, Wikileaks. foreignpolicy.com/posts/2010/12/7.

27   Clay Wilson, *Botnets, Cybercrime, and Cyberterrorism: Vulnerabilities and Policy Issues for Congress*. Washington, D.C.: Congressional Research Service, 2007, p. 7; Stephen Herzog, "Revisiting the Estonian Cyber Attacks: Digital Threats and Multinational Responses," *Journal of Strategic Security*, 2011, pp. 49-60; Jordan, *Hacking*, pp. 78-81.

28   Sean Bodmer et al, *Reverse Deception*, New York: McGraw Hill, 2012, pp. 39-40.

down access to computers, corrupts data, and cut off vital services such as electric grids, water pumps, and banking ATMs.[29]

With the assistance of cyber experts from Europe and America, the central government assembled an incident response team to employ countermeasures, with little success as the zombies adapted or were reprogrammed by the attackers to continue the attacks. Viewed by some as a "technically meager" cyber-attack, this same damage could have been employed by criminal hackers for a few hundreds of dollars. On May 10, Estonia was very near digital collapse. However, after protesting to NATO, the Estonian cyber team (ECERT), and 'vetted' Internet experts were able to slow the attacks and back track the attack to controlling computers in Russian — a clear hint was the code was written on Cyrillic-alphabet keyboards! The Russians denied any involvement, noting even if patriotic Russians had contemplated such an action there were no laws in Russia to prevent them from conducting "individual" actions.[30]

The increased ability of transnational players and networks to employ digital hacking tools will continue to be a significant challenge to nation-states as they strive to protect critical assets and computer systems. The use of globally dispersed unattributable computer systems has allowed the Internet to become a powerful asymmetric weapon in the wrong hands. Critical infrastructure and digital networks in both the public and private sector remain at risk. Defending national sovereignty in a growing borderless world, which is daily more interconnected in cyberspace, will remain a challenge. The cyber-attacks of 2007 on Estonia were a wake-up call and possible watershed event to raise awareness on the vulnerabilities facing the future.[31]

---

29   Clay Wilson, "Botnets, Cybercrime, and Cyberterrorism: Vulnerabilities and Policy Issues for Congress," Washington, D.C. : CRS, January 29, 2008; Martin C. Libicki, "Cyberdeterrence and Cyberwar," Santa Monica: Rand Corporation, 2009, pp. 15-20.

30   Hathaway, "Cyber Security," *Intelligencer*, Fall 2008, p. 35. Note: To ID the source of the attack, Estonia requested a bilateral investigation under the Mutual Legal Assistance Treaty (MALT) which Russia declined. The Russian were on safe footing because MALT is a paper tiger and has no mandatory enforcement mechanisms. Interestingly, the US did not press the case, noting that the cyber-attacks were most likely "carried out by politically motivated hacker gangs."

31   Carafano, *Wiki at War*, pp. 95-101.

Defend-the-Nation Team

Given the scale and resources, a nation-state attack would be the most disruptive, yet cannot be singled out as the only dramatic means to launch a cyber-attack. In the years since the 2007 attack on Estonia, there has been a tremendous increase in nation-state hacking and overt espionage. Incidents and attacks have compounded to an alarming rate. The prime leaders are US, China, Russia, Iran, and Israel. The motives of each vary, yet the overall goal is to gain an industrial, financial, and military edge. While the United States professes a defensive posture in the cyber realm, it is a certainty that, as noted by General James 'Hoss' Cartwright, the high ground in cyber operations is the degree to which a nation can be on the cyber offensive.[32]

The purpose for the creation of the US Cyber Command, while public relations talked of defense measures, is to be on the offensive and/or be prepared to be on the offensive when needed. In a rare moment of candor, US Cyber Command chief General Keith Alexander reported in mid-March 2013 to Congress that the military did have and would be expanding an active ability and mission focus to use and deploy offensive cyber weapons by "defend-the-nation teams — this is an offensive team." In so doing, he highlighted the surge of cyber attacks both on the US and allies, including the August 2012 attack on a Saudi ARAMCO, intrusions into the Wall Street banking and financial sectors, and hacking the 'critical' US power grids and infrastructure.[33]

---

32 Liff, *Cyber War*, 414-7.

33 White House, Presidential Directive 20, "Cyber Operations," October 2012; Carlo Munoz, "Obama authorizes cyber warfare directive," November 14, 2012, http://thehill.com/blogs ; Mark Mazzetti and David Sanger, "Security Leader Says US Would Retaliate Against Cyberattacks," *New York Times*, March 12, 2013; Ellen Nakashima, "Pentagon to boost cybersecurity force," *Washington Post*, January 27, 2013. See also DOD, DSB, "Resilient Military Systems and the Advanced Cyber Threat," pp. 15-18.

FIGURE 2-4

Suspected Chinese Cyber Attacks Reaction to Political or Cultural Event

Date	Event	Target	Comment
May 1999	U.S. accidental bombing of Chinese Embassy in Belgrade	U.S. government sites	Posted "down with barbarians"
August 1999	China-Taiwan tension	Taiwanese government web sites	Counter response to incident
April 2001	U.S spy plane crisis	Chinese "hactivists" deface over 1,000 U.S. websites	DDOS attack against CIA and Whitehouse
August 2001	China-Japan tension over Yasukuni Shrine	Japanese websites	DDOS attack
Fall 2006	Byzantine Haze	U.S. State Dept.	Spam-phishing Stole terabytes of data
April 2008	U.S.-China tension	Hacking to steal strategic information	Counter accusations
June 2008	GhostNet cyber espionage	The Dalai Lama	Search for information
April 2009	Penetration of U.S. electrical grid	Looking for vulnerability in SCADA	Leaving behind malware
March 2011	Espionage	Pentagon DoD	Theft of estimated 24,000 files
February 2012	Espionage	F-35 Fighter Plane Design	Stole classified technology

> **Project Gunman**
>
> A recently declassified example of Soviet high-stakes Cold War espionage, between 1976 and 1984, in the early era of Russian cyber warriors, reveals a devised an operation that resulted in a massive, long-term breach on the inter-workings of the US Embassy in Moscow. By modifying 16 IBM Selectric typewriters (considered an advanced electromechanical "computer" in its day) in key offices in the embassy, they had real-time access to US activity. The Soviets replaced the 'comb support bar' of the typewriters with a device that externally looked the same but was modified to enable the transmission in plain text of nearly every typed key stroke to a Soviet listening post. A tipoff from a "liaison service" exposed to a similar attack alerted the US, who was in disbelief of the breach due to their mindset and focus almost entirely on the Soviets' audio listening devices.[34]

Nation-State Reactionary (Defensive)

If the offensive rules of cyber war are vague, so too are the ROEs for a defensive response. Nation-states have the right to defend their interest, yet only now are policy makers considering the options to counter a cyber-event. The Putin government has made it clear in public statements that Russia would respond to a cyber-attack as an act of war and respond appropriately. The rhetoric is reminiscent of the Cold War nuclear policies that acknowledge no "first Strike," agreed to in the SALT I and II Treaties and the reduction of nuclear warheads.[35]

Given no international guide lines, except some academic referrals to the unratified Law of the Sea and previous nuclear treaties as a frame of reference, a cyber-event could escalate into a "Dead Hand" type policy from the Cold War era in USSR, which allowed a counter strike on the grounds of a strong perceived threat or any provocation on the survivability of the Russian state. Cold

---

34 DOD, DSB, pp. 23-5; NSA, "(U) Learning from the Enemy: The GUNMAN Project," NSA: Center for Cryptologic History, January 9, 2007, declassified May 2013.

35 Bracken, *The Second Nuclear Age*, pp. 1-23.

War strategies on 'containment' became a bit outdated and lacking in attribution in the face of a cyber-attack that cannot be fully identified. To bring the super powers into line, in early March 2013, the United States called for more cooperation on cyber issues to avoid a cyber-confrontation. The White House has called on China to open three prime aspects of cyber operations: public recognition of the urgency of cyber problems; a commitment to crack down on rogue hackers in China; and an agreement to take part in a dialogue to establish global standards, notwithstanding the fact that the Chinese have repeatedly claimed they do not hack other nations![36]

Nation-State Probe (Espionage) + Hackers

The cloak and dagger of espionage during the Cold War is not gone and dead. The past few years have seen some of the most aggressive efforts to collect top-secret military and industrial economic data in history. The only difference is that the spies and their agents and cohorts in the second oldest profession in the world have now gone high tech. Such espionage programs combine a collection of open source data, HUMINT, signal intelligence or SIGINT, and cyber operations. The Office of the Director of National Intelligence in late 2011 released the most detailed and assessment of the threats of pervasive adversaries, concluding that while some dozen countries target US information and technology, the most intense threat is from "Chinese actors . . . and Russia's intelligence service . . . the world's most active and persistent perpetrators of economic espionage . . . the proliferation of portable devices that connect to the Internet and other networks will continue to create new opportunities for malicious actors to conduct espionage."[37]

---

36 Hoffman, *Dead Hand*, pp. 13-40, 146-9; John L. Gaddis, *Strategies of Containment: A Critical Appraisal of American National Security Policy During the Cold War*. Oxford: Oxford University Press, 2005; Stephen J. Black, ed. *Russian Military Politics and Russia's 2010 Defense Doctrine*, Carlisle Barracks: SSI, March 2011; Mark Landler and David Sanger, "US Demands China Block Cyberattacks and Agree to Rules," *New York Times*, March 11, 2013: Liff, *Cyber War*, pp. 417-421.

37 White House. Office of the Director of National Defense, "Foreign Spies Stealing US Economic Secrets in Cyberspace: Report to Congress on Foreign Economic Collection and Industrial Espionage, 2009-2011," Washington, D.C.: October 2011; Spade, *Information as Power*, pp. 2-14.

Those that attack our system for intelligence are emboldened by the fact that cyberspace provides relatively small-scale operatives an opportunity to become players in economic espionage. Such attacks can be triggered by xenophobic sentiments such as the Chinese cyber-attacks on Japan stemming from historical animosity and nationalist feelings fueled from the World War Two mainland occupation by the Japanese army. Other examples include pro-Palestinian activist hackers attacking Israel in April 2013 with DDOS attacks, as well as the North Korean ongoing efforts to hack and disrupt computer systems in South Korea. Nation-states, often in well financed rogue criminal hacktivist groups, are able to build relationships to customize malware and remote-access exploits. Motivations range from pure monetary interest to political (nationalistic) and social agendas. And some disgruntled insiders can cause a massive breach of data by leaking data, such as WikiLeaks, Anonymous, and LulzSec.[38]

In addition to remote cyber means to collect data, the ongoing damage that is being conducted by insiders is tremendous. The damage possible by a "trusted agent" who is inside the firewall, such as an employee or vendor with a valid user name, password and regular access to company secrets and projects can be staggering. The most valuable attribution and hard to detect aspect of an insider threat is that they have gained access to "inside — trust."[39] The inside cyber threat falls into a number of categories:

Classic Insider — tasked to do damage by positioning in a specific organization and job function to carry out harm, either on the behalf of an espionage operation or on an individual basis.

---

38 James Ball, "WikiLeaks publishes Stratfor emails linked to Anonymous," February 26, 2012, www.guardian.co.uk/media ; Quinn Norton, "WikiLeaks Pairs with Anonymous to Publish Intelligence Firm's Dirty Laundry," February 26, 2012, www.wired.com/threatlevel/2012; "UK hackers admit plotting attacks on CIA," London: Reuters, June 25, 2012; Joshua Mitnick, "Hackers Hit Israel Over Palestinians," *Wall Street Journal*, April 8, 2013. See also R. Lennon, "Case Study of the Wikileaks Whistleblower," Dublin City University: December 10, 2010, pp. 1-13.

39 Robert F. Mills et al, "Insider Threat Prevention, Detection and Mitigation," in Kenneth J. Knapp, ed. *Cyber Security and Global Information Assurance*, Hershey: Information Science Reference, 2009, pp. 48-55.

- *Disgruntled Insider* — individual with the best intentions upon joining organization, but later becomes dissatisfied, resulting in the actor deciding to do damage due to grudge or retaliation.

- *Careless Insider* — generally, a well-meaning individual that due to poor training, improper access, random surfing on the system creates dangerous vulnerabilities — such action lead to inadvertently introducing malware, miss handles passwords, etc.

- *Espionage* — insider is directly linked to outside intelligence collector.[40]

> **Cyber-notes**: Our reliance on cyberspace stands in stark contrast to the inadequacy of our cybersecurity — we recognize that there may be malicious activities on DOD networks and systems *that we have not yet detected.*[41]

Defending against the insider threat is extremely difficult because those who commit these acts have been granted access and often such espionage goes undetected for years or decades. For example, the DOD operates over 15,000 networks and nearly 8 million computing devices across hundreds of installations in over 120 countries. And, not surprisingly, the most dangerous and hard-to-find insider-adversaries are those with legitimate access to systems and infrastructure, such as John Anthony Walker, a US Navy communications specialist who spied for the Soviet Union from 1967 to 1985. When caught and debriefed, Walker told his interrogators, "K Mart has better security than the Navy!"[42] The following breach released in a White House Report is a case in point:

---

40   CACI, Cyber Threats to National Security, September 2011, p. 11; London, "Made in China," *Proceedings*, April 2011. See also DOD, Department of Defense Strategy for Operating in Cyberspace, Washington, D.C., July 2011.

41   DOD, "Department of defense Strategy for Operating in Cyberspace," Washington, D.C., July 2011, p. 1

42   John Prados, "The Navy's Biggest Betrayal," *Naval History Magazine*, June 2010, www.usni.org/magazine Note: The DOD is concerned with three prime potential adversarial activities: 1) theft or exploitation of data; 2) disruption or denial of access or service, and 3) destructive action including corruption, manipulation, or degrade networks or connected systems.

Dongfan Chung was an engineer with Rockwell and Boeing who worked on the B-1 bomber, space shuttle, and other projects, and was sentenced in early 2010 to 15 years in prison for economic espionage on behalf of the Chinese aviation industry. At the time of his arrest, 250,000 pages of sensitive documents were found in his house. This is suggestive of the volume of information Chung could have passed to his handlers between 1979 and 2006. Chung was prosecuted only for the possession of these documents with the intent to benefit the People's Republic of China.

An interesting fact on the logistics of handling the physical volume of documents which would fill nearly four 4-drawer filing cabinets: with current technology, all data in the documents hidden in Chung's house would fit onto ONE inexpensive CD.

Note: On average, one page of typed text holds 2 kilobytes (KB) of data; thus, 250,000 pages x 2 KB/page = 500,000 KB, or 488 megabytes (MB). A data CD with the capacity of 700 MB retails for $.75, and a flash drive with a capacity of 4 gigabytes costs about $13.00.[43]

At all levels of government, military, and industry, the insider with authority to access and use data, coupled with the employee, researcher, or vendor intent do harm, is an ongoing threat. In mid-2012, one company pleaded guilty to gross violations of US Export Control Laws (imposed after the 1989 Tiananmen Square crackdown) after supplying control software and jet engine technology for over a decade to the Chinese military to build an attack helicopter. The company attempted to circumvent the law by working through a third party country, Canada, justifying what they did as a "calculated risk."[44] A more egregious example is the US Army PFC who had access and the ability to download, copy, and remove classified documents from his "secure" workplace — fueled the windfall gained by WikiLeaks in 2010. In addition to theft of data, an insider threat has a range of options to do harm, to include leaking data to the media, collecting passwords, obtaining vendor data, passing trade secrets and

---

43 White House, "Foreign Spies Stealing US Economic Secrets," p. 3.

44 Kate Linebaugh, "UTC Helped Build China's First Military Attack Copter," *Wall Street Journal*, June 29, 2012.

proprietary data to competitors or foreign intel services (FIS), and by simply deleting critical information. What is *your* security and access policy?[45]

> **Cyber-notes**: *hongke* or 'red hacker' — Chinese cyberwarrior motivated by patriotism to attack foreign digital systems[46]

China's intelligence service, by way of its diplomats, private citizens, and private companies, have systematic, active, ongoing intelligence operations in the US, as well as targets in Europe, Africa, and Latin America. These advanced persistent threats (APTs) target computer IT networks and software source code, utility grid systems, critical infrastructure, military R&D, manufacturing know-how, political intel, and the constant surveillance of both our domestic and international supply chain operations. The Chinese indignantly deny these charges — blaming non-government hackers or anti-Chinese elements in other countries including the United States.[47] The dynamics between the United States and China is driven by interdependency in trade and markets share; yet in terms of the emerging power of China, Beijing is threatened by the United States trying to limit military growth and intrigue in the Pacific region. The forward looking challenge by China will be in all aspects of the cyber domain. The annual US losses to IP theft are over $300 billion per year, comparable to the current yearly value of US exports to Asia. As global networks and the world become more wired in cyberspace, attribution remains especially difficult: — however, of the seven cases adjudicated in FY 2010 under the Economic Espionage Act, six involved a direct link with China.[48]

---

45 National Bureau of Asian Research, "The IP Commission Report on the Theft of American Intellectual Property," Washington, D.C.: 2013, pp. 1-3; "Crypto war 2.0," *The Economist*, November 8, 2014, p. 65.

46 Hannah Beech, "China's Red Hackers: The Tale of One Patriotic Cyberwarrior," February 21, 2013, www.world.time.com/2013/02/21/chinas-red-hackers

47 Desmond Ball, "China's Cyber Warfare Capabilities," *Security Challenges*, Winter 2011, pp. 81-103; Douglas Ernst, "China has power to shut down U.S. power grid with cyberattacks: NSA director," November 20, 2014, www.washingtontimes.com/news/2014/nov20/nsa-china

48 Ibid., p. 5.; Richard Clarke, "China's Cyberassault on America," *Wall Street Journal*, June 15, 2011; Spade, *Information as Power*, pp. 11-14; NBAR, "The IP Commission Report," 2013, p. 2

Cyber Blackout

For over a decade, Washington was silent on pointing a finger at the *hongke*, Chinese cyberwarriors, as the primary frontal attackers into American industry, governmental, and military systems. Finally, in May 2013, the Pentagon's in its *Annual Report to Congress* on the *Military and Security Developments Involving the People's Republic of China 2013* clearly noted that high volume of cyberattacks on the US in 2012 "appear to be attributable directly to the Chinese government and military... and these intrusions were focused on exfiltrating information... and these intrusions are similar to those necessary to conduct computer network attacks." And in consistent fashion, official sources in Beijing repeatedly denied any knowledge of cyberattacks on the United States.[49] The cyberwarfare capabilities of the Chinese are intended to augment military operations in three key areas:

1) Primarily to enhance data collection for intelligence and computer network attack purposes

2) Further to assist cyber tactic that can be employed to constrain an adversary's actions and slow response time by targeting network-based logistics, communications, and commercial activities

3) Serve as a force multiplier when coupled with kinetic attacks during times of crisis or conflict.[50]

---

49 Office of the Secretary of Defense, *Military and security Developments Involving the People's Republic of China 2013*, Washington, D.C.: DOD, May 2013, pp. 36-7. See also Associated Press, "Pentagon report for 1st time says China government, military responsible for US cyberattacks," *The Washington Post*, May 6, 2013.

50 Ibid., p. 36. See also Guangqian Peng and Youzhi Yao, *The Science of Military Strategy*, Military Science Publishing House, 2005 for details of Chinese thought and plans. See also CNBC, "Code Wars: American Cyber Threat," New York: May 26, 2011. Note: Since the Chinese cyber attacks of 2009, 'Night Dragon,' Jim Lewis of CSIS stated that espionage persist daily-hourly as massive amount of critical data... and design on US nuclear facilities, submarine programs, advanced jet fighters, electric grid and pipeline systems, and NASA has been exfiltrated.

Insider non-technical factors, characteristics and risk indicators for security threats –

+ Non-US cititzen   + Access to classified information
+ Major life change   + High level of computer skills and knowledge
+ Credit/debt problems   + System administrator rights and access
+ Intermittent work history   + Past or current arrest/criminal activity
+ Legal issues   + Strong interest in Blackhat community
+ Family/ marriage issues   + Political ideology[51]

Nation-State Defense:

Who will defend America from a cyber-attack? While there is much talk of, and even creation of, new cyber-focused units in the military and various agencies, the fact remains that the bulk of our anti-cyber resources, directed at all levels — national, state, and local — are consumed by the national level in two broad buckets. First in the primary emphasis and budgeting of technology-intelligence-espionage — in FY11-12 amounting to over $100 billion; and the second, hardening the military and security networks while developing the skills and capabilities to launch an offensive attack. Admiral Mike McConnell, former head of the NSA noted, "All the offensive cyber capability the US can muster won't matter if no one is defending the nation from cyber-attack." One analyst observed, "Cyber warfare is an arms race that cannot be won by defense alone."[52]

While clearly recognized as critical to the security of the nation, the problem of a coordinated defense and recovery efforts for the expansive systems of grids

---

51 J. L. Krofcheck and M. G. Gelles, *Behavioral Consultation in Personnel Security: Training and Reference Manual for Personnel Security Professionals*. Fairfax: Yarrow Associates, 2005. Note: the "political ideology" was added by the author.

52 James A. Lewis, "Cybersecurity: Assessing the Immediate Threat to the United States," House of Representatives Committee on Oversight and Government Reform, May 25, 2011; Scott J. Shackelford, "State Responsibility for Cyber Attacks: Competing Standards for a Growing Problem," Tallinn: Proceedings-Conference on Cyber Conflict, 2010, p. 200; S. W. Korns and J. E. Kastenberg, "Georgia's Cyber Left Hook," *Parameters*, Winter 2008, pp. 60-76.

in electricity, oil and gas, and water supply — which directly impact the local level — remains unresolved. While the technology and operations of the US military are being employed to protect the US military, which most definitely needs to be done in the wake of external hacking, computers at most other government entities (.gov), the nation's industrial, commercial and financial base (.com), and critical research (.edu) are not protected! This is partly due to the fact that still too few know of the full extent of the threat and ramifications of cyber-attacks.[53]

The NSA, US Cyber Command, and the joint services mission prior to 2010 was to defend DOD priorities, and there were few or no plans to defend civilian infrastructure, notwithstanding the fact that the military and government at all levels is vastly dependent on the private sector, and in no more important area that the utility-corporate network of critical infrastructure across the nation. As one observer noted, "Though it is called the 'Defense' Department, if called on to defend the US homeland from cyber-attack carried out by a foreign power, the half-trillion-dollar-a-year Defense Department would be useless." Thus, domestic defense and response has landed in the office of Homeland Security, who has organizational training abilities but no direct ability to counter, launch, or command a cyber-attack defense or offense at the points where assistance will be most needed, the community level.[54]

> **Cyber-notes**: cyber strategy — Deterrence is *achieved with offensive cyber*, some protected-commercial capabilities, and anchored with US nuclear weapons.[55] *emphasis added

By 2011, the DOD noted that the deterrence posture should consider the current vulnerability of the US economy and government institutions. Noting in a report to Congress, "Cyberspace is a critical enabler of the DOD military,

---

53   Clarke, *Cyber War*, p. 43; Martin Feldstein, "Everyone Should Pay for Cyber Defense," *Wall Street Journal*, April 23, 2012.

54   Clarke, *Cyber War*, pp. 44-5. See also DOD-JCS, "The National Strategy for Cyberspace Operations," Washington, D.C.: DOD, December 2006, classified as 'Secret' when issued, unknown date when status lifted.

55   DOD, DSB, p. 15.

intelligence, business and, *potentially, civil support operations.*"⁵⁶ The inclusion of 'civil support' is due to shifting policy calling for the government to partner with the private sector in what is being labeled the 'whole-of-government strategy.' The policy is based on five distinct and interrelated strategic initiatives: cyberspace is an operational domain, harden networks and systems, partner to develop a nationally integrated approach to cyber-security, build robust ties and information sharing with US allies, and enhance cyber workforce coupled with enabling rapid technological innovation.⁵⁷

The sum total for the deterrence of malicious activity in cyberspace relies on two principal mechanisms: denying an adversary's objectives in real time and, if necessary, imposing costs on an adversary for aggression. Motivated successful systems breaches can have catastrophic consequences and trigger cascading effects across critical infrastructure sectors. The report notes that the US "will discourage adversaries from attacking or exploiting our networks", but gives no solutions on how this will be done given stealth and attribution, and concludes that any state attempting such a strategy would be taking a "grave risk."⁵⁸

If our intent is to be prepared in this new cyber-age, and if the main goal of the state is to avoid war in general, it must maintain an offensive capability that is second to none and it must develop a robust and credible strategy of deterrence. Defending against threats to our security requires networks that are secure, resilient, and trusted. In so defending, any such threats could be perceived as American interference in our relationship with the PRC and their view in China of national security. Thus by 2010, the upper echelons of the Chinese military and Politburo agreed on one clear transformational objective to "continue

---

56 DOD, "Department of Defense Cyberspace Policy Report," Washington, D.C.: November 2011. Note: emphasis added.

57 Secretary Leon Panetta, "Remarks on Cybersecurity to the Business Executives for National Security," New York City, October 11, 2012, www.defense.gov ; DOD, "Department of Defense Strategy for Operating in Cyber Space," Washington, D.C.: July 2011; Mark R. Shulman, "Lead Me, Follow Me, or Get Out of My Way: Rethinking and Refining the Civil-Military Relationship," Carlisle Barracks: SSI, September 2012.

58 Ibid.; See also Greg Miller, "Pentagon establishes Defense Clandestine Service, new espionage unit," *Washington Post*, April 23, 2012 and Adam Entous, Pentagon Creates New Spy Service in Revamp," *Wall Street Journal*, April 24, 2012. Note: The DOD created the 'Defense Clandestine Service' with few details given.

efforts to transform military training [and deployment] based upon mechanized warfare to training based on information warfare" — cyber. However, posturing defense on raw strength and assurance of a kinetic response is one of the most important postulates of Chinese military strategist Sun Tzu; he states that if you want to prevent an attack of your enemy, you must show him all the disadvantages of such a decision.[59]

To accomplish this, the China National Defense policy states they will "leap-frog" military science and technical development and gain a leg up on all competition and potential adversaries by whatever clandestine means possible. It must always be remembered that on the global stage, there will always be a latent animosity between the United States and China. Among super-powers, this is in no way unique or surprising, and will be the defining basis of all relationships — diplomatic, commercial, technological, and military — now and into the next century. Both nations share a profound sense of national exceptionalism and a sense of entitlement among nations. And lately, China has been doing a better job of projecting a nationalistic pride and a broader role globally (though it is not completely accurate), without invoking the age-old threat of the formerly hostile "Chinese nationalism," and within bounds have become the poster-child for Joseph Nye's coining of global 'Soft Power.'[60]

Rogue State Assault:

A rogue state is equally problematic and at times more dangerous. The countries that fall into the category include Iran, North Korea, Syria, Cuba, Somalia, and Venezuela. There are three distinctive aspects that set rogue states apart in their threat level. First, there is little dialog and few enforceable treaties between the rogue players and the rest of the world. They each are isolated in some fashion

---

59 Department of Defense, "Strategy for Operating in Cyberspace," Washington, D.C.: DOD, July 2011; DOD, DSB, p. 15. See also Federal Ministry of the Interior, "Cyber Security Strategy for Germany," Berlin: February 2011.

60 William J. Lynn, "Defending a New Domain," Foreign Affairs, September 2010, pp. 97-109; Fritz, "How China will use Cyber Warfare to Leapfrog in Military Competitiveness,'" pp. 40-5. See also Scobell etal, Chinese Lessons from Other Peoples' Wars, Carlisle Barracks: SSI, November 2011; Wolf, "The Strategy Behind China's Expansion," Wall Street Journal, October 9, 2013.

from the mainstream, motivated by strong nationalist education and causes, anti-American doctrine, and/or religious fanaticism.[61] Furthermore, some rogue state have a survivalist mentality which emboldens them to maximize use of cyber options.

An evolving cyber threat is the wide use of 'spam.' While once viewed as a nuisance, the nature of spam has changed. India is the top source of spam distribution. Spam is used to broadly target phishing scams, styled to fool end users with "crafty social-engineering messages" that pose as legitimate business. Breaches have been further expanded to include fake banking alerts that prompt users to provide confidential data. In addition to banks, e-commerce sites as well as sites in healthcare, universities, governments, gamers, and the supply chain are increasingly more vulnerable. These threats, combined with the spread of open source social media, will continue to grow in volume and sophistication. IBM, in their detailed *X-Force 2012: Trend and Risk Report*, noted that 46% of security incidents occurred in the U.S as compared to 8% in the United Kingdom and 3% in Australia.[62]

Second, the rogue states are active in creating means to disrupt their précised enemies. This is primarily done by efforts to gain like-minded allies, such as Venezuelan efforts to influence Nicaragua and Bolivia; and Iranian and Russian support of Syria. A more troubling trend is the effort by Iran and North Korea to develop offensive cyber-attack capabilities and to weaponize nuclear fuels they otherwise claim are being used for peaceful purposes. Non-state actors operating within hostile nations, such as al Qaeda, Hezbollah and Hamas have also shown capabilities to employ cyber attacks. Russia, Iran, India, and China have all provided technical information and training.[63]

---

61 Ball, "China's Cyber Warfare Capabilities," pp. 92-97; Liff, *Cyber War*, pp. 409-412, 422-3.

62 IBM X-Force 2012: Trend and Risk report, March 2013, pp. 6-8, 43-8. Note: Nearly 50% of the relevant websites now link to a social network platform.

63 James M. Lindsay and Ray Takeyb, "When Iran Gets the Bomb," *Foreign Affairs*, March 2010, pp. 33-49. See also Charles Billo and Welton Chang, "Cyber Warfare: An Analysis of the Means and Motivations of Selected Nation States" Hanover: ISTS Dartmouth College, December 2004 and Paul Rosenzweig, *Cyber Warfare: How Conflicts in Cyberspace are Challenging America and Changing the World*, Denver: Praeger, 2013.

> **Cyber-notes**: Two-thirds of US firms report they have been the victims of cyber security incidents or information breaches.[64]

The third component is that each of the rogue states seeks recognition and justification for what they are doing. In so doing, they are willing to function as surrogate agents for other nations such as China or Russia — who will provide them financial aid, and technical assistance, as well as block Western efforts to curb disruptions in other nations or advance production of nuclear weapons.[65] Further ties include strategic raw materials such as Iran's daily supply of over 500,000 barrels of oil a day to China. Thus, the attitudes the rogue states harbor toward production of nuclear fuel, sourcing of raw materials, and the lack of transparency reflects the challenges with the rise of cyber threats. The employment of cyber espionage is critical to securing both the design data to supplement the existing programs, as well as to probe weaknesses in those they deem as enemies. These governments further empower, encourage, and threaten non-governmental persons and industries to do their cyber dirty work. By 2012, internet users in China reached over 500 million (the population of the United States is only 312 million), with many of these non-governmental Chinese home grown cyber-warriors, often referred to as 'netizens', internet citizens, motivated by government promoted nationalist causes and dogma.[66] The DOD, CIA, NSA, and DHS have maintained a high level of concern over the growing rogue threat, "while states have the greatest capabilities, non-state actors are more likely to initiate a catastrophic attack." Available intelligence released in the public domain demonstrates such states with hostile intent have and will continue to be monitored for the intentions and threats, yet the fact remains rogue states pose a clear and present danger.[67]

---

64 DLS, National Preparedness Report, March 12, 2012, p. 20.

65 Evan Ellis, *China-Latin America Military Engagement: Good Will, Good Business, and Strategic Position*, Caralsis Barracks: SSI, August 2011.

66 According to Steve Ballmer, CEO of Microsoft, as of January 2011 it was estimated that 90% of Microsoft users in the People's Republic of China use pirated software. www.networkworld.com/news/2-11/012111

67 Desmond Ball, "China's Cyber Warfare Capabilities," *Security Challenges*, Winter 20122, pp. 94-97; Wayne Ma, "Beijing's Oil Imports From Iran Rebound," *Wall Street Journal*, June

And some cyber attacks have immediate real-world implications, such as the April 23, 2013 tweet from the "Syrian Electronic Army" (with a strong likelihood of assistance from Iran) via the AP news outlet that the White House had been attacked and president Obama wounded! Of course, it was all false, yet the Dow crashed 143 points, causing the loss of some $136 billion in less than three minutes. The AP scrambled to reduce any hysteria, immediately tweeting "Please ignore the AP tweet on explosions, we've been hacked" and slowly the markets recovered once the bogus hackers were detected — a clear case of quickly identifying the attack and responding. Such an event could have devastating impact if it was planned to cascade across multiple markets, financial centers, and central banks.[68]

Rogue hacker intrusion:

What started in the early 1980s as amateur hacking, so-called 'script kiddies' trying to break into local computer systems among high school and college students for bragging rights and peer recognition, has ballooned into blatant criminal activity on a tremendously large scale. In Ken Thompson's early 1984 article on hacking, he stressed, "The acts performed by these kids are vandalism at best and probably trespass and theft at worst. It is only the inadequacy of the criminal code that saves the hackers from serious prosecution."[69] This earlier generation was weaned on Star Trek programs developed by Micromosaics Productions and Apple to give the user a hands-on look at interactive text simulation and programming. While amateur hacking continues to this day, the concern is over

---

22, 2012; Hai-Cheng Chu et al, "Next Generation of terrorism: Ubiquitous Cyber terrorism with the Accumulation of all Intangible Fears," *Journal of Universal Computer Science*, vol. 15, 2009, pp. 2391-2404; Sunny Le, "485 million Netizens Strong: The Demographics of China's Internet Rise," July 28, 2012, www.techrice.com/2011/china ;Nye, "Nuclear Lessons for Cyber Security?" *Strategic Studies*, Winter 2011, p. 22.

68   Steven Stalinsky, ""China Isn't the Only Source of Cyberattacks," *Wall Street Journal*, May 22, 2013; "Syrian Electronic Army linked to hack attack on AP Twitter," www.dailymail.co.uk/news , April 24, 2013. See also US House of Representatives, Committee on Financial Services "Cybersecurity: Threats to the Financial Sector," 112 Cong., 1st sess., Serial No. 112-60, September 14, 2011.

69   Ken Thompson, "Reflections on Trusting Trust," *Communications of the ACM*, August 1984, pp. 763. Note: Thompson's conclusion was that breaking into computer systems has had no social stigma attached.

the malicious attacks, seeking not fame but financial gain from banks and credit card companies as well as the next generation of private hackers that are driven by "social" and "political" motivations.[70]

In the compact monograph *Hacking*, Tim Jordon reminds us that, "Crackers are the transgressors of hacking" and hacktivism emerged in the mid-1990s, initially as a form of electronic protest:

> Hacktivism is produced by taking forward the collapse of a technological-social distinction in computer and network technologies and applying it to politics outside of the information-soaked spaces created by computers and networks. Hacktivism takes cracking and open source techniques and cultures and applies them to the politics that dominate the from pages of our newspapers — globalization, human rights, ecology — rather than the politics that dominate discussions in the backrooms of IT support.[71]

The cyber-crime groups, generally known as 'crackers,' have targeted the financial sector at all levels of entry. A decade ago, there was only adequate security for the trillions of dollars that flowed electronically in financial transactions and commerce, yet today one of the biggest expenditures of financial institutions is on systems protection and fending off thousands of anonymous criminal hackers per week. Russian criminals now profit more from cybercrimes than drugs. Furthermore, over 1,000 FBI advance cyber agents and forensic examiners are targeting cyber criminals forming private, trusted, and well organized groups to conduct a range of cyber-crimes. One example is malware embedded on chips to exfiltrate information from computer networks, which has resulted in a sharp rise in theft of personally identifiable information (PII), a key to future cyber hacking. And industry-wide reports disclose only the bare surface

---

70 Jordan, *Hacking*, pp. 29-31. See also Cavelty, *Cyber-Security and Threat Politics*, p. 21 and Paramount Pictures, Computer Software Division. *Star Trek: The Kobayashi Alterative*, New York: Simon and Schuster, 1985.

71 Ibid., p. 71.; CACI, "Cyber Treats to National Security," September 2011, p. 11. See also www.2600.com.

of the intrusions by these rogue individuals and groups hacking personal and financial systems worldwide.[72]

While dated by two decades, "Solar Sunrise," is a great case study and a story worth retelling. The rogue attack occurred from 1 to 26 February 1998 by three teenagers, one Israeli and two from Cloverdale, California is a classic case of an intrusion, notwithstanding the extent of their savvy and success, gone wild and very wrong. The script kiddies targeted an electronic assault on the elements of the Department of Defense, and the invasion was hidden through computer accounts in the United Arab Emirates, who had no role whatsoever. Using off the shelf code available from a university web site and gutsy persistence, the hackers exploited the operating system's vulnerabilities, to first determine if vulnerabilities existed — they did — and to implant a sniffer program to gather passwords and data and a backdoor program to retrieve the data once collected. All considered very basic computer hacking procedures in today's cyber world. But the kids were able the penetrate eleven US Navy, Marine Corps, and Air Force computer systems, as well as NASA and DOE sites worldwide, and made it appear the intrusions were coming from five countries. Given the fact that the US was involved in military action in the Persian Gulf, the government launched a "massive" international manhunt involving a dozen federal agencies to stem what some at CIA viewed as the initial stages of a cyber-attack by a hostile nation. — It proved not to be. In the end, the teenagers were arrested and pled guilty.[73] (Let's hope these kids are now working for us!)

---

72 Gordon M. Snow, FBI Cyber Division, "The Cybersecurity Threat," Senate Judiciary Committee, Subcommittee on Crime and Terrorism, Washington, D.C.: April 12, 2011, www.fbi.gov/news/testimony/cybersecurity . See also GAO, CYBERCRIME," June 2007 and Jackson, *Predicting Malicious Behavior*, pp. 15-22. See also Egmantec, Internet Security Threat Report: Threats for 2010, April 2011. The underground crime economy will pay anywhere from 7 cents to $100 for each stolen credit card number.

73 John A. Serabain, "Cyber Threats and the US Economy," Statement to Joint Economic Committee on Cyber Threats and the US Economy, Washington, D.C.: February 23, 2000, www.cia.gov/news-information ; Michael A. Vatis, "NIPC Cyber Threat Assessment," Statement to Senate judiciary Committee on Technology and Terrorism, Washington, D.C.; October 6, 1999. www.fas.org/irp/congress/1999

> **Cyber-notes**: DOD concern with the rogue attacker: while states have the greatest cyber capabilities, non-state actors are more likely to initiate an anonymous catastrophic attack[74]

While the DOD called Solar Sunrise "the most organized and systematic attack to date [2001], they and the Justice Department [due largely to the fact at the time statutory restrictions and void of cyber laws] dismissed the seriousness and claimed no classified information was compromised." Notwithstanding, prime US sites and systems were vulnerable. A report to Congress was a bit more blunt, noting there were no effective warning systems, intrusion detection system were insufficient, and the overwhelming government bureaucracy "hinders an effective and timely response."[75]

Comments from the postmortem of Solar Sunrise are telling. "We assumed it was an Iraqi attack," noted Richard Clarke, then national coordinator of security and counter terrorism at the White House, ". . . if two 14-year-olds could do that, think about what a determined foe could do?" And then, Prime Minister Benjamin Netanyahu, who fully cooperated with US law enforcement and intelligence agencies, "swelled like a proud father," when he learned one of the hackers was Israeli and said it was "damn good!"[76]

No longer adventurous script kiddies, the rogue hacker has evolved into a global cabal of interlinked chat-rooms, information sharing, data mining, defalcation of financial institutions, and organized crime. As an asymmetric platform, cyber favors the lone individual. And those loners can attract a following, such as Anonymous, WikiLeaks, the Web Ninjas, and LulzSec as well as a multitude of lesser-known hackers worldwide. These hackers or hacktivists have stepped well beyond simple insider bragging rights for cracking, escalating attacks for

---

74   Nye, "Nuclear Lessons for Cyber Security?" *Strategic Studies,* Winter 2011, p. 22

75   Hildreth, "Cyberwarfare," CRS, June 19, 2001.

76   William M. Arkin, "Sunrise, Sunset," www.washingtonpost.com March 29, 1999. Note: For an estimate of the economic impact of cybercrime see GAO, CYBERCRIME," pp. 15-18.

example, on the CIA, Rupert Murdoch's British newspaper empire, News International, and against Britain's Serious Organized Crime Agency (SOCA).[77]

One such loner, the Jester, is a rogue, self-styled doer of good, hacking against antagonists at Anonymous, militant Jihadist web propaganda sites, the Westboro Baptist Church in Topeka, Kansas (who harassed family members of deceased US military personnel), and the Libyan online press. In the case of Libya, Jester planted false news stories intended to break the support of troops and followers of Muammar Gaddafi. The Jester's ability to remain anonymous during 2011-2012, while competing underworld hackers work around the clock to out-him, as well as a multitude of government agencies, is concerning to many, resulting in one observer to noting, "this [cyber] domain is one that favors David over Goliath."[78]

A similar rogue conflict is a cyber exchange between Anonymous and the northern Mexican drug cartel, Los Zetas. Following the kidnapping of a member of Anonymous, the global hacking group, along with a cell in Acuna, a border City across from Del Rio, Texas, threatened that they would expose the location, personal information, and names of Zeta members. The kidnapped member was soon returned, but Anonymous has remained engaged in cyber operations against the Zetas. With both organizations concerned about their image and the secrecy of their operations, the stakes are high and potentially deadly. The role of Anonymous acting as cyber-vigilantes opens a new level of underworld crime and attacks.[79]

---

[77] "British LulzSec hackers admit CIA Cyber attacks," June 25, 2012, http://phys.org/news/2012 ; T.J. O'Connor, "The Jester Dynamic: A Lesson in Asymmetric Unmanaged Cyber Warfare," SANS Institute, December 30, 2011; The capture and conviction of the massive credit card cyber theft by the crime group known as "Western Express" is chronicled in Jeff Pohlman and Andrea Day, "Busted! Inside one massive cybercrime ring," September 12, 2013, www.finance.yahoo.comnews/busted . See also DA, New York County, press release, "Vadim Vassilenko and Western Express Plead Guilty to Laundering for Global Cybercrime Ring," www.manhattanda.org/node/3574 .

[78] T. J. O'Conner, "The Jester Dynamic: A Lesson in Asymmetric Unmanaged Cyber Warfare," Sans Institute, 2012; Breen and Geltzer, "Asymmetric Strategies as Strategies of the Strong," *Parameters*, Spring 2011, pp. 41-55. See also Dr. K, *The Real Hacking Handbook*, London: Carlton, 2011.

[79] Paul R. Kan, "Cyberwar in the Underworld: Anonymous vs. Los Zetas in Mexico," *Yale Journal of International Affairs*, Winter 2013; Kan, "Anonymous vs. Los Zetas: The Revenge

Cyber Blackout

So what has changed? The cyber game, the espionage, and the crimes have only escalated to become more ubiquitous and the vulnerabilities compounded. The ability to maintain deniability, lower risk, and cause disruptions is demonstrated by the Stuxnet worm.

Operation Olympic Games

In this regard, the Stuxnet worm attack in mid-2010 is the most dangerous cyber-attack to date — causing extensive destruction at an Iranian nuclear processing facility. While only a few nations have the ability to launch a Stuxnet-like attack, the cascading disruption of critical infrastructure could cripple any region or state. Created by the NSA in partnership with the CIA and Israeli intelligence, Stuxnet avoided detection for over five years. It was not just a piece of malicious code, but a sophisticated targeted mission, a cyber-attack. "By surreptitiously taking control on an industrial control link known as a SCADA (Supervisory Control and Data Acquisition) system, the sophisticated worm was able to damage about a thousand centrifuges used to enrich nuclear material."[80] Analysis of this attack and the copy-cats to follow will continue for years. Security is only as strong as its weakest link, and the best attackers will look for and go for the weakest link. Total cyber security is nearly impossible, as is noted by new robust hacking forays. In May 2012, the 'Flame' worm was made public, as extensive DDoS incidents appeared across the Middle East seemingly targeted against Iran.[81]

Indications are this is the fourth time, following Stuxnet, Duqu, and Wiper, that Iran has been targeted with sophisticated data-mining cyber viruses to attack

---

of the Hacktivists," June 27, 2013, http://smalwarsjournal.com ; Max G. Manwaring, "A 'New' Dtnamic in the Western hemisphere Security Environment: The Mexican Zetas and Other Private Armies," Carlisle: SSI, September 20019; Josh Buch, "Zetas have Anonymous Foes," *San Antonio Express-News*, June 1, 2013.

80   James Bamford, "The Silent War," *Wired*, July 2013, pp. 90-9. For a detailed account of Stuxnet see Kim Zetter, *Countdown to Zero Day: Stuxnet and the Launch of the World's First Digital Weapon*, New York: Crown Publishers, 2014.

81   David Martin, "Cyber Computer Wars [Flame]," New York: CBS Evening News, May 29, 2012; "Cyber-warfare: Seek and Hide," *The Economist*, June 9, 2012, p. 65; Lockhart and Gohn, "Utility Cyber Security," 2011, p. 4.

61

programmable logic controls at heavily fortified nuclear facilities at Natanz. The Flame virus was reported by the Kaspersky Labs in Russia, an IT security firm retained by the United Nations' International telecommunications Union (ITU) to investigate malware incidents. Cyber security experts in the field have concluded that the complexity and duration of the strike as well, as its spy capabilities, means it's more likely from a nation and not a rogue group, since there seems to be no clear monetizing function, such as bank penetration or defalcation and credit card theft. Earlier cyber intrusions have planted viruses to disrupt internal internet service, monitor the Iranian oil ministry, and launch computer espionage to transfer massive amounts of data. Flame, a windows-based cyber-espionage tool, is considered to be 20 times larger than the Stuxnet virus and special encryption hallmarks enable it to steal and store screen snapshots, log messaging conversations, and scan Bluetooth-active devices. The full extent of the damage may not be known for months or years. The *New York Times* reported sources close to Iran's leaders said, "That the virus was tantamount to an attack."[82]

In the wake of the media disclosures on US cyber programs, calls were made for an FBI investigation to determine who leaked 'Olympic Games.' In today's Washington, "The half-life of a hot secret is measured not even in days but in hours."[83] A string of US cyber related breaches to include top secret data on penetration of *al Qaeda* operations in Yemen, details of the search for and elimination of bin Laden, the use of unmanned drone (UAV) attacks on a secret "kill list", and the Stuxnet cyberworm disclosure raised red flags in Washington on how our security is handled and by whom. Senator John McCain, a former ranking member of the Senate Armed Services Committee, strongly protested the administration's "massive security breach" of ongoing operations that, if compromised, could put individuals and assets at risk.[84]

---

82   David Danger, "Israeli Worm Called Crucial In Iran Nuclear Delay," *New York* Times, January 15, 2011; Farnaz Fassihi and Paul Sonne, "Sophisticated Virus Infects Computers in Iran, Mideast," *Wall Street Journal, May 30, 2012;* Thomas Erdbrink, "Iran Confirms Attack by Virus That Collects Information," *New York Times,* May 30, 2012.

83   Graham Allison, "The Cuban Missile Crisis at 50," *Foreign Affairs,* July 2012, p. 16; Zetter, *Countdown to Zero Day*, pp. 308-370.

84   Senator John McCain, "Stuxnet Virus Info Leak," live Interview, Fox News: On the Record, 10:10 PM CST, June 12, 2012; Peggy Noonan, "Who Benefits from the 'Avalanche of

> **Cyber-notes**: Digital-quick transparency can unmask evils or unearth secrets. Information that is massed to protect us can quickly be used against us. Secrets meant to be seen by almost no one can in minutes be leaked to everyone. [85]

The leak of secure information on Stuxnet and related top secret projects has fueled broader discussion on controls for cyberspace that are not favorable to the United States. Activists are calling for a global forum, such as the United Nations and/or the World Trade Organization, to gather governments to negotiate a ban on developing cyber-weapons. The United States wants no part of a ban or regulation by third parties on cyberspace. In a related event, Google, who has been in a confrontation with Beijing since 2010, declared in early June 2012 that it would post online warnings to users whose systems, accounts, or computers are deemed to be targeted by what it believes state-sponsored cyber assaults, with following pop-up message: "Warning: We believe state-sponsored attackers may be attempting to compromise your account or computer. Protect yourself now."[86] Google's actions are counter to claims that creditable attribution is not possible in real time, resulting in the 2011 DOD Cyber Policy Report to Congress to conclude:

> There is currently no international consensus regarding the definition of a "cyber weapon." The often low cost of developing malicious code and the high number and variety of actors in cyberspace make the discovery and tracking of malicious cyber tools difficult. Most of the technology used in this

---

Leaks'?" *Wall Street* Journal, June 16, 2012. See also Sanger, *Confront and Conceal*, pp. 188-225 and James J. Carafano, *Wiki at War*, College State: Texas A&M University Press, 2012, pp. 120-1.

85 Carafano, *Wiki at War*, p. 14. See also, Sean Collins and Stephen McCombie, "Stuxnet: the emergence of a new cyber weapon and its implications," *Journal of Policing, Intelligence and Terrorism*, April 2012, pp. 80-91.

86 Gordon Crovitz, "Google Fights Back in China," *Wall Street Journal*, June 11, 2012, p. 11; "Free to Choose," *The Economist*, October 6, 2012, pp. 70-1.

context is inherently dual-use, and even software might be minimally repurposed for malicious action.

The interconnected nature of cyberspace poses significant challenges for applying some of the legal framework development for specific physical domains. The law of armed conflict and customary international law, however, provide a strong basis to apply such norms to cyberspace governing responsible state behavior. Significant multinational work remains to clarify the application of norms and principles of customary international laws to cyberspace... the development of norms for state conduct does not require a reinvention of customary international law nor render existing norms obsolete.[87]

To address the growing concern on cyber incidents, the US Senate tried and failed to pass a broad cyber law in August 2012 which addressed a number of key issues, ranging from liability to which agency or multi-level council would have the lion's share of responsibility. Agency turf battles between the DHS, DOD, FBI, NSA, and others could delay a final measure for some time. The White House, in response to the inaction of Congress exercised executive fiat to issue a Presidential Policy Directive 20 in late 2012, a classified document, which outlines protocols for the NSA and US military to thwart cyberattacks as well as the guidelines to launch an offensive attack. Full details are yet to be released.[88]

---

87 DOD, "Department of Defense Cyberspace Policy Report," November 2011, pp. 8-9. See also "Harry Reid's Virus," *Wall Street Journal*, November 16, 2012.

88 Presidential Policy Directive 20, White House, Washington, D.C.: October 2012; Ellen Nakashima, "Obama signs secret directive to help thwart cyberattacks," *Washington Post*, November 14, 2012; "White House Says No Data Were Lost in Cyberattack," *Wall Street Journal*, October 2, 2012; "Obama's Cyber Attack" editorial, Ibid, September 24, 2012. Note: release of PPD-20 coincided with DOD Secretary Pinetta's presentation in New York City on October 12, 2012, in which he discussed at length the cyber attack on ARAMCO operations in Saudi Arabia.

Cyber Blackout

> **Cyber-notes**: There is almost universal agreement that the US faces a catastrophic threat from cyberattacks by terrorist, hackers and spies. Even with the consensus about vulnerabilities in US networks, and with hundreds of billions of dollars at stake, Congress failed to pass cybersecurity legislation that was four years in the making and sponsored by both parties.[89]

The swift action by the White House on PPD 20 may in fact been an action long in the making. While we question the levels of our cyber security, the world-at-large also has intention on the future direction of the net. Without US Congressional action and quite possibly in response to the International Telecommunication Union (ITU) efforts at their Dubai conference to give sweeping powers to governments to censor the internet delays have gradually mounted. Late in 2012, a dozen countries, including America, voted down what amounted to a grab for a third party governance of the internet. These efforts to "politesse" the Internet, such as the nascent German Pirate Party focused on net-policy issues, will continue to gain an active voice among users and governments. Notably, it was the Internet activist, comprised of consumer groups, hackers, researchers, and those who call for transparency and demanded an open Internet protocol, who celebrated. [90]

---

89 Eric Engleman and Michael Riley, "Political Gridlock Leaves US Facing Cyber Pearl Harbor," www.bloomberg.bom, November 15, 2012. See also "Thousands Seen Dying if Terrorist Attack US Power Grid," ibid, November 14, 2012.

90 "Everything is connected," *The Economist*, January 5, 2013. See also Lawrence Lessig, *Code and Other Laws of Cyberspace*, Stanford: Basic Books, 1999; Yochai Benkler, *The Wealth of Networks*, New Haven: Yale University Press, 2007; Brett Frischmann, *Infrastructure: The Social Value of Shared Resources*, Oxford: Oxford University Press, 2012; and Editorial, President Obama, "Taking the Cyberattack Threat Seriously," *Wall Street Journal*, July 20, 2012. 'Hoss' Cartwright quote: Sydney Freedberg, "Military Debate Who Should Pull the Trigger for a Cyber Attack," May 22, 2012, http://defense.aol.com/2012/05/22

THREE
Supply Chain Meltdown

Gaining unauthorized advantage, control, and/or access to systems and the information they contain through manipulation and deployment of technology in proximity by cooperative/witting vendors, agents, hackers, or unilaterally at any point in the supply chain between the manufacturer, shipper, and end user.
Comprehensive National Cybersecurity Initiative

America has no effective system of supply-chain [security] checks.
The Economist, August 4, 2012

There are few aspects of our expanding technological driven world more co-dependent on cyber connectivity than the realm of global logistics — the multifaceted supply chain. Historically, US supply chains remained largely immune to threat because its most critical features were located in North America. During the past two decades, however, we moved from a just-in-time scheme and 'postponement' to a near virtually connected built-to-order response to buyers' needs. Globalization continues to compromise the supply chain's immunity. Sourcing of inputs to real time industrial drop shipments has transformed both today's Fortune 500 companies and their customers to become less manufacturers and more master assemblers. Manufacturers form a giant global ecosystem that has grown faster than the overall economy. The magnitude of this ecosystem is driven by innovative ideas, new technologies, the Internet, and mass markets. The world's factories and interwoven networks produce some 10 billion different products per year, all demanding access to global supply chain markers. In addition to the movement of raw materials, components and manufactured products, the supply chain includes a vast infrastructure network of pipe lines, ports, terminals, distribution hubs, railroads, transportation corridors, sea lanes, and air freight.[1]

Cyber-attacks on logistics centers and transportation nodes have raised a new level of awareness worldwide. Our supply chain systems are not secure because they were not designed to be secure. Thus, supply chain insecurity is both hard to detect and expensive to defend against. The advent of the modern day hacker and real time communications has changed the global security supply chain landscape.[2]

Assembly plants and the corresponding supply chain links of the future will strive to be more efficient (no idle inventory) and reduce cost as suppliers relocate to manufacturing centers. This realignment should reap lower prices for consumers. The lean supply chain has completely decentralized manufacturing as we have known it. Although leaner and faster, the global supply chain is more exposed to asymmetric threats. In 2012, nearly 75 percent of companies experienced at least one supply chain disruption.[3] Managing the risk of both natural disasters and manmade disruptions are critical components to secure the wellbeing of the U. S. economy. From Amazon's books-on-demand, to Boeing's special order aircraft, the logistical supply chain and real-time sourcing drives the world economy.[4] See chart 3-1

---

[1] Peter Marsh, *The New Industrial Revolution: Consumers, Globalization and the End of Mass Production*. New Haven: Yale University Press, 2012; "Manufacturing: The Latest Chapter," *The Economist*, September 15, 2012, pp. 79-80; Elisabeth Bumiller and Thom Shanker, "Panetta Warns of Dire Threat of Cyberattack on US" October 11, 2012, www.nytimes.com; Julie Sneider, "Railroads gear up to protect computers from hackers," September 2012, www.progressiverailroad.com . Note: Postponement-based supply chain is characterized by a combination of features, to include management of inventory carrying expenses, short customer lead times, uncertain demand, and demand for specialty design (built-to-order) or real-time modifications. The prime intent of postponement is a combination of flexibility and, customization, and cost savings.

[2] Georgia Institute of Technology, "Emerging Cyber Treats Report 2013," pp. 4-5, www.gtisc.gatech.edu; "The Physical Internet: A Survey of Logistics," *The Economist*, June 17, 2006, pp. 1-20.

[3] "Global Supply Chain Disruptions Increasing in Frequency, Consequences," January 10, 2013, www.securitymagizune.com

[4] Peter Finch, "Supply Chain Risk Management," *Supply Chain* Management, Vol. 9, 2004, pp. 183-196; Bill Powell, "The Global Supply Chain: So Very Fragile," December 12, 2011,

FIGURE 3-1: SUPPLIER DIVERSITY

Sources, Lead Time, and Suppliers

	Suppliers	Supplier Countries of Origin	Projected Lead Time	Total Sales
Boeing 787 Dreamliner	Tier One - 50 Tier Two - 289	22	Up to 7 years	$68.7 billion
Lockheed Martin F-35 Joint Strike Fighter	600	30	Up to 5 years	$46 bill total; $6 bill F-35
John Deere	30,000	65	6 months	$32 billion
Northrop Grumman USS Bush Carrier	Tier One - 150 Tier Two - 2,200	100	6 years	
General Electric Transformers	500,000	60	7-8 weeks*	$147 billion
Ford F-150	2000		12-14 weeks	$136 billion

*For a Distribution Transformer

http://tech.fortunr.cnn.com; Tersa Wu, et al, "A model for inbound supply risk analysis," *Computers in Industry*, 2006, pp. 350-365.

> **Cyber-notes**: rare earth metals — a collection of 17 chemical elements highly important to electronics and technological manufacturing and advancements, of which some 97% of these strategic metals are mined in China

The fragility of the complex global logistical network is measured in seconds, not days. Time is money. Due to the interconnected nature of the supply chain networks, the economic impact due to interruptions can be sudden and costly. These disruptions impact revenue, market share, and inflate cost. This was dramatically demonstrated in the disruption of the automotive industry demand for parts following the 2011 tsunami that struck Japan, earthquakes in New Zealand, and floods in Thailand. Referred to as a "Black Swan" event in Asia, the scale and wrath of these natural disasters exposed the vulnerabilities of a tight trans-global supply chain. Delays in shipments of unique components ranging from paint pigment to dashboard computers brought production and assembly lines to a halt. An estimated one-third of global hard disk drive production remains dependent on factories in Thailand. Any disruption impacts PC makers worldwide. Natural disasters demonstrated the weakness of the lean logistical supply chain.[5]

Super Storm Sandy in late 2012, while not a cyber-event, demonstrated how easy it is to disrupt a lean supply chain and how necessary it is to create contingency plans. The Northeast remained devastated long after the storm had passed, with critical supply chain infrastructure disrupted for weeks. In like fashion, cyber connectivity is today's backbone of the world's financial, investment, and logistical systems. The guiding principles going forward will involve a more robust approach to risk mitigation, on-shoring of manufacturing, and

---

5 Ben Bland and Robin Kwong, "Supply chain disruption: sunken ambitions," November 3, 2011; Ruud Bosman, The New Supply Chain Challenge: Risk management in a Global Economy," Windsor: FM Global, 2006, pp. 3-10; Joe Mullich, "The Resilient Supply Chain," *Wall Street Journal*, September 22, 2011. Note: The cumulative loss of the major natural disasters in 2011 — Japan tsunami/quake, Thailand floods, New Zealand quake, United State tornadoes, and Australia floods — alone was estimated at over $300 billion. Black Swan: surprise rare event(s) that have a disproportionate impact — *simillima cygro*.

better cooperation between industry and government at all levels to reduce, monitor, mitigate, and recover from threats and disruptions.[6]

Risk

Risk is a broadly discussed topic, yet for our purposes can be defined as three components: *threats*, measured by the degree of *vulnerability*, and resulting impact — *consequences*. Systems protection within the realm of these components shapes the effectiveness of detection and/or response on the profile of probability that a threat will occur. The identification and monitoring of a threat profile is only as strong as a system's underlying vulnerability, the weakest link that can be exploited and compromised with or without the knowledge of those penetrated. The vulnerability assessment for a system is the sum of probabilities for which a particular event is successful in inflicting the intended consequence — i.e. targeted system interruption, disruption, or failure. Herein lies the more complex result of the consequences of a cyber-attack. They can be launched in real time or planted not to be activated until a future time.

Most frustrating of all, these attacks are launched from mostly anonymous sources! The true measure of risk response and mitigation is the degree by which an organization knows its vulnerabilities, defenses, and resilience to possible consequences.[7]

Business risk comes in many forms. In the course of daily commerce, businesses can expect shifting markets, advancing technology, aggressive competitors, fluxuating pricing, changes in government regulations, and transportation delays. Network and infrastructure disasters arise from different sources whether by nature, manmade catastrophes, or internal sabotage. These three scenarios occur daily with little public notice or alarm. These disruptions tend to be localized, quickly contained, and gain little publicity, unless they last for a long

---

6 "Cyber attack bigger threat than Sandy," October 31, 2012, www.wkje.com.

7 Juha Hintsa et al, "Supply Chain Security Management: An Overview," *International Journal of Logistics Systems and Management*, January 2009, pp. 344-355; Paul Kleindorfer and Germaine Saad, "Managing Disruption Risks in Supply Chains," *Production and Operations Management*, 2005, pp. 1-16. See also, John A. Serabian, Jr, Statement to Joint Economic Committee on Cyber Threats and the US Economy, February 23, 2000, www.cia.gov/news

period of time. Today's supply chain risks are measured in terms of the 'physical flow' of goods and raw material. The customer expects reliable on-time delivery. Business has a long track record of managing such risk, yet few have fully prepared for a more massive disruption of cyber-attacks.[8]

CHART 3-2
Supply Chain Risk Matrix: External vs. Internal

EXTERNAL		INTERNAL	
Controllable	**Uncontrollable**	**Controllable**	**Uncontrollable**
Suppliers	natural disasters	IT security	market strength
Legal status	terrorism/war	product QC	accidents
Target Markets	national strikes	cost model	labor strike
Incorporation status	epidemics	staffing levels	staff turn-over
Site location	supply disruption	capacity	rogue hacker
Response plans	economic stability	safety	natural disasters
Cyber training	cyber-attack	risk assessment	cyber-attack

---

8   Covelty, *Cyber-Security and Threat Politics*, pp. 138-140; Hathaway, "Cyber Security," *Intelligencer*, pp. 31-36. See also Sandy Boyson, "The ICT SCRM Community Framework Development Project," College Park: Smith School of Business, University of Maryland, 2012.

Defining risk exposure is the first step toward improving and protecting the supply chain risk management (SCRM) decision awareness and process.[9] The measurement of SCRM risk correlates directly with a clear identification of the sources of risk. There are five sources of supply chain risk: process, control, demand, supply, and environmental. As SCRM becomes more dependent on the networked cyber domain, there is a pervasive link between IT risk and supply chain security (or lack thereof) and reliability. Given the fact that many of the IT network's security threats originate outside of the SCM organization, risk will be increasingly more difficult to monitor and guard against. Both foreign and domestic entities perform "unobtrusive cyber reconnaissance" to determine Internet-accessible computers and infrastructure. Thus, data mining (by criminal hackers, governments, corporations, and rogue hackers) targeting the supply chain network has become more precise. This precision results in both disruption and increased cost to guard against and/or repair damage. The resilience of the supply chain and its ability to adapt to threats will be the focal point of SCRM in years to come.[10]

Cyber-notes — undetectable — counterfeit hardware containing trojanized access built into the firmware or software loaded at the time of assembly, a foreign intelligence service or similar sponsored entity could gain the accesses they seek[11]

The expansive globalization of manufacturing matched by the explosive introduction of new products and the demands for shortened product life cycles resulted in longer supply lines and induced uncertainty. A recent extensive report of the US — China Economic and Security Review Commission stated its concerns bluntly on the potential risk of US portions of the supply chain:

---

9   Jarrellann Filsinger et al, "Supply Chain Risk Management Awareness,'" Armed Forces Communication and Electronics Association Cyber Committee, February 2012, pp. 1-13.

10 G.E. Smith et al, "A critical balance: collaboration and security in the IT-enabled supply chain," *International Journal of production Research*, July 2007, pp. 2595-2613; Martin Christopher and Helen Peck, "Building the Resilient Supply Chain," *The International Journal of logistics Management*, Vol. 14, Num. 2, 2004, pp. 1-13.

11 Krekel et al, "Occupying the Information High Ground," March 7, 2012, p. 89.

The pervasiveness of globally distributed supply chain networks means that virtually every sector of private industry has the potential to be impacted by compromise. The vectors into the telecommunications and integrated circuit (IC) supply chain specifically can come from either upstream (manufacturing channels) or downstream (distribution channels). Each vector presents distinctive opportunities, and also distinctive operational costs, to potential attackers.[12]

Cold War Disruption: The First Logic Bomb

In the Cold War era, predating the cyber era, espionage among the major powers ushered in ongoing efforts to address advantages over adversaries. The CIA, in an operation to sabotage Soviet industry and thwart spies, engaged in industrial espionage by duping Moscow into stealing booby-trapped software (the early birth of malware and the Trogan Horse). The US triggered a spectacular explosion in a Trans-Siberian gas pipeline exporting natural gas to Western Europe. The Soviets unwittingly stole US software programmed with built-in flaws to reset pump speeds and critical valve setting to produce pressures far beyond tolerances acceptable to pipeline joints and welds. Former Secretary of the Air Force Thomas Reed noted, "In order to disrupt the Soviet gas supply, its hard currency earning source from the West, and the internal Russian economy", the embedded software reset pump speeds. The project, personally approved by President Ronald Reagan in January 1982, exceeded all expectations. The resulting explosion from the ruptured pipelines created a worldwide scare that the Soviets had either detonated a nuclear device or had a massive nuclear accident. It was only a massive gas explosion carefully orchestrated by the US and monitored by satellite.[13]

---

12 US-China Economic and Security Review Commission, "Occupying the Information High Ground," p. 11. See also Hai-Cheng et al, "Next Generation of Terrorism: Ubiquitous Cyber Terrorism with the Accumulation of all Intangible Fears," *Journal of Universal Computer Science*, Vol. 15, no. 12, 2009, pp. 2391-2404.

13 Thomas Reed, *At the Abyss: An Insider's History of the Cold War*, New York: Random House Press, 2004, pp. 266-9; "Logic Bomb," seen in "Reducing Systemic Cyber security Risk," OECD/IFP Project, January 14, 2011, p. 24.

Risk reduction is expanding into a global problem demanding a review of norms and enforcement to limit attacks and disruption of systems in both the private and public sectors. In May 2011, the White House announced an "International Strategy for Cyberspace," outlining a proposed framework for better enforcement and deterrence of cyber threats. This framework included: international norms on state behavior, measures that built confidence and enhanced transparency, active and informed diplomacy and global interoperability, protection of digital infrastructure, reliable access, and the building of cyber security capacity and appropriate deterrence. Because the United States invented the Internet and dominated a majority of its technological advancements, many countries remain skeptical about the intentions of the United States.[14]

The Chinese quickly protested US calls for cyber standards, saying they were a mask to advance American technology and companies. Additional uproar related to a concern about enhanced capabilities and cyber deterrence of the military. Despite calls for international cooperation, US officials were slow to convince objectors who wanted to de-emphasize cyberspace as a 'warfighting domain' — which it has been clearly defined as in our national security policy. In the months following, the White House indicated the military role would be minimized and a cyberattack or response would only be used as a "last resort." To insure an environment of risk reduction demands a level of certainty. The rise of the cyber threats daily usher in more questions than answers, thus less trust and more uncertainty. While the White House strategy established a framework to open a dialog with other nations, it does not abate the persisting imperative to counter aggressive cyber threat to the global supply chain. The strategy failed to assign clear roles and responsibilities to particular government entities and address the private sector issues.[15]

---

14 White House, "Fact Sheet: The Administration's Cybersecurity Accomplishments," May 12, 2011, www.whitehouse.gov; IBM, "IBM X-Force 2012: Mid-Year Trend and Risk Report," IBM: September 2012, pp. 52-7. See also Jon Boyens et al, "Notional Supply Chain Risk Management Practices for Federal Information Systems," Washington, D.C.: NIST, March 2012, Draft NISIR 7622

15 White House, "International Strategy for Cyberspace." Washington: D.C., May 2011; Adam Segal, "Chinese Response to the International Strategy for Cyberspace," www.blogs.cfr.org/2011 ; David Sanger and E. Bumiller, "Pentagon to Consider Cyberattacks Acts of War," May 31, 20111, www.nytimes.com

> **Cyber-notes**: The future of an open, interoperable, secure and reliable cyberspace depends on nations recognizing and safeguarding that which should endure, while confronting those who would destabilize or undermine our increasingly networked world.[16]

The Weakest Link

Threats to the supply chain and primary security associate with the loss, vulnerability, or degradation of confidentiality, integrity, and availability of the organizations IT systems and networks. The design, manufacture, delivery, installation, repair, upgrading, and updating of the supply chain give adversaries ample intrusion points into all systems. This is compounded by the evolution and spread of wireless connections. Thus, an end-to-end process from raw materials to finished goods allows for a constant threat. Risk can be internal or external, although some risks are more controllable that others.[17] See Chart 3-2

The supply chain is one of the primary areas an adversary targets during the first line of attack. The supply chain becomes increasingly vulnerable, because it becomes more dependent on technology-enabled support. The targets are the countless unguarded weak links in computers and communications systems. The new reality in today's cyber environment is that electronic threats to sensitive data are increasing primarily because hackers are more tech savvy and targeted in terms of what and who they are attacking. The interlocked dependent nature of the supply chain networks make them subject to compromise and bring into question the lack of both hardware and software assurance. However, people, as an old security-industry adage runs, are the weakest link.[18]

---

16   White House, "International Strategy for Cybersecurity," May 12, 2011, p. 3.

17   CACI, "Cyber Threats to National Security: Countering Challenges to the Global Supply Chain," July 2010; US Senate, Report of the Committee on Armed Services, "Inquiry Into Cyber Intrusions Affecting U.S. Transportation Command Contractors," 113rd Congress, 2nd sess., 2014, pp. 7-33

18   "The Spook Speaks," *The Economist*, June 30, 2002, p. 67; Mullich, "The Resilient Supply Chain," *Wall Street Journal*, September 22, 2011; George Platsis, "The Real Vulnerability of the Cyberworld: You and I," www.usa.nationaldefensefoundation.org, February 29, 2012; Katie Hafner and John Markoff, *Cyberpunks*, New York: Touchstone Book, 1991, p. 61

Regardless of how detailed an organization's attempts to prevent security breaches, no systems are ever totally invulnerable. The key is the development of the most resilient system possible, ever ready to implement risk recovery plans that are both up-to-date and well-rehearsed. The increased dependence on foreign sources for computer systems and support networks tremendously weakens our system. Understanding the cracking process is very critical to understand the sequence of steps an intruder performs to penetrate a system. The process is age-old, only ultra-high-tech in today's world. The seven hacker penetration stages:

- Reconnaissance: gather information about the target system or network
- Probe and attack: probe the system for weakness and deploy the tools
- Toehold: exploit security weakness and gain entry into system
- Advancement: advance from an unprivileged account to a privileged account
- Stealth: hide tracks; install a backdoor
- Listening post: establish a listening post
- Takeover: expand control from a single host to other hosts on the network[19]

While the United States remains the global leader in R&D, it produces very little at home, with over 90 percent of computer systems and hardware produced off-shore. Correspondingly, 90 percent of the commercial-off-the shelf (COTS) information systems the DOD procures are assembled off-shore.[20] Private companies (contractors), the military, and agencies continue to buy and rely on architectures and systems that are neither secure nor resilient. They attempt to solve the cyber problems with retrofits with OTS products. The slippery slope to perpetuating vulnerable systems is daily compounded by an insecure

---

19 IBM X-Force 2012: Trend and Risk Report, March 2013, p. 20; http://www.lieb.com/Readings/IBMInfoWAR.pdf

20 "Threat Assessment," Information Warfare, http://cryptome.org/iwd-a.htm

approach to security, as noted by a recent US Naval Institute/CACI study and comments by Steven Chabinsky:

> The result has been a 'market failure' to the extent that the US can't afford the security necessary to survive in a system it created. Since competition for information technology systems is furious and capability is often considered over security, industry continues to develop insecure systems. Purchasers continue to select 'competitively priced' products with insecurity engineered in even while the US becomes increasingly less able to afford them from a security standpoint.[21]

> **Cyber-notes**: security prevention strategies — security architecture, patch management, intrusion detection and prevention, firewalls, active monitoring, anti-virus software, application security, data encryption, password policies, active process and exception management, education and security awareness, response and containment programs, and frequent assessments of vulnerabilities[22]

While Congress failed to pass a comprehensive cybersecurity legislation in late summer 2012, they did include critical cyber provisions targeted to statutory provisions of defense policy in the National Defense Authorization Act for Fiscal Year 2013 (NDAA) which President Obama signed into law on January 2, 2013, in light of the risks to national security in the area of data breaches and protection of cleared defense contractors (CDC) — by definition "a private entity granted clearance [by DOD] to access, receive, or store classified information for the purpose of bidding on contracts or conducting activities" for the armed forces. Thus, tighter cyber-penetration procedures and mandatory reporting would be required by late 2013. Such reporting will include three key items of information: a description of the technique or method used in such penetration, a sample of the malicious software (if discovered and isolated by

---

21   "Cyber Threats to National Security," p. 21.

22   Doniele Carlson, Kansas City Southern, "Railroad gear up to protect computers from hackers," September 2012, www.progressiverailroad.com

the contractor involved in the incident), and a summary of the information compromised due to the penetration.[23]

To address legal and privacy concerns, Congress further stated that new procedures must provide reasonable protection of trade secrets, commercial/ financial information, and personal data. However, information of a non-essential nature such as telecommunication and Internet service provider networks that merely transmit DOD information is not intended for the reporting provisions by contactors. Furthermore, Chinese companies Huawei and ZTE were specifically cited as "companies that present clear cybersecurity supply chain risks that the US Government must address."

Concerns with protecting cyber security and procurement with CDCs across the entire defense industrial base (DIB) were voiced by Congressional conferees, noting "that the DOD acquisition process and policies do not appear to have a defined role for Common Criteria." The NDAA does not create these requirements as statutory, yet these "sense of Congress" provisions suggests future action by Congress on additional cyber security issues, yet as one close observer noted, "political leaders appear to be paralyzed about meeting the needs for our cyber infrastructure and enterprises."[24]

On February 12, 2013, the same day the Cyber Intelligence Sharing and Protection Act (CISPA) was re-introduced to the House of Representatives, President Obama issued an executive order related to cyber security. The Executive Order will seek to provide a voluntary framework for businesses to follow to mitigate the effects of cyber-attacks. One expectation for the report revolves around a broader definition of what constitutes critical national infrastructure. The executive order gives the Secretary of Homeland Security the power to reassess and redefine US cyber priorities. In addition to national concerns on cyber-attacks, the broader concern involves critical distribution such as water, fuel, health care, and food at

---

23 National Defense Authorization Act 2013, 112th Cong., 2nd sess., H.R.4310, signed January 2, 2013. Note: Under section 939 the Secretary of defense is required to quarterly brief the Congress "on significant military cyberspace operations that were carried out by DOD in the preceding quarter."

24 National Defense Authorization Act 2013 – Conference Report, 112th Cong., 2nd sess., Report 112-705, December 18, 2012, pp. 829-838; James P Farwell, "Industry's Vital Role in National Cyber Security," *Strategic Studies Quarterly*, Winter 2012, p. 10, 18-21.

the regional and local level. Such concerns did not impress the Congress. After the House passed the CISPA for the second time on April 18, 2013, the bill stalled in the Senate, not even brought to the floor for debate and a vote.[25]

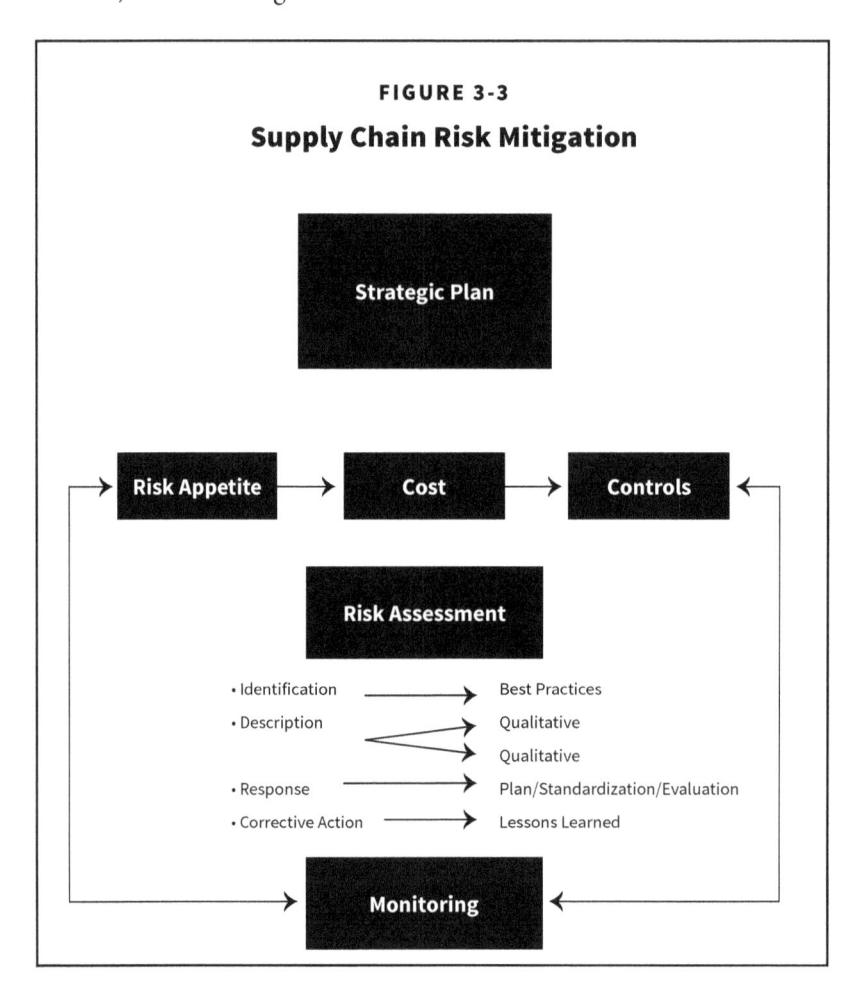

FIGURE 3-3

Supply Chain Risk Mitigation

```
                    Strategic Plan

    Risk Appetite  →  Cost  →  Controls

                    Risk Assessment

    • Identification    →   Best Practices
    • Description       →   Qualitative
                        →   Qualitative
    • Response          →   Plan/Standardization/Evaluation
    • Corrective Action →   Lessons Learned

                    Monitoring
```

---

25 Mathew Schwartz, "CISPA Cybersecurity Bill, Reborn: 6 Key Facts," February 14, 2013, www.informationweek.com/security/cybercrime/cispa. Note. Reintroduced House Bill H. R. 624, passed by a vote of 288-127, and was critized by the White House as lacking confidentiality and civil liberties safeguards. Very interesting response given the disclosures of the NSA monitoring CONUS communications and cracking encrytions.

Food Security

While a great deal of attention and time is given to 'high-tech' industries, there are concerns with the basic supply side to consumers at the community level that are cause for concern. There is no better example than the food distribution chain. Driven to reduce the cost of holding excess stock and to make more efficient use of working, the large scale companies in the grocery industry and their suppliers are driven by an ever demanding just-in-time manufacturing and delivery model. One such threat areas is food distribution.

Grocery store stock levels are constantly measured in real time. As long as the telecommunication and computer networks function, all is well. Even the shortest of interruptions in the supply chain can cause delays, spoilage, and potential havoc. A recent OECD study estimates that 80% of the grocery business in the United Kingdom is concentrated in 4-5 major supermarket suppliers. The just-in-time system in the UK means there is normally a 4 days' food supply available on the supermarket shelves at any one time — leading a Member of Parliament to note, "Britain is nine meals away from anarchy." This brash statement is further supported by the fact that the UK food supply is "almost totally dependent on oil." Nearly 95% of the food production and supply is oil dependent. If oil was suddenly cut off, the electric grid interrupted, and food deliveries delayed or stopped, London, which imports 81 percent of the seven million tons of food it consumes annually would have a grave cascading impact on the over four million consumers in the city.[26]

Over the past few years we have a vivid picture of the impact of the reduction in basic service and supplies following as natural disaster. Delays, service outages, shortage of gas and home heating oil, and transportation systems paralyzed in New York for weeks after Hurricane Sandy are only a snapshot of an all-out disruption due to a blended cyber-attack on a major metro area or region. Well-connected Estonia is a perfect example. The more 'connected' we are, the more vulnerable we are.

The tightness of the just-in-time supply chain and delivery interruption vulnerabilities coincide directly with the well-being and daily operations of the

---

26 Summers and Brown, "Reducing Systemic Cyber Risk," p. 20.

massive supply chains across the nation. Disruption in distribution and delivery can have a cascading impact across a broad range of sectors and regions, for example:

- Florida imports 100% of all gas and oil energy needs by pipeline, truck, and by ocean freight

- San Diego, California imports over 90% of its fresh water supply from out-of-state for a city/region of over1.3 million people

- Cushman, Oklahoma is the primary crossroads of oil and gas pipeline and transmission on the central region of the nation — a prolonged cyber-attack to the SCADA systems would impact distribution to over 35 states

- Petroleum refining is concentrated in only a few areas along the coast

- South Carolina state government was boldly hacked in October 2011, resulting in the loss of private personal and corporate tax records and data from 1998-2010 – the cost to the state is estimated to be over $40 million as of January 2013 and an yet unknown amount of disruption and cost to the private sector; similar attack occurred in Texas and Utah

- Over 70 percent of US export-import trade goes via 7 ports

Bring Manufacturing Home

While the global economy drives 85 percent of the parts to be shipped via suppliers to production floors worldwide, it is clear the United States will not reclaim all production it once had back to our shores — on-shoring. The cost alone would be prohibitive. Notwithstanding, companies are increasingly aware that to avoid risks and vulnerabilities, the solution is simple, return home (near-shoring) to be nearer to customers, IT and design centers, shipping centers, and US labor. One generally unwritten or unspoken reason is the broad theft of IP by off shore competitors. At one time the trend was to reverse engineer and copy to compete; now China wants the source code and encryption technology and generally will not welcome a foreign investor into the Asian market unless they surrender company core technology and knowhow.

This gradual shift will not fully break the trend of companies rushing to China to save on labor, only to have high turnover, training issues, higher inventory demands, compromised IP, and shoddy products. It does become a viable option to come home with at least a part of the production to service the North American market.[27] The risk will remain paramount no matter where companies, suppliers, and production facilities are located. As noted in a special report on China in *Barron's*: "Chinese research and development consists more of theft of intellectual property, industrial espionage, and cyber-attacks on Western companies than genuine collaboration with foreign concerns."[28]

> **Cyber-notes**: supply chain mapping — the diversified chip sourcing strategies geared to more rapid technology advancement extends the upstream supply chain for end applications considerably, potentially exposing the end product to greater opportunities for exploitation by an adversary with enough sophistication to 'map' the complete supply chain and identify points on vulnerability.[29]

Technonationalism

The supplier, at any stage of production, is a potential threat. Given the fact that most telecom systems are designed and manufactured in China creates a tremendous gap between secure networks and accountability. The source of both hardware and software requires repeated and robust inspection. The *Economist* clearly notes, "America has no effective system of supply-chain checks."[30] The

---

27 Bloomberg, "Supply Chain Cybersecurity," New York: April 10, 2012, www.bloomberg.com ; Barry Lawrence, "Bring Manufacturing Home Consortium," College Station: Global Supply Chain Laboratory, 2011: Jenel Stelton-Holtmeir, "Trends Points to Less Offshoring," *Modern Distribution Management*, February 25, 2012, pp. 1-4, www.mdm.com

28 Jonathan R. Laing, "Falling Star," *Barron's*, July 2, 2012, p. 23. See also "Investigative Report on the US National Security Issues Posed by Chinese Telecommunications Companies Huawei and ZTE," Permanent Select Committee on Intelligence, US House, 112th Cong, October 8, 2012, pp. 1-6.

29 Ibid., p. 85.

30 "Who's afraid of Huawei?" *The Economist*, August 4, 2012, p. 9; T. Zakaria, "US Blames China, Russia for cyber espionage," November 3, 2011, www.reuter.com.

prime concern is that networking systems and software could be used by Chinese spies to install eaves-dropping communications or 'kill switches' in systems and activate them in time of an attack. State sponsored firms, such as Huawei and ZTE who have customers in over 140 countries, provide a troubling scenario of agents eager to plant a Trojan horse by which to infiltrate foreign networks. Additionally, all the major computer, electronics, and IT fab/assembly firms headquartered in the United States manufacture offshore in China and other parts of Asia. Huawei in particularly was tied to both the Chinese government and the PLA. While this may allow for a competitive advantage in pricing, it also foretells a threat. Assuming the best is the road to being hacked. The US government and industry response to the Huawei case, appears to be indulging in what The Economist terms 'technonationalism,' and must develop better-enforceable standards for the supply chains to mitigate risk.[31] See Figure 3-5

Nowhere are enforceable standards more complex and threatening to the soft under-belly of the US economy and security than microelectronics sector. While we once manufactured most of our 'chips' in the United States, this trend dramatically shifted with the maturity of the microelectronics industry resulting in an increase in outsourcing of the fabrication of chips via off-shore subcontractors. Only about 20 percent of the chips currently in use were made in the US Industry pressure within the semiconductor industry for profits, volume production, and quality have forced manufacturers offshore, while still demanding products are delivered in near real-time. The complexity of the chip industry has resulted in global fragmentation of design, production, and sources, while increasing a race to the bottom to determine who will capture these lucrative markets. It enhances the possibility of rogue circuitry being implanted or hidden as malware at any stage of as systems manufacturing point. Increased complexity in the chip sector brings a corresponding increase in vulnerability — with 1 in 10 technology products or systems today have counterfeit parts or components with malicious codes embedded.[32]

---

31 "The company that spooked the world," *The Economist*, August 4, 2012, pp. 19-23; "Put on hold," Ibid., October 13, 2012, p. 78; US-China Economic and Security Review Commission (ESRC), "2012 Report to Congress," 112th Cong., 2nd sess., November 2012, pp. 163-4. Note: Huawei was founded in 1987 by Ren Zhengfei, a former officer in the People's Liberation Army, and operated in more than 140 countries with over 150,000 employees.

32 Bryan Krekel et al, "Occupying the Information High Ground," March 7, 2012, pp. 82-94.

FIGURE 3-4

Example of Off-Shore Concentration of Fabrication and Assembly

Manufacturer	Headquarters	Semiconductor Fab and Assembly
Fairchild	USA	China, S. Korea, Malaysia, US, Phillippines
Fujitsu	Japan	China, Japan, United States
GSI Technology	USA	Taiwan
Huawei Technologies	China	China
IBM	USA	Canada, Japan, United States
IDT	USA	Taiwan, United States
Intel	USA	China, Germany, Ireland, Israel, US
Intersil	USA	China, Netherlands, US
Lattice	USA	China, Japan, S. Korea, Taiwan, Malaysia
Motorola	USA	Mexico, Malaysia
National Semiconductor	USA	Maylasia, United Kingdom, United States
NEC	Japan	China, Japan
Pericom Semiconductors	USA	China, Taiwan
Pulse Electronics	USA	China
Samsung	South Korea	China, S. Korea, United States
STMicroelectronics	Switzerland	China, France, Italy, Morocco, Malaysia
Texas Instruments	USA	China, Germany, Japan, United States

Source: Krekel et al, "Occupying ....," pp. 83-4.

> **Cyber-notes**: the complexity of our weapons platforms and systems may be cutting-edge; they are also very vulnerable, for example the U. S. Navy carrier model of the F-35 Joint Strike Fighter has over 3,500 integrated circuits.[33]

A number of emerging of cases of technonationalism have surfaced in recent years as Chinese suppliers to western nations have progressively embedded their technology into critical communications systems that bring into question a variety of security issues. The potential for conflict between a commercial imperative such as communication and national security, as a result of increasing private ownership of the telecommunication sector and CNI combined with globalization are now problems. For example, questions have been raised in London about the decade long relationship between British Telecom (BT) with China's Huawei. The relationship began in 2004 when the process for considering national security issues and concerns was insufficiently lacking. The risk assessment overlooked then should not prevent or delay a full assessment on the impact to CNI. Huawei has strongly responded that they are acting in good faith in spite of perceptions of compromised security issues and stand to have reputational concerns and financial implications. In a special report released by the Intelligence and Security Committee in London, it was concluded that there is disconnect between the UK's inbound investment policy and national security, stating:

> The Government's duty to protect the safety of its citizens should not be comprised by fears of financial consequences, or lack of appropriate protocols ... a lack of clarity around procedures, responsibility and powers means that national security issues have risked, and continue to risk, being overlooked.[34]

---

33 US-China ESRC, "2012 Report to Congress," p. 161.

34 United Kingdom, Intelligence and Security Committee, "Foreign involvement in Critical National Infrastructure: The implications for national security," London: Parliament, June 2013, pp. 1-27; James Blitz, "UK security committee 'shocked' over Huawei contract with BT," *Financial Times,* June 6, 2013.

Robust Measures

As the supply chain globalizes, specialized bodies of expertise are developing across a section of industries to address specialty components of SCM: specialized software, hardware, communications systems, and systems-integration functions. As Sandy Boyson, logistics expert notes, "At present, no readily identifiable large-scale end-to-end risk management model exists that cuts across the various functional areas of the Information Communications technology (ITC) supply chain."[35] Notwithstanding, Boyson's Supply Chain Management Center group identified two broad capabilities focused guidelines to urge logistics management toward robust supply chain and a more comprehensive means to integrate processes end-to-end from acquisition to disposition:

- Defense in breadth should be extensive: it covers the whole end-to-end ecosystem of customer/acquirers, integrators, suppliers and key processes between them.

- Defense in depth should be intensive: it covers risk governance; systems lifecycle management including design, risk assessment and supply base modeling/auditing; and operations management.[36]

The concern worldwide is that cyber threats are becoming more frequent, persistent, and sophisticated. The increase in hand-held devices, the ease of access to smart meters, cloud computing, and very low awareness level of the general public on the full impact of cyber-attacks only heightens vulnerabilities. While companies continue to enhance firewalls, monitoring, and anti-virus software, a multitude of outdated systems and poor recovery plans further complicate security matters. Malicious software and spam (decoy emails known as 'spear phishing') is rampant, and unchecked. Hackers have subverted the design function to surreptitiously send malware to unsuspecting users where the attack

---

35   Boyson, "The ICT SCRM Community Framework," p. 6. See also NAVSEA, "Culture of Cybersecurity Awareness and Compliance," Strategic Business Plan: 2013-2018, Washington, D.C.: 2013.

36   Ibid., pp. 6, 65-90; Eric J. Byres, "Defense in Depth: A single cyber defense is the weakest form of cyber protection," Automation It, November 2012. See also Jeffery R. DiBiasi, "Cyberterrorism: Cyber R Prevention vs. Cyber Recover," Monterey: Naval Postgraduate School, December 2007.

exponentially increases the infection vector for malware penetration, greater data loss, and systems damage. Security systems will soon include requirements for mandatory data encryption, biometric security and multi-factor authentication. Manufacturers are daily going on the offensive to protect products and IP by designing components to render inoperable IP stolen through cyber means. The information and data developed by the companies are using the highest grade encryption as well as marking electronic files through technology such as "meta-tagging," beaconing," and "watermarking." Vigilant measures to plug vulnerabilities, as well as robust disaster management and recovery plans are an ongoing challenge.[37]

The cascading set of problems threatening the United States will test both the breadth and depth of any response that addresses both the vulnerabilities and mitigation of threats. While there has been some return of industrial manufacturing to the US, both these firms and other sectors will continue to source (import) raw materials and component parts and systems from foreign sources. In 2012, the US imported over $2 trillion worth of products from more than 150 countries. Given the increased reliance of networked systems and the Internet, it will be increasingly difficult to insure end-to-end reliability. The following areas along the supply chain are examples of concern and very exposed to manipulation or cyber-attacks:

Over 90% of rare earth materials critical to a broad cross section of high-tech systems are imported from China.

Over 80% of the raw material that are used by US pharma manufactures are imported; and of these imports only an estimated 12% are inspected and secured from the foreign source to the US customer.

Over 21 million containers annually arrive in the United States by sea, truck, and rail from over 150 countries; and less that 3% are fully inspected.

---

[37] Adam P. Liff, "Cyberwar: A New 'Absolute Weapon'? The Proliferation of Cyberwarfare Capabilities and Interstate War," *Journal of Strategic Studies*, June 2012, pp.401-428; Thomas J. Holt, "Exploring the Economic of the Malicious Software Market," seen in Tarek Saadawi, et al, *Cyber Infrastructure Protection*, Carlisle: SSI, May 2013, pp. 17-52; Geoffrey A. Fowler, "A Series of Cyberattacks Points to Sites Inside India," *Wall Street Journal*, June 24, 2013; NBAR, "The IP Commission Report," 2013, p. 81.

RFID hand held devices, the standard for tracking cargo, trains, and livestock are tagged and tracked worldwide allowing for disruption in the supply chain.

Over 30% of the 'black box' components used in aviation, aerospace, military, and naval applications are imported.

Over 90% of all global ocean sea freight is handled by non-US flagged vessels.

Over 60% of fish, vegetables, and fruit (some $20 billion) are imported for US domestic markets; and less than 2% are inspected.

Security concerns over the rise of 'cloud computing' — one of the most significant shifts in IT in a generation — surrender on site servers for remote sites open to nefarious use, as well as anonymous access to unauthorized files and systems.

A critical element that has not received enough attention is the understanding and employment of robust authentication and attribution mechanisms to protect critical resources and data. Authentication information can play a major role in systems security and attribution. Who is responsible for the attack and which assets should be target when retaliating? What is the threshold for retaliation and does it rise to the level of an act of war? This is often glossed over by policymakers as too much and too expensive — or too political! While seemingly a localized hacking attack and little or no attribution, the massive attack on the South Carolina department of revenue which exfiltrated vast amount of data was the failure to upgrade and encrypt systems proved costly. Managers should ensure policies and procedures exist to secure a high level of assurance (LOA). Digital identity and security measures into today's cyber environment require a trusted "proofing" protocol, a pre-authentication step in which the user and the identity provider exchange reciprocal authenticators. And there is no sector more lagging in the adoption of authentication than critical infrastructure and supply chain channels.[38]

---

38 Joshua Gruenspecht, "Cyber Security and Identity: Solutions for Critical Infrastructure that Protect Civil Liberties and Enhance Security," seen in Saadawi, et al, *Cyber Infrastructure Protection*, May 2013, pp. 139-182; Vincent Joubert, "Five years after Estonia's cyber attacks: lessons learned for NATO?" National Defense College, Rome: *Research Paper*, May 2012, p. 3. See also IBM, "IBM X-Force 2012, pp. 60-72.

Cyber-notes: The US DHS ran a test to see how hard it would be for hackers to gain access to computer systems. Staffers secretly dropped UBS flash (or thumb) drives in the parking lots of government buildings and private contractors. Of those picked up, 60% plugged the drives into office computers, and if the drive had an official logo, 90% were installed.[39]

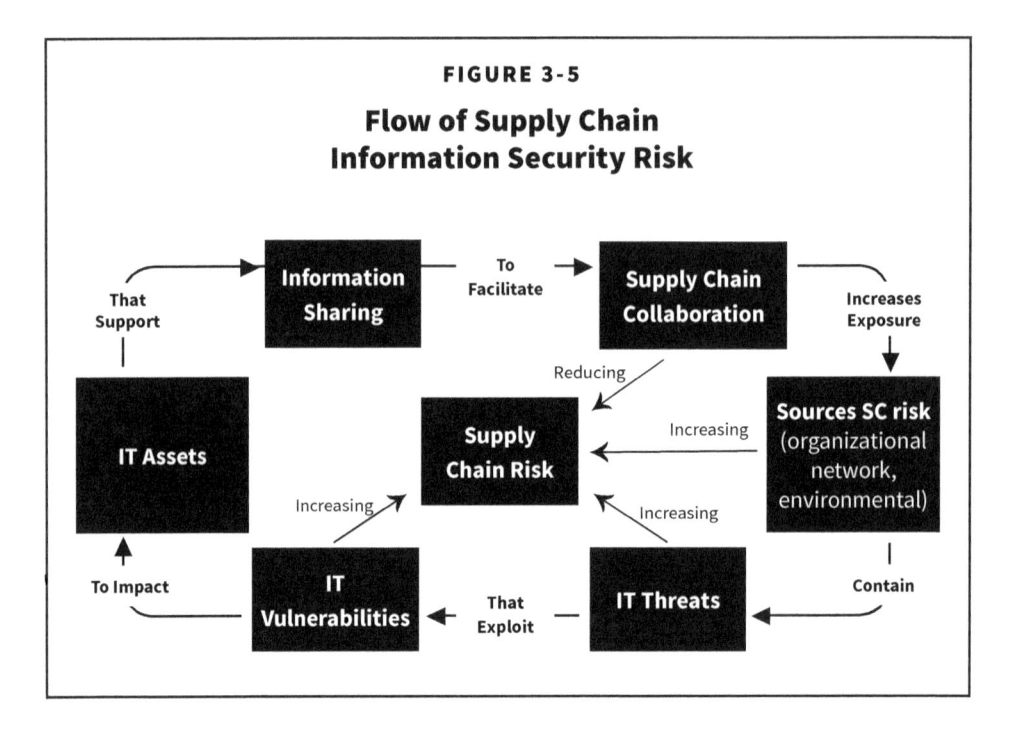

FIGURE 3-5

Flow of Supply Chain Information Security Risk

While much attention has been placed on the wired and network side of security, viruses and malware, the old fashioned physical side of deterrence must be addressed with a stronger focus than just making sure the main entrance gate of a facility is guarded. While all companies, government agencies, hospitals, utilities, and universities are subject to intrusion, the many points on entry along a global supply chain offer a host of attack opportunities. One ongoing vulnerability is the intruder that walks and talks their way into a facility by just following a

---

39 Paul Hyman, "The Dangers of Unsecured USB Drives," August 18, 2013, www.cioinsight.com

legitimate employee into the building as they offer to hold the door open. Such walk-in attacks, gaining access to computers, passwords, and employee data, can be instigated by fake identities, pretext phone calls, vendor access, or covert surveillance — beware of the pizza man who wonders the hall ways looking for a delivery! Often times, critical information is not protected and an intruder with a thumb drive can be highly effective in data theft. To combat this casual, yet serious form of intrusion, companies have hired security firms to prepare and test their employees for such social-engineering attacks. One of the safest practices is to ban all thumb drives, and allow no visitor without advanced screening to enter a critical facility with either a laptop computer or a cell phone.[40]

No matter how well an organization attempts to prevent security breaches, no system is totally free from vulnerabilities, and every system can be breached and compromised in some way. The question is the resilience of the system and the ability to identify the threat and then recover. Since supply chain security is defined in terms of assured data entry, storage, and delivery of physical and digital goods and services — risk recovery plans must be in place, real time, up-to-date, and very well-rehearsed to be of any sufficient recovery. It must be further remembered that cyber threat and hackers have no boundaries. The government is not the solution. It should a partner and run in parallel with efforts to combat threats. Thus, layered defenses; increased training and participation by employees, vendors, and IT providers; and close collaboration with government agencies — public-private partnerships — will become more critical as the threats increase in sophistication and volume.[41]

---

40   Ibid.; Christopher Matthews, "Cyber Gets Physical," *Wall Street Journal*, August 19, 2013; Greg Millman, "Some CEOs Open door to Hackers," Ibid., May 22, 2013; Y.S Enoch, et al, "Mitigating Cyber Identity Fraud using Advanced Multi Anti-Phishing Technique," *IJACSZ*, vol. 4, no. 3, 2013, pp. 156-164. Note: iPhones, iPads, and Andriod devices are UBS-compatible and can store up to 64 gigabits of data!

41   Platsis, "The Real Vulnerability of the Cyberworld: You and I," NDF: February 29, 2012; IBM X-Force 2012: Trend and Risk Report, March 2013, pp. 62-83; Yossi Sheffi, *The Resilient Enterprise*, Cambridge: MIT Press, 2007, pp.10-15, 90-1, 126.

> **Cyber-notes**: the cyber domain — defined broadly, the cyber domain cannot be devoid of the inevitable contentions that arise when competing interests consolidate around different principles and priorities and then collide when actors with different intents and capabilities seek to pursue their objectives.[42]

One of the most difficult hurdles to overcome to insure increased security is the fostering of an environment of collaboration among companies and government agencies. Most companies have established working relations with long term suppliers and vendor services, and assume to be protected by NDAs, IP protection (as well as nonproprietary models of knowledge rights[43]), and non-compete arrangements. In contrast, companies in direct competition are reluctant to fully cooperate, partly because of market competition, but also many are hampered by anti-trust, copyright, and privacy laws as well as IP protection. The lack of meaningful international laws or accords on economic espionage has allowed cyber-espionage to operate in a "legal black hole." Much needs to be done to bring forward more cooperation, yet the main impediment is government regulatory uncertainty and oversight. Global firms strive for resilience and long term supply chain dependence, further highlighting the need for layered response, clear identification of a true threat versus baseline activity, enhanced collaboration, and most importantly, a culture of awareness, and in the event of disruptions, effective communication and confidence in a rapid return to normal operations. The ever tightening and daily more demanding supply chain will forever challenge fool-proof resilience.[44]

---

42 Choucri, *Cyberpolitics in International Relations*, p. 125.

43 Ibid., p. 83.

44 Sheffi, *The Resilient Enterprise*, pp. 69-70, 118; David P. Fidler, "Tinker, Tailor, Soldier, Duqu: Why cyberespionage is more dangerous than you think," *International Journal of Critical Infrastructure Protection*, 2012, pp. 28-9. See also Office of the National Counterintelligence Executive, "Foreign Spies Stealing US Economic Secrets in Cyberspace: Report to Congress on Foreign Economic Collection and Industrial Espionage, 2009-2011," Washington, D.C.: October 2011.

FOUR
When the Lights go Out: Cyber Threats to Critical Infrastructure

Cyberspace has fundamentally transformed the global economy. Cyberspace is the new frontier — the new domain — full of possibilities to advance security and prosperity in the 21st century. And yet, with these possibilities, also come new perils and new dangers. These threats are real and they exist today. A cyber-attack perpetrated by nations, state or violent extremist groups could be as destructive as the terrorist attack on 9/11. Such a destructive cyber-terrorist could virtually paralyze the nation.

Imagine the impact an attack like that would have on your company or your business. For example, we know that foreign cyber actors are probing America's critical infrastructure networks. They are targeting the computer control systems [SCADA] that operate chemical, electricity and water plants and those that guide transportation throughout this country. We know of specific instances where intruders have successfully gained access to these control systems.

We also know that they are seeking to create advanced tools to attack these systems and cause panic and destruction and even the loss of life. Let me explain how this could unfold. An aggressor nation or extremist group could use these kinds of cyber tools to gain control of critical switches. They could, for example, derail passenger trains or even more dangerous, derail trains loaded with lethal chemicals.

They could contaminate the water supply in major cities or shutdown the power grid across large parts of the country. The most destructive scenarios involve cyber actors launching several attacks on our critical infrastructure at one time, in combination with a physical attack on our country. Attackers could also seek to disable or degrade critical military systems and communication networks. The collective results of these kinds of attacks could be a cyber-Pearl Harbor, an attack that would cause physical destruction and loss of life. In fact, it would paralyze and shock the nation and create a new, profound sense of vulnerability.

Secretary of Defense Leon J. Panetta
October 11, 2012

The recent remarks of former Secretary Panetta highlight the tremendous amount of concern and attention on the identification and protection of critical infrastructure and key resources (CIKR). For decades, as we felt insulated from outside terrorist attacks, security was sacrificed for the economy of operations, expanded market demands, and low cost service. Outside of government regulations on safety, monopolies, and interstate trade — growth and market share have been the engine of the big four infrastructure services: electricity, telecommunication, water, and oil and gas. Prior to 9/11, infrastructure was generally taken as a given, and few other than the military and local base operations raised the question of what should be protected and how. Our nation had been insulated from homeland disruptions and "attacks." While there have been veiled incidents against the homeland, such as espionage threats and penetration of US war production during World War I and German U-boat patrols in the Gulf of Mexico off New Orleans during World War II — the last time we were attacked at home was two centuries ago, during the War of 1812, when the British burned the White House. This all changed on 9/11, as cyber expert Ted Lewis notes: "The devastation of 9/11 demonstrates that attacks on the infrastructure can result in massive casualties, sizeable economic, political, and psychological damage, not to mention damage to the American psyche."[1]

While there are a dozen critical infrastructure sectors, the National Infrastructure Protection Plan (NIPP) lists 18 (See Figure 4-1). Protection of each critical component is paramount, yet the element that is the most important to the overall economy, security, and safety of the nation is the electric grid. Electricity is the lifeblood of today's modern world and a prime necessity for all citizens. It powers economies, consumer conveniences, national security, critical telecommunications, and the industrial production/supply chain ability to deliver competitive advantages to global markets. Given the efforts to provide sector specific cyber information and procedures, there is a "plethora of guidance available" to manage and protect our critical infrastructure.

> **Cyber-notes**: Security is only as strong as its weakest link. The best attackers know instinctively to look for that weak link.

Each element of our overall infrastructure is vitally important; the cascading impact of local and regional failure of electrical power will impact all primary services — especially water, telecommunication, and oil and gas. The vastness of the country has resulted in the evolution of the interconnection of the power grid, connecting over 3,000 power providers and generating more than 800 megawatts transmitted over more than 210,000 miles of transmission lines — all valued at over $1.1 trillion. Thus, in this review of the critical infrastructure, each critical sector will juxtapose a position against the role electricity has in the delivery, safety, security, and impact of any event that would diminish and disrupt overall service. The first detailed assessment of the scope of the challenge to protect and ensure resiliency and continuity was issued in the 2009 NIPP.[2]

---

1 Ted G. Lewis, *"Critical Infrastructure Protection in Homeland Security,"* Hoboken: John Wiley& Sons, 2006, p. 6. See also White House, Presidential policy Directive — PPD-8: National Preparedness, Washington, D.C.: March 30, 2011 and Henry Landau, *The Enemy Within: The Inside Story of German Sabotage in America*, New York: Putan Sons, 1937.

2 Homeland Security, National Infrastructure Protection Plan. Washington, D.C.: 2009. Note: In terms of actions dealing with infrastructure and cyber there are some 20 laws in statute, over 25 Homeland Security Presidential Directives, and a half dozen presidential executive

Disruption of the electric power grid can happen at a number of points, yet the most critical is at the site of generation, followed next by its transmission to customers. While both are important, the ability of a cyber-attack to penetrate the SCADA (Supervisory Control and Data Acquisition) systems that control electric production and delivery, some of which have outdated security features, presents a significant vulnerability. (See Figure 4-2).[3]

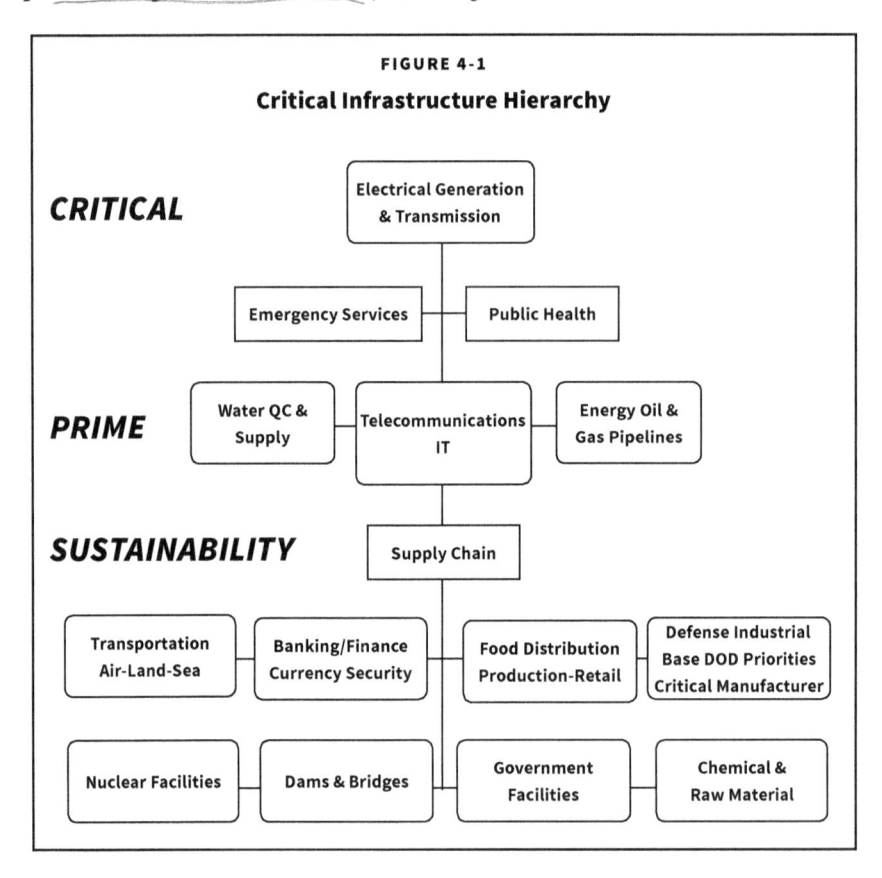

FIGURE 4-1
Critical Infrastructure Hierarchy

CRITICAL — Electrical Generation & Transmission; Emergency Services; Public Health

PRIME — Water QC & Supply; Telecommunications IT; Energy Oil & Gas Pipelines

SUSTAINABILITY — Supply Chain; Transportation Air-Land-Sea; Banking/Finance Currency Security; Food Distribution Production-Retail; Defense Industrial Base DOD Priorities Critical Manufacturer; Nuclear Facilities; Dams & Bridges; Government Facilities; Chemical & Raw Material

---

orders. See also GAO, "Critical Infrastructure Protection," Washington, D.C, December 2011, pp. 7-8, 46-7.

3 US House, Subcommittee on Emerging Threats, Cybersecurity, and Science and Technology, "The Cyber Threat to Control Systems: Stronger Regulations are Necessary to Secure the Electric Grid," 100 Cong., 1st sess., October 17, 2007 (hereafter, 'House Cyber Threat report'). Note: SCADA encompasses several types of 'control systems' that typically remotely control critical infrastructure devices and operate processes in the electricity, oil and gas, and water industries.

Figure 4-2
Ten Common SCADA Vulnerabilities

Common Vulnerability	Reason for Concern
* Unpatched published known vulnerabilities	Most likely attack vector
* Web Human-Machine Interface (HMI)	Supervisory control access
* Use of vulnerable remote display protocols	Supervisory control access
* Improper access control/ authorization	SCADA functionality access
* Improper authentication	SCADA access
* Buffer overflows in SCADA services	SCADA host access
* SCADA data/command manipulation	Supervisory control access
* SQL injection	Data historian access
* Use of IT protocols with clear-text authentication	SCADA host access
* Unprotected transport of application credentials	SCADA credentials gathering[4]

The bad guys have far too much access to power providers, because of our SCADA and metering vulnerabilities, and opportunities for a cyber-attack. Hackers and cyber-spies, from both nation-states and rogue groups probe for the weakest link. They have already successfully penetrated our power grid at a number of locations that we know of and likely at locations we do not know about. While rogue actors continue to explore ways to hack systems, the threat to the electrical power grid and other key infrastructures across the country long ago moved from amateur incidents to intentionally state-sponsored disruptive

---

4   DOE, Idaho National Labs, "Vulnerability Analysis of Energy Delivery Control Systems," September 2011, p. v-vi. See also Lior Tabansky, "Critical Infrastructure Protection against Cyber Threats," *Military and Strategic Affairs*, November 2011, pp. 61-78.

events and terrorism. According to the National Security Agency (NSA), both the Russian and Chinese intelligence networks have repeatedly probed the US electric power grid for vulnerabilities. Thus, one of the most concerning aspects of cyber-attacks on the grid is that most 'advanced persistent threats' (APT), have completely evaded detection. If and when a threat is detected, positive source attribution, the scope of attack and intent is often difficult.[5]

Advanced Persistent Threats — APTs

The range of attackers includes state-sponsored hackers, and the breadth of targets includes intelligence gathering and high-value targets across many industry sectors and types of critical infrastructure. The scope of the APT is measured by the available resources and determination of the attacker. One element of persistence is the ability to adopt the attack to the security profile of the target and neutralize access in order to extract data or disrupt critical infrastructure. Thus, this makes defending against APT's very problematic. The Director of the Counter Threat Unit of Dell Secure Works, Barry Hensley, noted, "The tools, procedures and other controls used to defend commodity security threats are often ineffective against targeted APTs. When actors are focused on a specific target, they customize and adopt their tactics, techniques and procedures to predict and circumvent security controls and standard incident responses."[6]

Such APT attacks can occur over months and years as the attacker responds to counter measures and explores security lapses. Once the hacker has gained access to the network, it is very difficult to rid the network of the intrusion. Stuxnet, Shady Rat, and Night Dragon are examples of highly successful APTs. The resourceful and adaptive adversaries generally have very specific targets and, when planned and encouraged by a nation-state actor, many times are executed by decentralized agents of the state. And the move to enhanced smart

---

5   Verton, *Black Ice*, pp. 39-54; Bob Lockhart and Bob Gohn, "Utility Cyber Security: Seven Key Smart Grid Security Trends to Watch in 2012 and Beyond," Pike Research, 4Q 2011. See also Le Xie, "False Data Injection Attacks in Electricity Markets," *IEEE Proceedings*, 2010, pp. 226-231.

6   Quote seen in GTCSS, "Emerging Cyber Threats: Report 2012," p. 10, www.gtisc.gatech.edu

grids and cloud computing, while hyped as the 'next best thing', is also the 'next' great target for adversaries.[7]

Evidence of the cascading impact of APTs is the release in mid-February 2013 of report compiled by Mandiant Security Systems, a private company that works to clean up the impact of cyber-attacks. The report, APT1, documents the systematic cyber theft of hundreds of terabytes of data from at least 141 organizations, 87% of which conduct business in English, spanning 20 major industries. The report singles out, with details, the operations of the People's Liberation Army's cyber unit known as Unit 61398. With a staff of perhaps thousands of hackers and IT personnel, many very proficient in English, the unit is located in the suburbs of Shanghai. This Chinese espionage organization is comprised of over 900 Command and Control servers hosted by 849 distinct IP addresses, known as 'fully qualified domain names' or FQDNs, in 13 countries. The main purpose is to hack and steal critical data and designs. The Mandiant report has helped to awaken concerns at the highest level of the US government. Left to continue, the US and its English speaking allies are daily more susceptible to a crippling cyber-attack. Lessons and expertise crafted in the 61398 attacks on industry are prime training for a potential multifaceted threat against our smart grid systems that control electrical, oil and gas, communications, and water systems.[8]

---

7   Ibid., pp. 10-12; Zetter, *Countdown to Zero Day*, pp. 308-358.

8   Mandiant, "APT1: Exposing One of China's Cyber Espionage Units," February 2013, pp. 1-60; David Sanger et al, "Chinese Army Unit is Seen as Tied to Hacking Against US," *New York Times*, February 18, 2013; Julian Barnes et al, "US, China Ties Tested in Cyberspace," and editorial, "China's Online Thieves," *Wall Street Journal*, February 20, 2013. See also Bryan Krekel, Patton Addams, and George Bakos, "Occupying the Information High Ground: Chinese Capabilities for Computer Network Operations and Cyber Espionage," US — China Economic and Security Review Commission, 2012; Ian Easton and Mark A. Stokes, "China's Electronic satellite Developments: Implications for US Air and naval Operations," Project 2049 Institute, 2011. See also Steven Stalinsky,"China Isn't the Only Source of Cyberattacks,' *Wall Street Journal*, May 22, 2013.

> **Cyber-notes**: grid vulnerability: "With one well-placed keystroke, American could be plunged into darkness and chaos through the damage to our electric grid. Foreign enemies are employing Web warriors to attack our way of life, and it's time that our actions respond to the potential threat."[9]

In spite of the new 'smart grid' programs — new digital electricity networks — required by the Federal Energy Regulatory Commission (FERC) and supporting agencies, we are as a nation still highly exposed to ATPs. This is primarily because the utilities use commercial software operated over the Internet that has not been fully vetted and protected.[10] The smart grid is intended to open a new era beyond traditional grid interconnection and technologies — to enhance systems to be more flexible, accessible, secure, and reliable.[11] Notwithstanding, concern has been expressed by power industry that coordination between agencies has been lacking and some have questioned whether FERC has the technical or intelligence-handling expertise to oversee the hardening of the grid. Furthermore, there is a lack of enforceable cyber requirements and standards for major pieces of the bulk power system, to include investor-owned utilities (IOUs), municipally-owned utilities, and rural electric cooperatives; mandates regarding the interoperability of the smart grid are costly and challenging. Blackouts from catastrophic electric power systems failure would have

---

9 Rep. Ed Markey, D-Mass., in Josh Hicks, "House Democrats' report says power grid is vulnerable to cyber attack," *Washington Post*, May 22, 2013 at www.washingtonpost.com/blogs/federal-eye. See also full report, Staff of Cong. Edward J. Markey and Cong. Henry A. Waxman, U. S. House, "Electric Grid Vulnerability: Industry Responses Reveal Security Gaps," Washington, D.C.: May 21, 2013.

10 Testimony of Joseph McClelland, Director, FERC, before the US House, Committee on Homeland Security, Subcommittee of Emerging Threats, Cyber security, and Science and Technology, Washington, D.C., September 12, 2012. Note: In terms of recommended grid-security guidelines there are two regulatory bodies: the industry-run North American Reliability Corporation, NERC and the Federal Energy Regulatory Commission, FERC, which reviews and gives final approval.

11 Y. Yang et al, "Impact of Cyber-Security Issues on Smart Grid," Belfast: 2011, pp. 1-7; Rebecca Smith, "Power Shortage Vexes Texas," *Wall Street Journal*, June 5, 2012.

significant cascading financial loss across the broader economy. An interdisciplinary approach to security measures is imperative.[12]

Since some utilities do not think they are targets for monetary defalcation, espionage, or Internet theft, they fail to recognize the risk. The electric power industry (to include nuclear facilities) is undergoing profound changes to address security concerns. Currently it is estimated that energy companies that do invest in computer/systems security are able to prevent about 70 percent of known cyber events. Increased spending, replacement of old systems, and employee training help reduce exposure, yet, there will always be threats. Despite the replacement of older equipment with 'digital devices,' exposure to hackers still remains a threat. Anywhere there is a digital system — from the generation plant to the smart meters to the home controls — the system is vulnerable to an ever-growing set of motivated and highly-skilled attackers. The sophistication of new malware attacking systems, including zero-day attacks, control systems rootkits, and software has shown it is difficult to prevent and/or detect attacks. The simplest intrusions may be the most damaging. For example, new systems that allow home owners to remotely set their thermostats are a direct portal for hackers to penetrate. Furthermore, there is only modest sharing of cyber information between private utilities and government agencies.[13]

---

12 Brian Wingfield, "Power-Grid Cyber Attacks Seen Leaving Millions in Dark for Months," February 1, 2012, www.bloomberg.com; James Lewis, ed. "Cybersecurity Two Years Later," January 2012, pp. 4-7. See also House Cyber Threat Report, pp. 7-29 and Huma Khan, "Cyber Attack on US Electric Grid 'Gravest Short Term Threat' to National Security, Lawmakers Say," May 31, 2011, www.abcnews.go.com.

13 Alvaro A. Cardenas, et al. "Attacks Against Process Control Systems: Risk Assessment, Detection, and Response," *ASIACCS '11 Proceedings*, March 2011, pp. 355-366; Gail Reitenbach, "Regulators Cannot Move Fast Enough to Protect Grid, FERC Warns," September 12, 2012, www.powering.com ; Brian Wingfield, "Power Grid Cyber Attacks," February 1, 2012.

FIGURE 4-3

Inventory of Critical Infrastructure

Energy	5,800 power plants 824, 847 oil and gas producing sites
Transportation	5,179 public airports 140,000 miles of active railroad with 21,178 passenger miles 600,000 bridges & tunnels 2.5 million miles of pipelines 361 airports
Telecommunications	2 billion miles of fiber and copper cable 14,000 radio & 1,700 television broadcasting facilities 252,000 cell phone towers 293 million wireless subscribers
Agriculture and Food	2,200,930 farms 28,000 food processing plants
Water	1048 federal reservoirs 14,780 public wastewater treatment facilities
Public Health	5,754 registered hospitals
Emergency Services	19,791 EMS agencies
Banking and Finance	7,280 FDIC insured institutions
Postal and Shipping	151.5 million delivery sites
Key Assets	87,265 historic places 104 commercial nuclear power plants 84,000 dams 1,500 government-owned facilities

Cyber Blackout

FIGURE 4-4

A robust cyber security defense-in-depth strategy includes:

- Concise and accountable command and control guidelines
- Well defined and monitored boundary for controls of cyber authorizations
- Robust authentication, authorization, and accounting controls
- Restricting physical access to ICS network and devices
- Established risk tolerance and risk methodology: threats and vulnerabilities
- High level cyber policies, procedures, authentication, and standards
- Documented purpose, functions, sensitivity, and capabilities of each function
- Clearly crafted roles and responsibilities for cyber incident response
- Implementing a network topology for the ICS that has multiple layers
- Secure assessment of organizational affiliations, access rights, and privileges
- Ensuring that critical components are redundant and are on redundant networks
- Operating standards that provide defense in depth and defense in breath
- Clear requirements for implementing controls and cyber-attack response
- Robust operational standards for addressing high-impact risk
- Effective monitoring and measurements of cyber security programs[14]

To date, an alphabet soup of government agencies that have compiled extensive reports, data, and technical briefs; driving the creation of regulations and oversight that cost the industry millions of dollars. Since most of the grid is owned by the private sector, there has been a natural push back to invest adequate funding to keep pace with security requirements. Safety is paramount and has been a world-class hallmark of the industry. As such, the security aspects, due to cost and oversight, have not kept pace with the increased threats. A number of risk management models have been developed to define techniques and methodologies to assess cyber-security risk. Our electricity providers across the nation deal daily with risk, yet few have ever dealt with a cyber-attack. Thus, many questions remain — has management defined risk constraints, does each organization have a risk tolerance profile, do they know their cyber security requirements and have they organized them accordingly, and is there a creditable and flexible plan for recovery.[14]

---

14   DOE, "Electricity Subsector Cybersecurity Risk Management Process," Washington, D.C.: DOE, May 2012.

> **Cyber-note**s: Cyber deterrence has to be repeatable because no feasible act of cyber-retaliation is likely to eliminate the offending state, lead to the government's overthrow, or even disarm the state. Thus, a state could attack, suffer retaliation, and live to attack another day.[15]

When the lights go out over a wide area of the country as a result of a cascading cyber-attack, there will be little concern for mission or vision statements, financial limitations, legislation, or stockholders. Elaborate outlooks promoting a 'holistic' approach will be useless. The prime objective will be to safely assess the problem, defend against the threat, if possible, and restore service. Thus, the most important objective of the industry working with government agencies at all levels is, and always will be, to first 'frame the risk' as clearly as possible — given all the best data, training, and intelligence available; second, conduct a 'risk assessment' which is short hand for "what are the priorities?"; and third, given the assessment of the situation and priorities, determine what will be the 'response' or recovery time objective (RTO). In a classic sense, risk management is the process of risk avoidance, mitigation, sharing and/or transference. What may initially appear as an isolated cyber-attack on a local system, could, without the ability of the operators to act fast enough, cascade into a statewide or regional outage. In other words, a "systems" attack, could not only create damage and disruption to the grid, but escalate into widespread physical damage as vital services shut down and routinely sustainable basic services such as transportation, water, food supplies, and telecommunications are disrupted.[16]

Risk-based Decisions

Framing the risk depends on assumptions about the threats — how likely is the occurrence, can the initial impact be quickly measured, and what is in place to protect our perceived vulnerabilities. If a tree falls across a power line, the

---

15 Libick, "Cyberdeterrence and Cyberwar," p. 31.

16 DOE, Electricity Subsector Cybersecurity Risk Management Process, p. 26; Brian Wingfield, "Rower-Grid Cyber Attack Seen Leaving Millions in Dark for Months," February 1, 2012, www.bloomberg.com/news; See also Texas Public Utility Commission, "Report on Electric Grid Cybersecurity in Texas," Austin: PUC, November 2012, pp. 15-20.

disruption is quickly noted, traced to the location, the grid is rerouted, and crews are dispatched to service the outage. Procedures are in place and action taken. In the case of a cyber-attack, employing a Trojan horse or sleeper virus could go unnoticed for days or weeks laying the seeds of corruption and doing unnoticed damage. The risk tolerance could be mishandled or misinterpreted because of false positive and false negative responses to system checks, and operators crippled by the speed of the disruption once it starts. In the event of such a catastrophic event, there will be only two key elements to addressing the attack and responding in kind. First and foremost is a 'trusted relationship' between all the players, both public and private, addressing the event. These relationships need to form long before an incident in order to properly facilitate experience, training exercises, cyber education, and constant communication. The second critical element is communications: point-to-point over secure lines between vendors, those with interconnections to the system, and government agencies is paramount. Those with communications access should be based on a prequalified access control list (ACL). For example, security protocols need to be in place in writing and easily accessible long before an incident to allow third parties and vendor access to sensitive data and systems. When the lights go out, so to do the cell towers, land lines, and given the presence of EMP — radio frequency traffic can also be disturbed.[17]

Once in the environment in which the risk-based decisions must be made and a detailed realistic and a credible framework established, the next level is to substantiate the assumptions of the framework with a risk assessment. Though the SCADA systems are not directly a part of the Internet, increasingly the private sector and corresponding government agencies have explored systems-wide architecture to link SCADA systems with IT and web access. The obvious goal is to identify all vulnerable threats to all IT systems, interconnected electrical subsectors, and SCADA connections. Given the likelihood of a cyber-event at all levels, an organization must have credible real-time plans to address the priorities response, tools and methodologies to assess and address the risk. If such an event hits the power grid over a large region, the prime factor could cause the assessment and forward planning to be obsolete if there are unplanned constraints (i.e. physical loss of substations, placed on the normal process of

---

17   McClelland, FERC, testimony to US House, September 12, 2012; Libicki, "Cyberdeterrence and Cyber War," pp. 11-36.

recovery). For example, if there is a major disruption in the grid, this could cause loss of communications, delays in getting the proper technicians to critical sites, and a cascading result in major delays in the supply chain and delivery of critical components to maintain or repair systems.[18]

> **Cyber-notes** : security and the smart grid: It remains to be seen how the industry will guard the security and privacy of the data while also integrating smart metering data into the utility smart grid analytics frameworks.[19]

Incident response to a cyber-attack on the electric grid or sub-system will need an organization-wide response. Determination of the attack and resulting damage will be driven by the ability of all responders to mitigate the impact. A clear and informed assessment of the situation must occur followed by the development of alternatives to correct and defend against the attack. If in fact there is multi-level attack, regionally or in a specific area, the response could be a mixed approach to both the cyber damage and the resulting physical damage due to disrupted systems. At this stage, the government at all levels must engage in the response, as well as those decision makers at the level of the threat and the demands to triage the events. Good intelligence and damage assessments along with real time communication will be critical to the response. Local responders and electric operators RTO (recovery time objective) may not have the full picture and magnitude of larger regional cyber disruptions that would in turn delay resources being allocated to the local level for recovery. As noted above, supply chain constraints and recovery of basic services could cascade to impair the response.[20]

To ensure a robust response to a cyber-attack, there needs to be a very clear chain of command to address the levels of priorities needed to combat the threat and insure recovery. Command and authority that is driven by those responsible is imperative. There is always a concern that the experts who solve and lead the

---

18   Carafano, *Wiki at War*, p. 120. See also House Cyber Threat Report.

19   Kevin Cornish, "Smart Grid and Intelligent Infrastructure," 2012 Strategic Directions in the US Electric Utility Industry, Overland Park: Black & Veatch, 2012, p. 51

20   DHS, *National Cyber Incident Response Plan*, Interim version, September 2010, pp. 26-9.

response and recovery will be undercut by those interjecting political clout or perceived authority — generally resulting in confusion, uniformed pronouncements, and costly delays in addressing the situation. The classic example of the folly and ineptness of the local, regional and state political structure to properly address large scale emergencies was Hurricane Katrina. While attribution of a cyber-attack is important to federal officials, the immediacy of action takes low priority unless it is directly related to the immediate recovery of defense against an imminent attack. Nevertheless, fresh forensic evidence is important, as long as it doesn't interfere with the first responders and recovery efforts.[21]

Thus, a better understanding of the means and impact of a cyber-attack should be key in training civilians, employees, elected officials, or responders who could and will come in contact with the results of a cyber-attack. Although volumes are written on these topics, awareness of the cyber threat must be conveyed in the clearest terms possible. The awareness is not for computer programmers, but for those who drive policy and respond to cyber incidents.[22]

Foot Printing

The first step to hacking a system or network is to gather information. Attackers systematically glean data and information from whichever 'door' they can find open or unprotected. Like a burglar in the dark of night casing a break-in opportunity, cyber attackers accumulate a systematic footprint of an organization, site, or component of the grid by completing a detailed profile on the organization's security posture. The ultimate strategies of a covert attack is to sift through the data to develop a list of intrusion detection systems, domain names, specific IP addresses, access control functions, and possible passwords. Such information is often found in open access sites across the Internet. Following a data probe, hackers can refine footprint information by identifying related companies, phone numbers, email addresses, and reviewing privacy policies. One of the best backdoor means of gathering data is developing a list of web servers and

---

21 Ibid., Appendix A: B3—4, C1-2. See also Texas PUC, "Report on Electric Grid Cybersecurity in Texas," pp. 21-25.

22 Libicki, "Cyberdeterrence and Cyber War," pp. 91-115.

links related to the target. The more enticing the information, the easier it is to focus a hackers attack.[23]

Driving the modernization and reliance of the electrical grid was the passage of the Energy Independence and Security Act of 2007 (EISA) that required a number of federal agencies, led by FERC, the National Institute of Standards and Technology (NIST), and the Department of Energy (DOE). The bulk of the cyber-security was assigned to NIST to develop a framework for protocols and standards, and by January 2011, eleven cyber-standards had been developed for the smart grid. However, the threats to the critical infrastructure in transmission and distribution systems have not been reduced or fully managed but instead are growing more and more complex. The range of threatening cyber exploits from possible rogue hackers, espionage, or terrorists in our daily more wired world have only compounded.[24] Those who intend an attack are able to mix and match a deadly combination of system damaging "cyber exploits", resulting in interruptions, such as:

Cross-site scripting	Denial-of-service	Phishing
Logic bomb	Distributed DOS	Worm
Passive wiretapping	SQL injection	Trojan horse
Zero-day-exploit	War driving	Virus

Preparing for a cyber-attack or major disruption of the grid has been a priority of both the bulk power system (BPS) of the electric industry and scores of government agencies. To review the level of effectiveness of cyber incident response plans, NERC hosted a nationwide security exercise, GridEx 2011, in November 2011. Modeled after the DHS Cyber Storm exercise, the scenario allowed participants to respond from their normal work stations in real time. Some 48 utilities and two dozen government and regional entities were involved in a two day exercise to validate the readiness of the electricity sub-sector. The after action

---

23   Oliver Kusut, et al, "Malicious Data Attacks on Smart Grid State Estimations: Attack Strategies and Countermeasures," IEEE Proceedings, 2010, pp. 220-5; Stuart McClure, et al, *Hacking Exposed: Network Security Secrets and* Solutions, Osborne/McGraw-Hill, 1999, pp. 5-28

24   "Cybersecurity: Challenges in Securing the Modernized Electricity Grid," GAO 12-507T, Washington, D.C.: February 2012.

Cyber Blackout

report indicated that on par entities possess effective cyber incident response plans, yet need to enhance protocols and response guidelines (i.e. command and control). Within the industry, there were significant 'horizontal' communications, yet poor vertical information sharing with NERC and government agencies remained a problem. Utilities took appropriate steps to secure the grid, however the industry needs to ensure response protocols address a coordinated cyber threat.[25]

The greatest threat to the electrical grid is the aging SCADA control systems and the lag in updating these systems to prevent a cyber-intrusion. Assessing vulnerability, determining the best risk mitigation means, and managing the resources to reduce vulnerability is largely the responsibility of the entity that owns and operates infrastructure.[26] The ability of organizations to provide strategic information and security investments may be compromised based on the funding and resources available. Many companies continue to fail to recognize cyber intrusions in their IT/SCADA systems and often allocate limited resources to lesser threats.[27] Thus, the penny wise and pound foolish approach retards industry attempts to reduce cyber-security vulnerabilities. Real and present threats have seemed to elude both the industry and consumers who call for more access, lower rates, and growth. The nature of these demands increased the number of exploitable entry points, coupled with the introduction of new yet unknown vulnerabilities as systems are either only updated or replaced. The biggest vulnerability lies with the overall connectivity, both internally and with surrounding systems and networks of so-called shared information. This gives potential adversaries the incentive to hack — driven in the final analysis by — the challengeelectricity! The sources of 'cyber threats,' either unintentional or intentional, vary by source, intent and expertise:

---

[25] Jacob Kitchel, "2011 NERC Grid Security Exercise After Action Report Review," May 27, 2012, http://blog.industrialdefender.com/?p=1271

[26] Carafano, *Wiki at War*, p. 224. See also Steve Kroft and Graham Messick, "Stuxnet," *60 Minutes*, March 4, 2012 and DOE, INL, "Vulnerability Analysis of Energy Delivery Control Systems," September 2011, pp. 1-162.

[27] Ted DeZabala, "Cyber Crime: A Clear and present danger," Deloitte: Center for Security & Privacy Solutions, 2010, pp. 3-7. See also Melissa Hathaway, "Five Myths About Cyber Security," Mosaic: The New New Internet, 2009.

FIGURE 4-5
Sector-Specific Agency and CIKR Sectors

Sector-Specific Agency	Critical Infrastructure and key Resources
Department of Energy	energy, generation, refining, distribution
Department of Defense	defense industrial base and sourcing
Department of Agriculture	food and agriculture
Dept. Health and Human Services	healthcare and public health
Department of Treasury	Banking, Finance, currency
Environmental Protection Agency	water and wastewater systems
Department of Interior	national monuments and icons
Department of Homeland Security	
Cyber Security	IT and Communication sectors
Transportation Security	postal and shipping Transportation systems and infrastructure
U.S Coast Guard	maritime security
Federal Protective Service	government facilities
Infrastructure protection	emergency services, commercial facilities, critical manufacturing, chemical sectors, dams, and nuclear reactors, materials
Director of national security	critical intelligence

Bot–network operator	Criminal Groups	hacker
Insider's	nation-states	phishers
Spammer's	spyware/malware	terrorist[28]

Incident attacks on the power grid are only seldom reported, yet data indicated that 'reported' SCADA systems attacks in the industry have increased from three in 2009 to twenty-five in 2011. Across federal agencies, 'reported' cyber incidents have increased 680 percent over the past six years. The FBI has hundreds of energy related cases under investigation ranging from sophisticated hackers of large amounts of power through smart meters, largely by remotely changing the power consumption recording settings with software commonly available on the Internet, to phishing attacks collecting customer data. Moreover, the August 2003 northeast power blackout, due to an over loaded transition line making contact with trees, caused the failure of 508 generating units at 265 power plants across eight states, which cascaded from Ohio through the east coast and up to Canada. Were these cyber related? Could advanced cyber systems, such as SCADA, have prevented the incidents?[29]

Given the fact that as the FBI investigates cyber incidents, the Department of Homeland Security (DHS) has been designated by federal policy to 'lead, integrate, and coordinate' efforts to protect the cyber-critical infrastructure. The task to date has been overwhelming and gaps in ensuring safe systems and networks abound. The nexus between government and industry that is addressing a secure grid is hindered by a coordinated approach to voluntary standards. The current fractured regulatory environment and continued debate over compliance instead of comprehensive security, partnered with the lack of security features built into systems and a poor culture of shared information within the industry, make it difficult to ensure cyber grid systems. A parallel problem exists with tracking illicit financial transactions where new ways to acquire and share information is needed. In this new high tech age, the electricity industry does

---

28 Clay Wilson, "Computer Attack and Cyberterrorism: Vulnerabilities and Policy Issues for Congress," CSR Report, April 1, 2005, www.history.navy.mil/library

29 "Cybersecurity: Threats Impacting the Nation," GAO 12-666T, Washington, D.C, April 2012, pp. 9-11. Note: According to US-CERT 'reported' cyber incidents have increased from 5,503 in FY 2006 to 42,667 in FY 2011.

not have clear traceable metrics for evaluating cyber security and incidents, for example, basic items which would measure the effectiveness of security controls for blocking and detecting a cyber-attack.[30]

> **Cyber-notes**: the privacy hurdle — there is no political consensus, at least in the United States, on how to strike the balance between preserving privacy and preventing criminal activity.[31]

FIGURE 4.6

CFATS Risk-Based Performance Standards

Restricted-Area Perimeter	Secure Site Assets	Sabotage
Screen and Control Access	Deter, Detect, and Delay	Theft and Diversion
Shipping, Receipt, Storage	Cyber	Response
Monitoring	Training	Personal Surety
Threats, Vulnerabilities, or Risk	Officials and Organizations	Elevated Threats
Significant Security Incidents	Report Incidents	Records

The Challenge:

The general public has little or no concept of the fragility of the electrical grid system across America. In August 2012, a blackout hit northern India leaving

---

30 "Cybersecurity" Challenges in Securing the Electricity Grid," GAO 12-926T, Washington, D.C.: July 2012. See also GAO, "Critical Infrastructure Protection," Washington, D. C., December 2011.

31 Christopher Bronk et al, "The Dark Side of Cyber Finance," *Survival*, April 2012, p. 139.

600 million people — nearly twice the population of the United States and ten percent of the world's population — in the dark. This is the largest known blackout in history in terms of population. Delhi commuters discovered "electricity [is] the life blood of an economy."[32] What was reported as an "unprecedented grid failure as a result of negligence and incompetence" is the first of massive rolling blackouts that will likely impact the less industrialized world in years to come, as they are often mired in debt, operating outdated power production facilities, and facing daily growing shortages of coal and natural gas. As demand for critical resources out strips supply, it is little wonder that the Chinese, also stretched to capacity, are globally sourcing tremendous hordes of oil, coal, and natural gas.

To date, customers in America expect, and have received, a level of reliable service unequal in any other country. Electrical companies, which are more than ninety-five percent owned by private industry, work to maximize service, increase efficiency, and by so doing — enhance the revenue curve to generate profits. In so doing, the electrical industry has heavily focused investment and new technology in advanced metering infrastructure (AMI), which is driven by vendors, and not focused on industry control systems (ICS). The realm of vulnerability by the increased points of entry in the high-tech smart meter is growing daily. One industry analysis concluded: "The utility cyber security market will be characterized by a frantic race to gain the upper hand against the attackers."[33]

Without extensive security, smart meter technology is only as good as the next major systems intrusion and attack. The systems today are not secure. The magnitude and stealthiness of the Stuxnet worm by highly motivated attackers on the Iranian nuclear SCADA systems is a troubling case in point.

---

32 "Blackout Nation, *The Economist,* August 4, 2012, pp. 10-1, 35-6; Cassell Bryan-Law, "U.K. Blocks Extradition of Alleged Hacker," *Wall Street Journal,* October 17, 2012.

33 Lockhart and Gohm, "Utility Cyber Security," 2011, p. 1; Amol Sharma et al, "India's Power Network Break Down," *Wall Street Journal,* August 1, 2012; Gardiner Harris, "Power is restored Across India After Crippling Blackout," *New York Times,* August 1, 2012: Russell A. Green, "India outage illustrates infrastructure woes," *Houston Chronicle,* August 2, 2012. Note: India in 2012 had an estimated population of 1.22 billion, of which 300 million have no access to electrical power, and at least an additional 300 million have only sporadic access.

The electrical grid is only as strong as its weakest link. The Stuxnet code and others look for the weakest link when testing digital defenses. Most, for now, have evaded detection. Compounding the protection of the electric grid and smart system is the fact that there are no enforceable smart grid security measures anywhere in the world for power distribution grids. For example, current US NERC, Critical Infrastructure Department (CID), NIST, DHS, Control System Security Program (CCAP) guidelines apply only to transmission and generation. Incredibly, for the prime security sector in our nation — the safety and availability of electricity — there are no enforceable standards and at best a labyrinthine of guidelines and recommendations. In spite of the increasing threat of cyber-attacks, as well as ongoing calls for increased security measures, the Congress has not provided any government entity with the necessary authority. As a result, industry invests in cyber security only when the bottom line is threatened.[34]

The NERC Security exercise in 2011 was designed to review and prepare the bulk power system (BPS) for a disruptive cyber incident. The exercise demonstrated that gaps did exist. For example, there need to be clear protocols to rapidly and accurately distinguish between a common operational issue and a major cyber-attack. The primary areas of concern dealt with establishing a verified means to communicate (due to lack of confidence in conventional systems), timely information sharing, and physical intrusions into BPS infrastructure which can have grave cyber implications. Thus, the linkage between the cyber and physical elements need to be addressed in parallel. This will reinforce the critical importance of maintaining and testing a Cyber Security Incident Plan well in advance of any incident. The findings and lessons learned, termed 'hotwash,' will prove valuable to enhancing future exercises and hardening the grid.[35]

---

34   Ibid., pp. 2-6; NERC, "2011 NERC Grid Security Exercise: After Action Report," March 2012.

35   NERC, "2012 NERC Grid Security Exercise," pp. 1-17; Yan Sun and Haibo He, "Understanding Cascading Failures in the US Power Grid," Cybersecurity Symposium, University of Rhode Island, 2011. See also James Kimmance, "Infrastructure Risk & Resilience," BCI Workshop, Bristol, 2011.

The cooperation of private sector providers of electricity, vendors, and government agencies at all levels continues to be critical to a continued robust approach to risk. All three entities share a common concern to protect system data from unauthorized access, disruption, and modification. The keys going forward include establishing clear protocols for data security, and integrity of information; while simultaneously protecting the confidentiality of private information, ensuring data availability to authorized users on a timely basis, and maintaining safe and secure operations. One of the most detailed and user-friendly cyber-security documents to address issues and actions concerning the national electrical grid with recommendations for the protection of the SCADA is the Idaho National Laboratory report *Vulnerability Analysis of Energy Delivery Control Systems*. The ultimate goal of SCADA cyber-security is to reduce risk. Understanding the exposure to attack can reduce the probability that a threat can exploit a vulnerability — thus, reducing the consequences of such an incident.[36]

> **Cyber-notes**: opaque transactions — technology-facilitated transactions can be designed to be invisible; alternatively, they can be designed to be visible but anonymous.[37]

Poison Ivy

In addition to the electric grid, there are clearly a number of critical sectors that have a major impact on our defense's industrial base. Oil and gas, water, and telecommunications are sectors that are more widely recognized by the public. However, the chemical industry (due to its special nature) is less in the main stream — until there is a problem or accident. Over the last century, the chemical industry has for the most part been self-regulating, adhering to the

---

[36] DOE, INL, "Vulnerability Analysis," pp. 1-150; NPPD Assistant Secretary Roberta Stempfley and NCCI Director Larry Zelvin, statement to House Committee on Homeland Security, "Facilitating Cyber Threat Information Sharing and Partnering with the private Sector to Protect Critical Infrastructure: An Assessment of DHS Capabilities," Washington, DC: May 16, 2013, www.dhs.gov/news/2013/05/16 . See also Executive Order 13636 and PPD-21, February 2013.

[37] Bronk et al, "The Dark Side of Cyber Finance," p. 130.

regulatory guidelines coming from the states and eventually nationally from the EPA. In terms of security for chemical operations, other than individual company efforts to secure a facilities perimeter with verified access procedures, there had been little (except during World War II) nationwide concern until the Chemical Facilities Anti-Terrorism Standards (CFATS) of 2007. These standards for high risk chemical operations, which expired in October 2012, were considered both overly burdensome and complicated. Efforts are underway for a public-private effort to streamline these regulations and provide a policy solution that enhances the security of the chemical industry.[38]

Chemical safety is a paramount concern to the United States. A broader global concern surfaced with the deadly Union Carbide gas leak in Bhopal, India in December 1984. To date, that event, which left thousands dead and many more injured, is the worst industrial accident in modern history. Threats of chemical terrorism increased following the 1993 bombing of the World Trade Center and the 1995 sarin gas attack in the Tokyo subway system. Thus the CFATS, which predates the 9/11 attacks, was augmented following the creation of DHS with a requirement that the industry develops a vulnerability assessment and establishes risk-based performance standards on all facilities, including the production, handling, and/or storage of high-risk chemicals and raw materials. As of September 2011, there were an estimated 38,000 chemical related facilities in the United States, of which 7,000 were considered a high-risk designation in a DHS review.[39]

Threats to the chemical industry are very real. Between July and mid-September 2011, 48 chemical and defense contractors were victims of coordinated cyber-attacks traced to China. Company systems were infected by malicious software known as "Poison Ivy" — deemed a Remote Access Trojan (RAT) targeted at control of a machine and systems. Experts determined that this was part of a five-year-long hacking plan against more than 70 governments and corporations, known as "Operation Shady Rat." The prime purpose of these sustained

---

[38] Jessica Zuckerman, "Chemical Security in the US: CFATS Regulations too Complex," *Backgrounder*, August 14, 2012, www.report.heritage.org/bg2718

[39] Ibid.; Joseph Straw, "The Skinny on CFATS," *Security Management*, www.securitymanagement.com

attacks, according to a Reuter's interview with a security expert, was likely industrial espionage aimed at collecting technology and intellectual property.[40]

In spite of the failed efforts by Congress to pass cyber legislation in 2012, the White House has stepped forward with executive orders address the cyber issue. Following a directive to increase the sharing of "classified" information among state, local, tribal, and private entities, the White House due to repeated and growing cyber intrusions into critical infrastructure, released an executive order on February 12, 2013 to "improve critical infrastructure cyber security." The spirit of the executive order is clearly toward cyber security directing reevaluation and improved regulation, but the EO did not provide any federal agency with additional statutory authority with which to address the risks — that can only be accomplished by an act of the US Congress.[41]

To manage the growing turf war over who is the primary government agency for cyber security, the order included a coordinated focus by the Attorney General, Secretary of Homeland Security, and the Director of National Intelligence to establish procedures to enhance cyber security programs for "all critical infrastructure" — where a "cybersecurity incident could result in catastrophic regional or national effects on public health or safety, economic security, or national security." The executive order, which is short of direct action and long on voluntary initiatives, was not expected to have guidelines in place until late summer 2013. The order contemplates a revised risk-basis assessment to identify critical infrastructure cyber threats. In the meantime, a diverse group of government agencies involved remain engaged "in the consultative process" that

---

40   Jim Finkle, "New Cyber arrack targets chemical firms: Symantec," October 31, 2011, www.reuters.com; Joe McDonald, "Cyber-attacks on chemical companies traced to China," November 1, 2011, www.usatoday.com; "US Chemical Companies Hit by Chinese Hackers," November 1, 2011, www.cnbc.com

41   Markey and Waxman, "Electric Grid Vulnerability,", May 21, 2013, pp. 7-9. Note: A measure of industry-government grid-lock is that it has taken six years for 25 recommended NERC cyber standards to be used, with only a few standards were incorporated into "CIP Version 5" that may or may not become mandatory in 2016!! By May 2013, FERC had approved only nine CIP reliability standards developed and recommended by NERC.

daily is increasingly more politicized and less response to the national security of the nation.[42]

Thus, community leaders should increase their knowledge of cyber-threats and how to respond to minimize loss and restore critical systems. While Hurricane Sandy that hit the upper East coast in late October 2012 was a natural disaster and not a cyber-event, the massive storm did highlight the damage and cascading impact of over 8 million customers without electricity.[43] When the lights go out — there is a corresponding impact on fuel and water supplies, health care services, transportation systems, and communications. And a cascading cyber-attack that cripples the electric grid could in fact have a much longer period of disruption.

Kenneth Van Meter, GM of Energy and Cyber Services for Lockheed Martin, stated that, "By the end of 2015 we will have 440 million new hackable points on the grid. Every smart meter is going to be a hackable point… if you can communicate with it, you can hack it."

---

42 White House, Executive Order. "Improving Critical Infrastructure Cybersecurity." Washington, D.C., February 2013 and Choucri, Cyberpolitics *in International politics*, pp. 143-6. See also Executive Order 13549, "Classified National Security Information Program for State, Local, Tribal, and Private Sector Entities (SLPTS)," Washington, D.C.: August 18, 2010; Jason B. Jones, "The Necessity of Federal Intelligence Sharing with Sub-federal Agencies," *Texas Review of Law & Politics*, Vol. 16, no. 1, pp. 175-210; and Andrew B. Serwin, "President Obama Issues Executive Cyber Security Order," February 14, 2013, www.securitymagazine.com

43 George Pataki, "In Sandy's Wake, Time to Upgrade the Power Grid," *Wall Street Journal*, November 26, 2012.

FIVE
Communities: Cascading Chaos

Who is likely to make suitable provisions for the public defense, as that body to which the guardianship of the public safety is confided ... which, by the extension of its authority throughout the States, can alone establish uniformity and concert in the plan and measures by which the common safety is to be secured?
Alexander Hamilton: *Federalist Papers No. 23*
December 18, 1787

The impact of a destructive cyber attack on the civilian population would be even greater with no electricity, money, communications, TV, radio, or fuel (electrically pumped). In a short time, food and medicine distribution systems would be ineffective; transportation would fail or become so chaotic as to be useless. Law enforcement, medical staff, and emergency personnel capabilities could be expected to be barely functional in the short term and dysfunctional over sustained periods. If an attack's effects cause physical damage to control systems, pumps, engines, generators, controllers, etc., the unavailability of parts and manufacturing capacity could mean months to years are required to rebuild and reestablish basic infrastructure operation.
Defense Science Board, DOD,
"Task Force Report." January 2013, p. 5.

John A. Adams, Jr.

CHART 5.1
Community Cyber Security Maturity Model

LEVEL 1 Initial	LEVEL 2 Advanced	LEVEL 3 Self-Assessed	LEVEL 4 Integrated	LEVEL 5 Vanguard
• Minimal cyber awareness	• Leadership aware of cyber threats, issues and imperatives for cyber security and community cooperative cybertraining	• Leaders promote org security awareness; formal community cooperative training	• Leaders and orgs promote awareness; citizens aware of cyber security issues	• Awareness a business imperative
• Minimal cyber info sharing	• Informal info sharing/ communication in community; working groups established; adhoc analysis. little fusion ormetrics: professional orgs established or engaged	• Formal local info sharing/ cyber analysis. Initial cyber physical fusion; informal external info sharing/cyber analysis and metrics gathering	• Formal info sharing/ analysis, internal and external to community; formal local fusion and metrics, initial external efforts	• Fully integrated fusion/analysis center, combining all-source physical and cyber info; create and disseminate near real world picture
• Minimal cyber assessments and policy & procedure evaluations	• No assessments, but aware of requirement initial evaluation of policies & procedures	• Autonomous tabletop cyber exercises with assessments of info sharing, policies & procedures, and fusion; routine audit program; mentor externals on policies & procedures, auditing and training	• Autonomous cyber exercises with assessments of formal info sharing/ local fusion; exercises involve live play/ metrics assessments	• Accomplish full-scale blended exercises and assess complete fusion capability; involve/mentor other communities/entities
• Little inclusion of cyber into Continuity of Operations Plan (CDOP)	• Aware of need to integrate cyber security into COOP	• Include cyber in COOP; formal cyber incident response/recovery	• Integrate cyber in COOP; mentor externals on COOP integration; formal blended incident response and recovery	• Continue to integrate cyber in COOP; mentor externals on COOP integrations; formal blended incident response and recovery

Source: White, Community Cyber Maturity Model, IEEE: 2011

No single actor has all the necessary tools and resources to respond completely to a major crisis. We are a nation in transition, both demographically and technologically. Our population has tripled to more that 310 million over the past century. A century ago, over 60 percent of the population was urban and 39 percent was considered rural. By 2010, the nationwide census placed over 80 percent of Americans in growing urban areas. Urbanization, the speed of communications, and the near real time concentration and delivery of products and services, has in one regard induced more connectivity, while at the same time cyber vulnerabilities. Yet, despite the vast technical advancements and efforts at all levels of government and the private sector as well as abundant resources to develop and respond to a cyber-threat, a seamless effective unified solution still seems to elude us.[1]

A Battlefield without Borders

One of the primary impediments that should be of major concern to local leaders and responders is the ongoing diffused authority and capability across multiple levels of government and agencies coupled with the sheer size and complexity of inter-jurisdictional authorities across the nation. The cascading impact of a major cyber-attack against critical infrastructure would, even though at the local level first responders are well trained and motivated, be overwhelming. In a report addressing the systematic reduction of cyber risk, the OECD noted, "A pure cyberwar, (wherein only cyberweaponry is deployed) is unlikely. Future wars and the skirmishes that precede them will involve of conventional or kinetic weapons with cyberweaponry acting as a disrupter or force multiplier." Notwithstanding, a cyber-attack at the level of a nation state can and will cause long-term damage to our national security, infrastructure, businesses, and individuals.[2]

---

1   H. Steven Blum and Kerry McIntyre, *Enabling Unity of Effort in Homeland Response Operations*, Carlisle Barracks: SSI, April 2012, p. ix.

2   Peter Sommer and Ian Brown, OECD, "Reducing Systemic Cybersecurity Risk," OECD/IFP project: January 14, 2011, pp. 13-14, 55-68. Note: DNI Director James Clapper in mid-March 2013 noted that an ultra sophisticated cyber-attack capable of wiping out major nationwide computer networks are "remote." See in Siobhan Gorman, "US Steps Up Alarm Over Cyberattacks," *Wall Street Journal*, March 13, 2013.

Natural disaster events give a window into the scale of damage and recovery needed and the response needed to address a blended attack of cyber and conventional means. As was seen with the delays, confusion, political infighting, and mishandling during a crisis like the Katrina Hurricane in 2006, which was not a cyber-related event, there was a complete breakdown at the state and local level of the chain-of-command, poor prioritization of vulnerabilities, little or no situational awareness, lax information sharing, and delayed triage of all aspects ranging from evacuation of hospitals to the role of the local law enforcement — all highlighted and accented by "politically-motivated bickering" that delayed a unified response. Only after the Army was placed on the ground, did a coordinated response begin. A recent study on "Unity of Effort" captures the essence of the concern:

> In many disaster situations, including the largest and the most dangerous, the ability to field a seamless, unified, robust response from government and private sector entities is still out of reach. The problem at its heart is not lacking resources and capabilities, but in being unable to bring them to bear at the right time and place, and in the right combination, to achieve effective results. [3]

> **Cyber-notes**: The Nation is highly reliant upon interdependent cyber systems, yet stakeholders have an incomplete understanding of cyber risk and inconsistent public and private participation in cybersecurity partnerships.[4]

Community leaders and citizens alike should be concerned. The lessons learned seem not to be a priority. Of course, in our dynamic nation, the citizens and government at all levels face directly or indirectly other pressures that seem to put the planning, risk assessment and countermeasures on the back burner. For the past decade, the war on terror, active US military engagements in the Middle East, and a comparative sluggish economy and double digit unemployment has captured the political focus. To be sure, a response to our vital interest globally is indeed critical to our national security. But herein lies the greater threat to our communities, shallow planning at the local and state level, combined with a

---

3   Ibid., pp. 1,3.

4   HLS, National Preparedness Report, March 30, 2012, p. iii.

Cyber Blackout

notion that the federal government would provide the primary response, which they will and should, creates an expectation that cannot be fulfilled in the event of a massive cyber event that collapses even ten percent of the power grid in any section of the nation. See figure 5-1.[5]

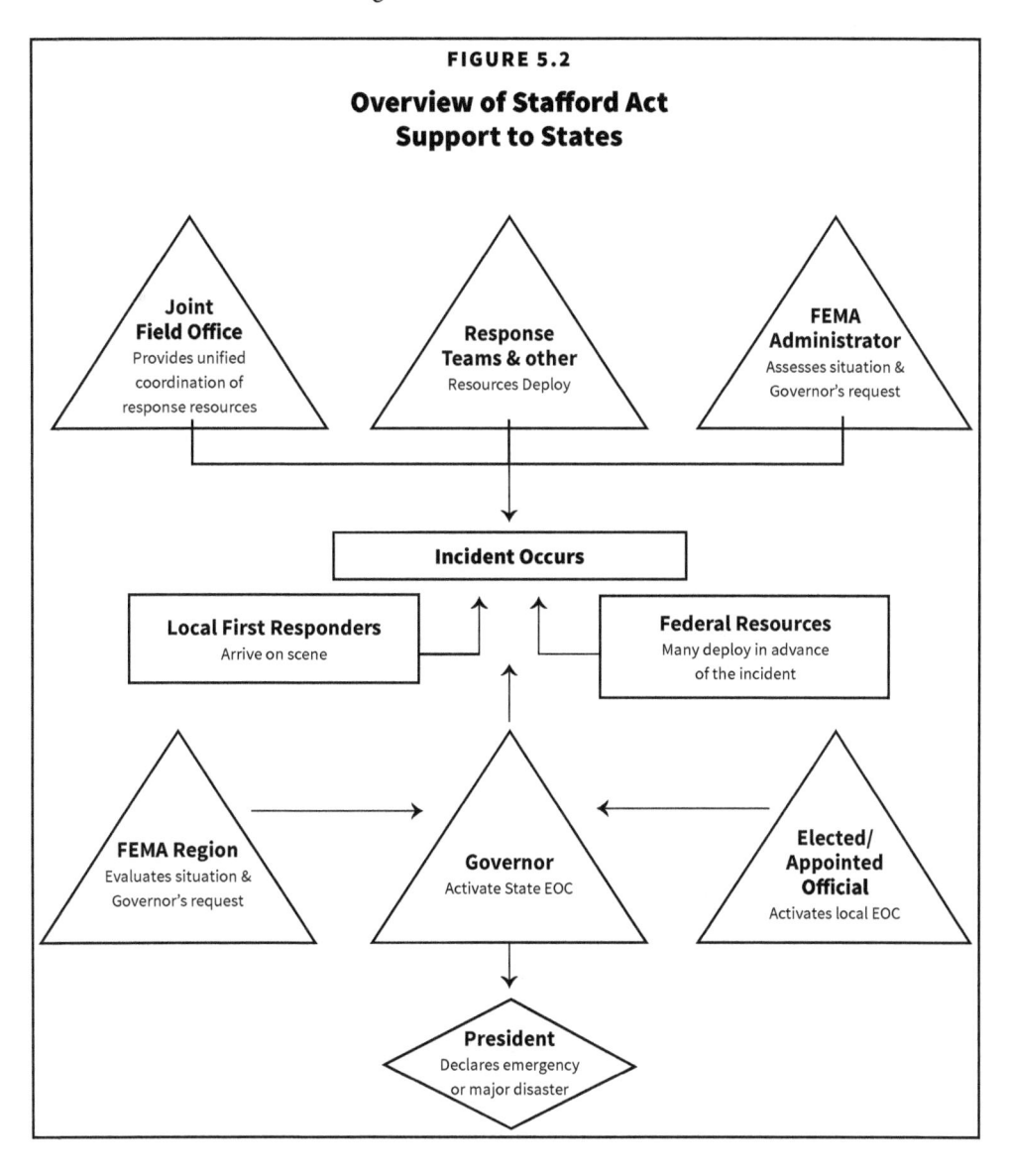

FIGURE 5.2
Overview of Stafford Act Support to States

Joint Field Office — Provides unified coordination of response resources

Response Teams & other — Resources Deploy

FEMA Administrator — Assesses situation & Governor's request

Incident Occurs

Local First Responders — Arrive on scene

Federal Resources — Many deploy in advance of the incident

FEMA Region — Evaluates situation & Governor's request

Governor — Activate State EOC

Elected/Appointed Official — Activates local EOC

President — Declares emergency or major disaster

---

5   Warren B. Rudman, et al. *Emergency Responders: Drastically Underfunded, Dangerously Unprepared*. Washington, D.C.: Council on Foreign Relations, 2003.

Even with the extensive after action assessments and reports following 9/11; Hurricane's Katrina, Ike, and Charley; the BP Gulf of Mexico oil spill; and massive fires in the West; we have left our nation vulnerable and unprepared.[6] The hundreds of reports, Congressional hearings, NGO studies, and Presidential Executive Orders have reviewed the disaster response issues, but have failed to insure a unified action plan.[7] And by the fall 2010, an extensive study by a DOD appointed panel on the support of civilian authorities after certain incidents, concluded: "There is currently no comprehensive national integrated system to respond to either natural or manmade disasters . . . planning among Federal agencies and other levels of governments is fragmented and nonstandard, and there is no formal process by which State plans can inform Federal planning and vice versa."[8]

Governance, Risk Management, Trust

While responders in the United States are the best trained and equipped in the world, most states and local communities have little or no experience in cyber security or the processes to respond to cyber-crime or terrorism. Referring a cyber-problem resulting from a cyber-attack to the "IT" department is not the solution. One reason for this disconnect with first responders and cyber incidents is that natural disasters, as well as fire and storm incidents, have been the prime focus of training and response — not cyber attacks. Most first responder incidents are local in nature. Cyber incidents do not fit into the traditional

---

6 US Congress, "Report by the Select Bipartisan Committee to Investigate the Preparation for and Response to Hurricane Katrina," *A Failure of Initiative*, Washington, D.C: GPO, 2006; US Congress, *The 9/11 Commission Report*, Washington, D.C.: 2012. Note: In a period from August 2004 to October 2005, Florida had landfall of six Cat 3 hurricanes: Charley, Francis, Ivan, Jeane, Dennis, and Wilma.

7 White House. George W. Bush, Homeland Security Presidential Directive, PD-8, 2003.

8 Steve Abbott et al. *Before Disaster Strikes: Imperatives for Enhancing Defense Support of civil Authorities*, DOD, Washington, D.C.: GPO, September 15, 2010. Note. The focus of the panel was on CBRNE — Chemical, biological, radiological, nuclear and high yield explosives; and did not focus on cyber incidents.

scenarios found in current first responder training. The mindset and training of responders is to deal with what they can "see, feel, and touch."[9]

The national response to natural disaster assistance dates from the 1950s Civil Defense network and the passage of the Disaster Relief Act of 1974. Over the past four decades there has been a growing dialogue between the federal government and state and local political leaders and responders on how best to address disasters. The prime goal of these efforts has been to encourage states and localities to develop their own comprehensive preparedness and recovery plans. For some time it was unclear whether a "major disaster" included a pandemic event or a cyber-attack that was not attributable to fire, flood, natural disaster, or explosion. The key component of these efforts has been to train and ensure enhanced intergovernmental coordination and communication. At the heart of any disaster response is the assurance that there is timely command and control.[10]

In 1988, the Stafford Act amended the act of 1974 and expanded the demands for more cross-government interaction and the establishment of a means to determine when a presidential disaster declaration should be triggered. Furthermore, direct physical and command assistance was authorized through the Federal Emergency Management Agency (FEMA), soon followed by the Emergency Management Assistance Compact in 1996. Further enhancements were added to the disaster response protocols when Congress passed the Disaster Mitigation Act in 2000 and, following the 9-11 attacks and the creation of the Department of Homeland Security (2002), two presidential directives, HSPD-5 and PPD-8, which have been added to address terrorist attacks, pandemics, catastrophic natural disasters, and cyber incidents. The National Counterterrorism Center (NCTC) was added by a presidential executive order in 2004. The Presidential Policy Directive PPD-8 issued by the White House on

---

9   Gregory B. White, "The Community Cyber Security Maturity Model," IEEE: 2011, pp. 173-8: Interview with Scott Terry, KE/TEEX/ College Station, March 13, 2013.

10   William C. Banks, "The Legal Landscape for Emergency Management in the United Sates," Washington, D.C.: New America Foundation, February 2011, pp. 5-9.

March 30, 2011 was the first effort to name 'cyber attacks' as a threat and as a part of the national disaster framework.[11]

Beginning in the fall of 2012 and into early 2013 the number of cyber-attacks against public and private initiatives escalated into to thousands of cyber-attacks. Mandiant's report of over 140 US corporations penetrated by cyber-attacks, most likely from Chinese, followed by Russian and Iranian sources; focused more attention on the subject but little substantive action. Congress's failure to pass a bill to establish protocols and cybersecurity standards for protecting critical infrastructure in August 2012 was followed by both a presidential executive order addressing the cyber threats and placing emphasis on the level and severity of the attacks. The Obama administrations campaign to draw attention to unprecedented scale of cyber threats and national vulnerabilities gradually took on a more urgent tone. "It's hard to overemphasize its [cyber] significance," Director of National Intelligence James Clapper said, "the capabilities put all sectors at risk — from government and private networks to critical infrastructures." The era of cyber threats is no longer a nuisance but a real problem that has quickly shifted from mere cyber-crimes or rogue hackers to one of well-funded nation-state 'cyber espionage.'[12]

As nation states get bolder in probing our computer networks and security capabilities, more cyber-attacks will occur. As noted by Mandiant, China, for example, has an entire military unit directed at attacking US systems — public, private, and military. One case that demonstrates the cascading impact of a massive cyber attack is the hacking of the South Carolina Department of Revenue in late 2012. A combination of aggressive cyber attackers, blended

---

11   Ibid., pp. 10-20; Robert T. Stafford Disaster Relief and Emergency Assistance Act, 42 USC., 5121-5206, (Public Law 93-288) as amended; White House, Homeland Security Presidential Directive/ HSPD-5, February 28, 2003 and Presidential Policy Directive/ PPD-8, March 30, 2011.

12   Siobhan Gorman, "US Steps Up Alarm Over Cyberattacks," *Wall Street Journal*, March 13, 2013; Mark Landler and David Sanger, "US Demands China Block Cyberattacks and Agree to Rules," *New York Times*, March 11, 2013; White House, "Remarks by Tom Donilon, National Security Advisor to the President, Washington, D.C.: March 11, 2013; Jody R. Westby, "We Need new Rules for Cyberwar," *New York Times*, March 1, 2013, www.nytimes.com/roomfordebate/2013/02/28 . Note: In addition to comments made by the president, Clapper and Donilon; General Keith Alexander, commander of the US Cyber Command also expressed strong public concern for cyber security.

Cyber Blackout

with outdated computer equipment, poor security procedures, and political oversight that did not understand how to protect public data, often delaying protection based on funding or misinformation, resulted in the compromise of massive amounts of confidential tax records and public data.

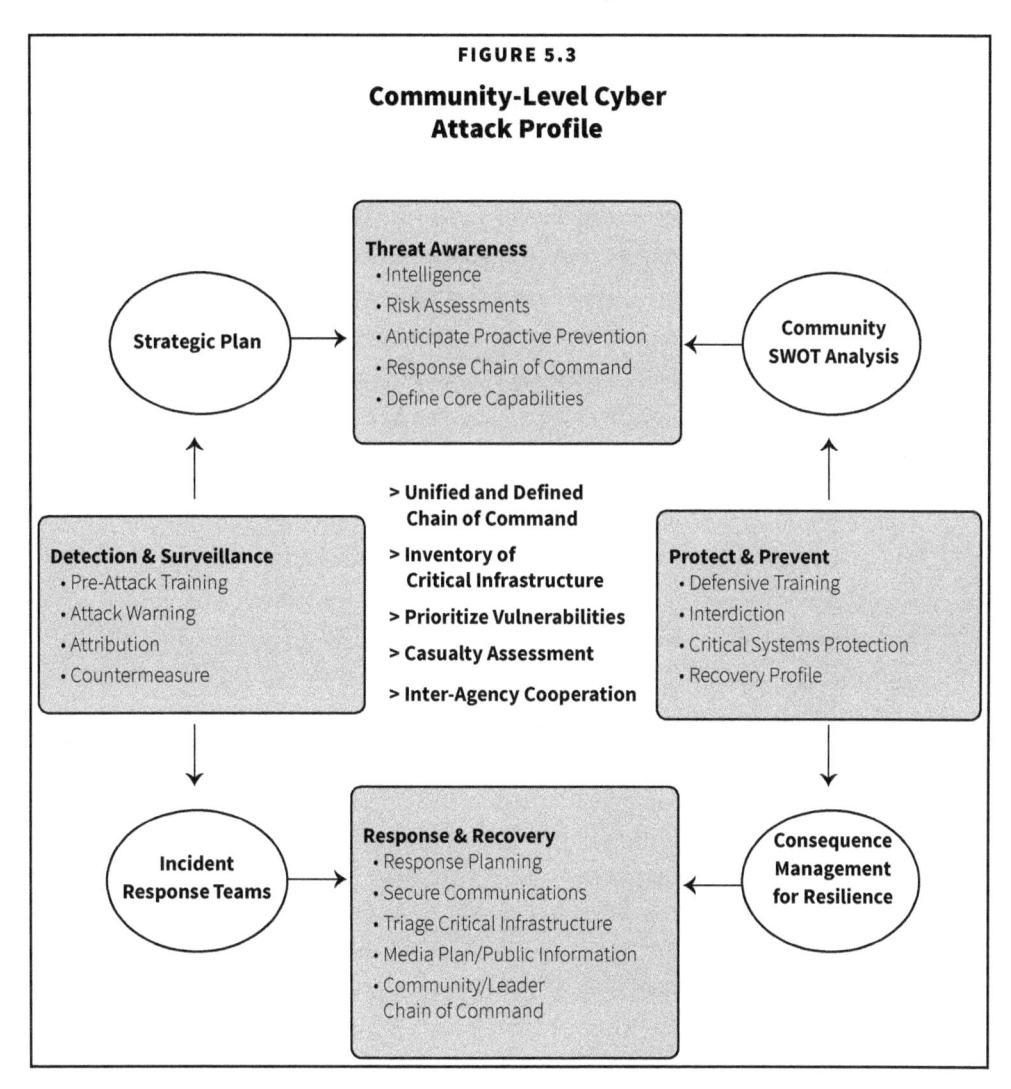

FIGURE 5.3

Community-Level Cyber Attack Profile

Threat Awareness
- Intelligence
- Risk Assessments
- Anticipate Proactive Prevention
- Response Chain of Command
- Define Core Capabilities

Strategic Plan

Community SWOT Analysis

> Unified and Defined Chain of Command
> Inventory of Critical Infrastructure
> Prioritize Vulnerabilities
> Casualty Assessment
> Inter-Agency Cooperation

Detection & Surveillance
- Pre-Attack Training
- Attack Warning
- Attribution
- Countermeasure

Protect & Prevent
- Defensive Training
- Interdiction
- Critical Systems Protection
- Recovery Profile

Incident Response Teams

Response & Recovery
- Response Planning
- Secure Communications
- Triage Critical Infrastructure
- Media Plan/Public Information
- Community/Leader Chain of Command

Consequence Management for Resilience

> **Cyber-notes**: a cyber-security compromise of communications equipment used for transmission line management could lead to cascading failures across portions of the electrical grid.[13]

On Click Away From Cyber Attack

As the media filled the nightly news reports and blogs during late 2012 with a running report of the fate of the federal 'fiscal cliff' and the Congress waffled on passing a cyber-security bill, governments at the state level were gearing up for upcoming 2012-13 legislative sessions and budget challenges. Tight on fiscal resources and challenges, a laundry list of demands in Medicare, education and infrastructure enhancements were at the top in many states, including a promise of brighter days — until the evening of August 16, 2012 when South Carolina was subject to an extensive cyber-attack.

The computers of the South Carolina Department of Revenue (SCDOR) were hit by a determined hacker, triggering what may have been the most extensive state-level cyber strike in the US on public sector systems. Stories and debriefs are numerous on the national cyber strike in 2008 against the country of Estonia, oddly about the same size as South Carolina, as well as the state computer servers in Utah and Texas which were hacked in 2011, and a federal intrusion during mid-2012 which attempted to take down the Economic Development Administration (EDA) computer network at the US Department of Commerce. Furthermore, attacks on the private financial and corporate sector computer sites accelerated in 2012 to the highest of cyber-attacks to date.[14]

The attack on South Carolina continues to impact operations at the state and a mounting level of claims by those who were exposed by loss of confidential data. What went wrong and could this have been prevented or mitigated?

---

13 DOE, "Electricity Subsector Cybersecurity," May 2012, p. 18. See also, Rebecca Smith, "California Grids for Electricity Woes," *Wall Street Journal*, February 27, 2013.

14 South Carolina, Department of Revenue (DOR), "SC DOR Responds to Cyber Attack, Will Provide Credit Monitoring and Identity Theft Protection to Taxpayers," Columbia: October 26, 2012; Robbie Brown, "South Carolina Offers Details of Data Theft and Warns It Could Happen Elsewhere," *New York Times*, November 20, 2012.

In an October 26, 2012, a press release the South Carolina Department of Revenue (SCDOR) announced that over 3.6 million tax records and social security numbers, 3.3 million bank accounts, 700,000 business accounts, 387,000 credit and debit cards dating back to 1998 were exposed and exfiltrated by an extensive cyber-attack. Two weeks earlier, the DOR had been notified by the US Secret Service that the breach occurred, followed by notification of state and federal law enforcement agencies. DOR contracted with Mandiant, a private computer security firm, who uncovered cyber probes that began in mid-August and lasted for eight weeks until a containment plan was implemented on October 26. The cat was out of the bag![15]

The South Carolina attack, which could have come from across town or the other side of the world, has been attributed to an unknown international source. It is likely forensics will never fully know who launched the intrusion. Given the ability to bounce from computer to computer or a chain of computers, known as a "botnet" or "zombies", attribution in cyberspace may be the single most difficult challenge to bring the hackers to bay.

The ease of entry by hackers into the DOR computer systems was amplified by outdated 1970s vintage computer equipment, poor firewalls, and a general low level of cyber security awareness at all levels of government and management. Mandiant reported that the agency's computers were compromised by sending state employees spam-email that contained embedded malicious (phishing) links. Clicking on the link unwittingly activated the malware and gave the hackers a clear path to user names, tax data, and passwords. The initial report by Governor Nikki Haley indicated that employees mismanaged passwords and access to sensitive tax data, and that the state did not have a procedure to encrypt social security numbers and tax ID data — because it was not required by the IRS to encrypt data![16]

Given the magnitude of this event, it was likely not a minor, one-off attack. It is interesting to note in the aftermath of a cyber-attack, with approximately

---

15   Andrew Shain, "HACKED: Your Questions," *The State*, November 3, 2012 and "$25,000 password system could have halted SC hacking, November 28, 2012, www.thestate.com

16   Mandiant, " South Carolina department of revenue: Public Incident Response Report," November 20, 2012, www.mandiant.com ; "Senate subcommittee to examine S.C. security breach," *Charleston Business Journal*, November 9, 2012.

74.4 GB of data stolen and 44 DOR system data bases compromised, how an effort by some was made to down play the assault. During the hacker reconnaissance activities of the DOR, the attackers used at least 33 unique pieces of malicious software for data theft. The South Carolina attack was an extensive cyber-attack.[17]

Think of it this way. What would have been the reaction from the media, FBI, legislators, and citizens if burglars would have backed up to the back door of the Department of Revenue at midnight, busted the locks, and loaded a half-dozen trucks with all the tax records from 1998 to date, along with addresses, social security and tax ID numbers! The cyber-attack is in every way more serious, given the fact the stolen data can be electronically and instantly, sold, forwarded, and used.

Outdated state and local computer networks are among the most vulnerable in the nation. This, coupled with aging control systems, known as SCADA, for electric grids, water treatment plants/distribution, and infrastructure, means states and communities should be concerned with threats and have higher awareness of possible attacks from cyber hackers. Such intrusions are only a matter of time. No system is impregnable.

Since the massive data breach was announced in October, 2012 the governor and state officials have scrambled to manage the damage as well as public and legislative outcry for accountability. More safeguards should have been in place at DOR. However, until the massive attack and meltdown, security allocations for computer security in South Carolina were either cut or delayed. While there have been a number of reports that a preventative $25,000 dual password system most likely would have prevented or mitigated the attack on 6.4 million citizens, the fact remains that no action was taken to upgrade the vintage computer systems and equipment at SCDOR.[18]

---

17 South Carolina General Assembly, Bill 334, www.scstatehouse.gov/sess120_2013-2014/prever/334 . Note: It is interesting to note that Bill 334 cast blame on the SCDOR for "failure to protect taxpayers," "declined technology services, including cyber security services," and failed to "encrypt taxpayers' personally identifiable information;" with NO reference to the shortfall in legislative funding!

18 South Carolina, "Credit Monitoring Products Agreement," with Experion, confidential, October 25, 2012.

In 2006, the DOR priced encrypting data at a cost of $5 million, but the state chose to follow only minimum IRS standards for protecting tax information — which did not require encryption. In 2011-12 the agency sought $14.4 million to upgrade computers that included encryption of data, but the request was cut by the House budget committee. Furthermore, key computer security staff positions at DOR went unfilled for over a year, complicated by the fact that state salaries offered for such key positions did not compensate at the same level as the private sector. The cost to the state of South Carolina since the October 2012 cyber attack has been over $23 million, including $1.2 million for security forensics, legal fees, and public relations; a $12 million contract with Experian for taxpayer credit monitoring and fraud insurance, $5.6 million to encrypt data, and $1.3 million for taxpayer notification. Some estimates indicate the total cost to the state will be over $30 million by yearend 2013; and an extra $7.3 million per year to maintain the new cyber security changes. South Carolina Finance Chair, Senator Hugh Leatherman is noted to have taken a "dim view of what the real cost would be to fix the damage," noting, "I really believe this: whatever this initial cost is, is simply the down-payment on a very long process." Thus, states and local government should learn from this case that computer systems are one click away from a cyber-attack![19]

> **Cyber–notes**: Spending does not equal security — "many organizations allocate significant resources to technological security measures, but neglect simple, inexpensive measures such as patch management, log analysis, privilege restrictions, password expiration, and termination of former employees' access through a robust deprovisioning process."[20]

The exposure to all level of government is due to the fast moving nature of vulnerabilities of cyberspace, and secondly, a void of clear laws and new aggressive cyber security guidelines. Where do you draw the 'line' in the open uncontrolled

---

19 Kathy Lohr, "'We Didn't Do Enough' To protect S.C. Tax records," NPR, November 21, 2012, www.npr.org ; South Carolina, "Amendment dated November 9, 2012: Credit Monitoring Products Agreement," November 9, 2012; Andrew Shain, "SC agency gets $20 million loan to pay hacking costs," December 13, 2012, www.thestate.com ; "Cyber security bill in Senate, lawmakers worry about hacking's impact," http://cpf.cleanprint.net/cpf

20 Deloitte, "Cyber Crime: A Clear and Present Danger," p. 9

cyber domain? The legal community and policy makers have been engaged in an expanding debate attempting to qualify cause-and-effect, establishment of attribution, jurisdiction, and what constitutes an attack. Currently the United States government has no coordinated policy that articulates the parameters of cyberspace in terms of a hostile intent against the nation or a state's infrastructure. The Congress failed to pass a cyber-law last year, which was followed by the White House issuing a confidential Presidential Directive on cyber rules of engagement. Not having clearly defined policies assists those nation states and especially rogue hackers, most of which are not held accountable, to flourish. Rogue-state hackers have leveraged up their skills to pursue their own political, cyber theft, and espionage ends.[21]

Cyber policy is long overdue and currently based on outdated laws and old technology, leading the Commission on Cyberecurity to conclude: "Many of us fear that we will see no action on cybersecurity absent some overwhelming crisis, which will produce unnecessary draconian legislation." [22] Until a clear national policy on the cyberspace threat is further defined — state and local governments need to address the real time cost and security measures to mitigate cyber threats with improved equipment, professional staffing, and training of all employees. And in the case of finger pointing at the IRS or any other agency, the lesson is very clear that the governing never mistake or confuse regulatory compliance with the timely priority to insure adequate information security at all levels of government.[23]

Governors Haley's simple but important admonition is a wakeup call: "Every state needs to be looking at this... It is a new part of any governor's role to make sure the data is secure." The DHS in the 2013 National Preparedness Report confirmed these concerns, noting that "states continue to have a low confidence

---

21 CSIS, "Cyber Security Two Years Later." Commission of Cybersecurity for the 44th Presidency, January 2011, pp. 13-14.

22 Ibid., p. 13.

23 Mathew J. Schwartz, S.C. "Security Blunders Show Why States Get Hacked," December 14, 2012, www.informationweek.com/security/attacks ; IBM, "IBM X-Force 2012: Mid-year Trend and Risk Report,' IBM: September 2012, pp. 1-106.

in their ability to protect against cyber threats." Accessing and securing data via open source and public data looms large.[24]

OSINT: Intricate Mosaic

The soft under belly of the cyber world has and will be the ease of access to mega-volumes of data at the stroke of a key. More than any time in history, the Internet has allowed ready access to vast amounts of knowledge, systems processing power, near instantaneous connectivity, and public information. This access has allowed for further surfing of both public and private data, often deemed to be safeguarded. Fueling the creation of data have been Linkedin, Twitter, MySpace and Facebook. Beware what you post or tweet — it is and will be in cyberspace forever. What passes as chatting sites are indeed a window on social trends and preferences that prove valuable to those that profile and "data-mine." Information sharing in terms of being more sociable has the looming potential to reduce and compromise both privacy and confidentiality. And the rampant growth of hacking, identity theft, defalcation of financial centers, credit card theft, and espionage. This is the era of OSINT — open source intelligence.

> **Cyber-notes**: OSINT — open source intelligence — acquiring information from overt and publicly available recourses and data and analyzing such data to produce actionable intelligence.[25]

There is no social media site, web site, or system that is not vulnerable to hacking. You will be attacked! Organized criminals are extremely adept at identifying and targeting social, business, and government networks and blogs. The information is at their fingertips. For example, with an estimated 400 million Facebook account worldwide, many of the online users with lax security habits and poor judgment in their posting present an open target for OSINT. Additional sources of OSINT that offer vast intelligence possibilities includes

---

24 DHS, "National Preparedness Report," March 30, 2013, p. 25. Note: State Chief Information Security Officers (CISOs) cited lack of funding and skilled staff as the top barriers to improving cybersecurity capabilities.

25 Richard Best and Alfred Cumming, "Open Source Intelligence (OSINT): Issue for Congress," Washington, D.C.: Congressional Research Service, December 5, 2007, pp. 5-7.

culling presentations at international technical conferences, foreign patents, foreign university research and libraries, newscast, photos, geospatial information (e.g. maps, drawings, commercial imagery products), as well as foreign government publications and reports. Much of which is collected at a very low cost. In past years, open-source data and reports were used mainly by intelligence analysts, by groups like the OCS — Open Source Center — at the Central Intelligence Agency, police departments in large cities, industrial groups, political campaigns, newspaper reporters, and the military.[26]

The State of South Carolina intrusion began with an old-fashion reconnaissance by gathering passive information in publicly open sources. Staff org-charts, news releases, newspaper reports, and even parking lot data can be used to identify targets and weaknesses to hone a cyber-attack — all part of an underground cyber economy that has "evolved around stealing, packaging, and selling information." This initial collection of data, combined with active social media sites and public records are the hacker's gateway to attack. A Deloitte cyber crime report noted that among "trends that demand a bold response" included the fact that, "Cyber criminals are leveraging innovation at a pace which may target organizations and security vendors cannot possibly match."[27]

Information does not have to be secret to be valuable. Open source analysis has always been important. The major shift today is the sheer volume and the development of sophisticated software and technology to manage, sort, and delivery is a timely fashion. With the convergence of two dynamic industries — media and information technology opened up the rise of big data and the 'cloud.' The accumulation of big data is promoted as a means to help with weather forecast, as a resource to fight rare diseases, tracking consumer purchasing patterns, and speed data processing.[28] For example, the OCS at CIA produces over 2,300 instances of reports, translations, analysis, video compilations and geospatial

---

26 "CIA mines 'rich' content from blogs," www.washingtontimes.com/news/2006 , April 18, 2006; Peter Eisle, "Today's spies find secrets in plain sight," *USA Today*, April 1, 2008. Note: The OSC at CIA has the capabilities to translate in over 80 languages, source media analyses, and review rare cultural dynamics.

27 Deloitte, "Cyber Crime: A Clear and Present Danger," p. 5.

28 Kenneth Cukier and Viktor Mayer-Schonberger, "The Financial Bonanza of Big Data," *Wall Street Journal*, March 8, 2013.

intelligence daily to address short-term needs and longer-term issues. Some estimates indicate that the amount of mushrooming digital information double every two years, and is expected to reach 8 zettabytes by 2015. Thus, in the hacker-espionage world, big data combined with stolen secrets, diplomatic reports (such as the WikiLeaks disclosures in 2012), and technical collection, OSINT constitutes what one former deputy director of intelligence termed the "intricate mosaic" of intelligence. [29]

Open source intelligence tools to aggregate data are available and many at little or no cost. OSINT is using and will mushroom with the mining of credit card data, GPS tracking in phones, travel via plane ticket information, face recognition software (now in use in the private sector, but soon to be ramped up at all government levels, first with the FBI in 2014 to track existing criminals database), and the most ubiquitous source personal posts and information on such sites as Facebook and Linkedin. As the data compounds, so too does the applications to harvest OSINT to include such programs as CaseFile, Spokeo, Drawbridge, Flurry, Creepy, Maltego, and FoxOne. Creepy, for example, can be downloaded to track social networks such as Twitter and Flickr in order to target the user's location my pinpointing locations on a map using geo-tagged data, as well as exposing every shared image. By clustering data, this program can be used to pinpoint a person's workplace or residence. In contrast, the Maltego application is a forensics tool to analyze real-time relationships between people, groups, websites, domains, and networks. Searches can acquire detailed data and access affiliations of the targeted user's online activities. And for those hacking to access financial data, Spokeo digs deep to target both online and offline sources.[30] And Drawbridge has figured out how to follow people without embedded 'cookies' — by watching "the notifications for behavior patterns and

---

29 Stephen C. Mercado, "Sailing the Sea of OSINT in the Information Age," www.csi-publications/Vol48no3/article05 ; "Data mining is tool in disease fight," *Houston Chronicle*, August 11, 2013; Tam Harbert, "Cloud-Based Storage," *Wall Street Journal*, December 18, 2012. Note: A "zettabyte" of data equals a trillion gigabytes, roughly equivalent to the amount of data captured on 250 billion DVDs.

30 Jim Ray, "Tool Review: Maltego," December 18, 2008, www.networkworld.com/community/print/36529; M. Smith, "Famous Patriot Hacktivist the Jester Shares Battle Chest of OSINT Tools," October 28, 2012, Ibid., 81688; Thomas J. Holt and Max Kilger, "Know Your Enemy: The Social Dynamics of Hacking," May 28, 2012, pp. 1-17, www.honeynet.org; "Firewalls and firefights," *Economist*, August 10, 2013, www.economist.com/news/business.

uses statistical modeling to determine the probability that several devices have the same owner and to assign that person an anonymous identification."[31]

The Cloud

There has been a rush by government and industry to embrace 'cloud' computing. And in terms of speed, handling larger volumes of data, and internet efficiencies, the cloud, where companies rent computing power rather than run their own data centers, is the next step. But it is also the next target. As more and more data and service providers co-locate in the cloud environment, cyber-attacks will rise. The compression of data, accurate tracking of the infrastructure within the cloud will (not can) result in greater collateral damage to non-intended victims by hobbyist hackers, organized crime, and corporate and nation-state espionage, solely because they were co-located in the cloud. Centralization and concentration of data only narrows the target for the attacker. One infamous hacker notes, "Putting everything into a single box will only make it easier for hackers."[32]

NIST defines cloud computing as:

> A model for enabling ubiquitous, convenient, on-demand network access to a shared pool of configurable computing resources (e.g., networks, servers, storage, applications, and services) that can be rapidly provisioned and released with minimal management effort or service provider interaction.

The cascading impact that security items, health records, personal data, and financial records will be prone to mismanagement and fail to protect data and records. Further complicating the security of the cloud is the ongoing conflict with the speed of the private sector to move toward such new technology and

---

31 Clair C. Miller and S. Sengupta, "Selling Secrets of Phone users to Advertisers," *New York Times*, October 6, 2013.

32 Paul Zimski, "Cloud computing faces security storm," www.computerweekly.com/Cloud-computing . See also Ana Cantu, "The History and Future of Cloud Computing," *Forbes.com*, December 12, 2012, www.forbes.com/sites/dell/2012/12/20.

disconnection with government agencies, regulations and oversight due to a void of leadership, expertise, budgeting, and realization of the threat that is poised by such advancements. Of prime concern is the rise of mobile access. Many DOD requirements for cloud security surpass off-the-shelf cloud security platforms, yet given the move to reduce budgets further questions security over the long-term.[33] The only government sector that is attempting to keep pace is the intelligence community — the so-called 'whole-of-government' in reality is disconnected and lags behind evolving cyber developments. The rise of private OSINT search engines is a good case in point.[34]

> **Cyber-notes**: performance measures — The government's strategy documents include few milestones or performance measure, making it difficult to track progress in accomplishing stated [cyber] goals and objectives. The lack of milestones and performance measures at the strategic level is mirrored in similar shortcomings within key government programs that are part of the government-wide strategy.[35] GAO 2013

---

33   CIO, DOD, "Cloud Computing Strategy," Washington, D.C.: July 2012, pp. 1-27; Greg Bensinger and Spencer E. Ante, "Amazon Wins Over IBM in CIA Row," *Wall Street Journal*, October 8, 2013.

34   CSA, "The Notorious Nine: Cloud Computing Top Threats in 2013," February 2013, www.cloudsecurityalliance.org/topthreats/ ; Cloud Security Alliance, "Top Threats to Mobile Computing," 2012, www.cloudsecurityalliance.org. See also A. Paventhan, "Cyber Security Challenges in Cloud," ERNET: India, June 7, 2013; "10 ways cloud computing is revolutionizing aerospace and defense," www.cloudcomputing-new.net/blog-hub/2013/aug/19 . Note: The threats to the cloud include: data breaches, data loss, service traffic hijacking, insecure interfaces and APIs, DOS, malicious insiders, cloud abuse- using the cloud to break an encryption, insufficient due diligence, and the hazards of shared technology vulnerabilities. The DHS with the creation of the National Cybersecurity Protection System (NCPS) has been tasked with devising an integrated system for intrusion detection to defend government IT infrastructure from cyber threats. See DHS, "National Cybersecurity Protection System," DHS/NPPD/PIA-026, Washington, D.C.: July 30, 2012 and DOD, CIO, "Cloud Computing Strategy," Washington, D.C., July 2012.

35   GAO, "Cybersecurity: National Strategy, Roles, and Responsibilities Need to be Better Defined and More Effectively Implemented," GAO: Washington, D.C., February 2013, pp. 1-3. See also "Federal Cloud Computing Strategy," February 2012, www.cio.gov/documents/Federal-Cloud-Computing-Strategy.pdf

In whatever medium data is kept, it generally holds the best practice is to secure the data, not the devices. The value is in the data, yet all too often the investment and concern is in the hardware. The cloud is data-centric and highly vulnerable. In mid-August 2013, the Department of Energy informed it employees by email that hackers had attacked the DOE human resources system and gained access to payroll and personal data as well as social security numbers of some 14,000 current and former employees.[36] And a short time later DOE leaked information, that much like the state of South Carolina, the prime reason for the hacking attack was sloppy procedures, poor data management, and neglect. DOE systems are grossly outdated, unpatched, and easy pickings. Fundamental security of data was ignored, including basic steps to prevent a breach. This is most concerning given the fact that DOE has oversight of 30-plus facilities and national laboratories — some of which deal with high level nuclear secrets, including Los Alamos National Laboratory. Too much time has been spent on outdated policies and not enough on hands-on cybersecurity skills and deterrence procedures.[37]

> **Cyber-notes**: Cloud threats: If a multitenant cloud service database isn't designed properly, a single flaw in one client's application could allow an attacker to get at not just that client's data, but every other clients' data as well — the measures you put in place to mitigate one can exacerbate the other.[38]

---

36 DOE, "Cyber Incident," Memo, August 14, 2013 seen at http://blogs.wsj.com.cio/2013/08/15

37 Mathew Schwartz, "Department of Energy Cyberattack: 5 Takeaways," August 27, 2013, www.informationweek.com/security/attacks ; cyberinfo@hq.doe.gov and www.ftc.gov/idtheft

38 "9 Top Threats to Cloud Computing Security," February 25, 2013, Tech Watch www.infoworld.com/print/213428

Panoramic Paranoia: How to foil snoopers[39]

Vulnerability		Solution
Browsers	Will pick up malware from Websites	Use reputable browser, install Adblock, HTTPS Everywhere and Do Not Track extensions
Other software	May contain backdoors	Use open-source software with symmetric-key encryption, update regularly
Passwords	If short or in dictionary, they're crackable	Try something like: L$x1ngt0n_ B@ggehot_Ch@r1gn$* *sample only
Mobile phones	Can be switched on remotely	Turn off, take out battery, then keep in fridge
Computers	Anything connected to the internet is vulnerable	Use a typewriter
Webcams	Can be turned on remotely and undetectably	Cover when not in use
Keyboards	Keylogging software can copy everything	Use mouse and onscreen keyboard to type passwords, play music to disguise keysounds
Screens	Radiation can leak contents to distant observers	Install shielding equipment, or line office with lead

---

39 Taken in part: "Cracked credibility," *Economist,* September 14, 2013, p. 66 and NSA.

Speech	Bugs are cheap and tiny, distant laser	Have important meetings naked, microphones can pick up conversations in newly ploughed field, at night, from vibrations of windows or plastic cups in howling gale; failing that, draw curtains, sweep for bugs, mutter, and avoid direct factual references.

The cloud environment and the search engine vendors are here to stay. The challenge will be enforcing the fundamental security protocols to secure the internet and the vast amounts of data. Trouble looms ahead if basic security steps and oversight are not implemented. The rush to save cost often results in more, not less, risk. The economic climate is causing many to want cheaper access to the cloud, but not pay for the needed security measures to ensure safety. *Computer Weekly* stressed the absolute need for the customer and owner of the systems to exercise a high degree of operational awareness and security to ensure their machines are up-to date, and to embrace the basics: "minimize administrative privilege, support enforcement of the rule of least privilege, and absolutely stay on top of vendor patches."[40]

The threat of lax cyber security is further compounded by rogue clouds that intercept and/or copy confidential data. Hackers, the military, government, competitors, and criminals all want a piece of this information. Both government and the private sector are navigating the compliance complexities and the security need to protect data. First and foremost, there must be clear protocols for who can access data and when. This is directly tied to a clear awareness of which data is sensitive and proprietary, followed by where the data resides in the cloud. Once identified and located, the protection of information should be done by encrypted data. Commercial sources of encryption are available via such free apps as 'Wickr' that encrypts text, voice and video messages, and other recent start-ups offering data protection include Koolspan, Seecrypt, and Silent Circle. It will not be long before all data will be required to be encrypted as a baseline and by more robust measures such as military grade 256-bit AES.

---

40   www.computerweekly.com/Cloud-computing

The user organization must keep the keys that encrypt and decipher under the narrow control of the principle user organization, not a broker, not third party systems analyst, or comingled with routine data. And for long-term resiliency, have a robust cloud malware detection system in real-time to screen all information exchanges — inbound and out-bound. Don't assume anything.[41]

Active Cyber Defense: prevent, detect, respond

The key to cyber security is that we cannot expect to have security integrity doing what we have done in the past. Passive cyber defenses that rely on off-the-shelf fire walls protection and minimum perimeter sensors to prevent intrusions are prime targets for more sophisticated hackers to attack. Proactive action that engages the adversary head-on before and during a cyber-incident is needed now more than ever.

The level of technological sophistication demonstrated by highly motivated criminals and state-sponsored espionage efforts, daily outpaces the efforts of business and government to mitigate these cyber intrusions. State-sponsored cyber-attacks continue to go undetected, with on study by Mandiant in 2012 noting, "Only about 6 percent of organizations detect advanced attackers via internal methods ... the median number of days from first evidence of compromise to identification of the attack was 416 days!"[42]

The best defense is a good offense. George Kurtz of CrowdStrike noted the fundamental flaw in dealing with cyber intrusions is that "Most spend too much time trying to work out what hit them and far too little trying to understand

---

41   DOD, "DOD IT Modernization," Fact Sheet, www.DODcio.defense.gov/ITModernization ; Pravin Kothari, "Cloud computing: how can companies reduce the security risk?" June 13, 2013, www.theguardian.com/media-network-blog/2013 ; Paul Wagenseil, "Cryptopalypse' Now: Looming Security Crisis Could Cripple Internet," TechNewsDaily, August 21, 2013; "Six security issues to tackle before encrypting cloud data," www.computerweekly.com/news/2240180087 ; Eric J. Byres, "Defense in Depth," AutomationIT, November 2012.

42   Irving Lachow, "Active Cyber Defense: A Framework for Policymakers," Center for North American Security, February 2013, pp. 1-3; Mandiant, "M-Trends 2012: An Evolving Threat," 2012.

the motivations of their attackers and how to counter future assaults."[43] This has not always been the train of thought in the cyber industry, since some view offensive operations as somehow controversial, even as their systems and IP are being exfiltrated by hackers. Oddly enough, this active cyber defense approach is exactly what the NSA and other foreign governments are exercising to slow down advanced persistent threats and protect critical data and infrastructure, with the NSA recognizing the motivation of attackers, in their 2013 SIGNET Computer Network Operations work plan, is to "Insert vulnerabilities into commercial encryption systems, IT systems, networks, and endpoint communications devices used by targets."[44] Agency efforts include inserting back doors into commercial products and breaking the encryption code, and monitoring communications — both at home and abroad. However, such intrusion and "hack backs" or other preventive measures to take the fight to the hackers are viewed by some as aggressive. Furthermore, there has been some delay by the private sector to engage in this practice due to unclear legal ramifications and definitions regarding whether or not that counts as a firm actively thwarting attacks.[45]

> **Cyber-notes:** active cyber defense — a synchronized, real-time capability to discover, detect, prevent, analyze, respond, and mitigate threats and capabilities.[46]

---

43 Quoted from, "Firewalls and firefights," August 10, 2013, www.economist.com/news/business/21583251

44 "Secret Documents Reveal N.S.A. Campaign Against Encryption," Budget documents, SIGNET Enabling Project, marked Top Secret, seen at www.nytimes.com/interactive.2013/09/05/us/documents .

45 James Ball et al, "Revealed: How US and UK spy agencies defeat internet privacy and security," September 5, 2013, www.theguardian.com/world/2013/sep/05/nas-gchq ; Elien Nakashima, "When is a Cyberattack a Matter of Defense?" February 27, 2012, www.washingtonpost.com/blogs/checkpoint . See also Defense Security Service, "Targeting US Technologies 2012: A Trend Analysis of Reporting from Defense Industry," DOD: November 12, 2012; Jody Westby, "Caution: Active Response to Cyber Attacks Has High Risk," November 29, 2012, www.forbes.com/sites/jodywestby/2012.

46 DOD, "Department of Defense Strategy for Operations in Cyberspace," July 2011, p. 7.

Advanced cyber-attacks do not occur in a vacuum, but instead involve a number of advanced and active stages in advance of targeting a victim. Contemporary conventional cyber defense approaches that are vulnerability-focused processes largely presuppose the attackers have the upper hand and advantage. Data indicates over 80 percent of cyberattacks are turned away, yet the remaining 20 percent could do massive damage. The APTs indeed are the aggressor, picking who, where, and when to strike. Oddly enough, it should be apparent to all that at any time, any system is subject to hacking. Over the last couple of years, a more active approach has been devised by a process known as the cyber kill chain (CKC), "a systematic process to target and engage an adversary to create desired effects." Developed at Lockheed by Eric Hutchins and his EBS Team, CKC challenges the conventional network defense tools to identify and stop or mitigate APTs to optimize detection of an event by grouping attack stages together to allow early detection. In the course of contemplating and executing a cyber attack, there are a number of stages an attacker plans. The seven phase continuum, styled to be an end-to-end process described as a 'chain', is vulnerable given that the interruption of any one link will disrupt the entire process. It is a clear and proactive means to stop or minimize an attack in its earliest stage.[47]

The cyber kill chain approach employs a proactive approach to stopping or limiting advanced attacks. The kill chain is depicted by the progressive phases of a cyber attack from inception or recon through to active incident response:

Cyber Kill Chain

RECON	Deliver	Control	Maintain
	Weaponize	EXPLOIT	Execute
Proactive Detection and Mitigation		Incident Response and Mission Assurance	

---

47 E. M. Hutchins, M. J. Cloppert, and R. M. Amin, "Intelligence-Driven Computer Network Defense Informed by Analysis of Adversary Campaigns and Intrusion Kill Chain," Proc. 6th Int'l Conf Information Warfare and Security, 2010, pp. 113-125, www.lockheedmartin.com/content/dam/lockheed/data ; Charles Croom, "The Cyber Kill Chain: a Foundation for a New Cyber Security Strategy," *New Frontier*, August 2010, pp. 52-56.

Preparedness Consortium

National efforts to address vulnerabilities ranging from weapons of mass destruction to cyber-attacks has been augmented by a network of centers nationwide to address all level of concern and training at the public and private sectors.[48] Established by Congressional mandate in late 1998, further reconfirmed in Public Law in 2001, and reauthorized by DHS in 2007, a consortium of seven members now has the role to enhance the preparedness of federal, state, and local first responders and reduce vulnerabilities in all manner of catastrophic all-hazard events. Training and emergency management exercises ranging from chlorine chemical containment to emergency response training for the staff of the New Orleans Superdome prior to the February 3, 2013 Super Bowl XLVII. These public-private groups and sponsoring institutions each has a special mission in terms of emergency preparedness, incident management, and security training.[49]

---

[48] DHS, "National Preparedness Report," March 30, 2013, pp. 24-6.

[49] "TEEX/NERRTC Partners with DHS Office of Infrastructure Protection," *Socorro: The NDPC News*, Fall 2012., www.ndpc.us/consortium

Figure 5-4
National Domestic Preparedness Consortium[50]

CDP	Center for Domestic Preparedness	Anniston, Al.

- WMD, incident prevention, healthcare/ public health response

NERRTC	National Emergency response and Rescue Training Center	Texas A&M

- Incident mgnt, risk assessment, cyber security, public works, hazmat

EMRTC	Energetic Materials research and Testing Center	New Mexico Tech

- IT, energetic materials, petroleum recovery, explosive materials

NDPTC	National Preparedness Training Center	University of Hawaii

- Natural hazards, urban planning, critical infrastructure, economic recovery

NCERST	National Center for Emergency Response in Surface Transportation	Pueblo, Co

- Transportation and testing, railway

NNSA	National Nuclear Security Administration: Rad/Nuc	Las Vegas, Nevada

- Prevention, deterrence and response to radiological/ nuclear attacks

NCBRT	National Center for Biomedical research and Training	LSU Baton Rouge, La

- Law enforcement, biological threats, food defense and agriculture

---

50 www.ndpc.us/consortium

SIX
Cyber Triage & Trends

Trusted actors and trusted networks must be established before crunch time, the terrible moment when the dogs of war are straining at their chains.
James J. Carafano
Wiki at War – 2012

Cyberspace's dynamic nature must be acknowledged and addressed by policies that are equally dynamic. There are no generally accepted cybersecurity standards, and there is no generally applicable liability system to account for failing to meet those standards.
Steven P. Bucci
Heritage Foundation

Cyberspace will never be completely secure.
The Economist — July 12, 2014

The cyber-security threat is an unquestioned national security interest that the US is not prepared or equipped to address. — The nation needs cyber domain awareness before there is a major incident — and thus must convey the urgency, complexity, security at point of entry, and cyber-related insider threat. Securing cyberspace is extremely difficult in real-time because the architecture of the Internet was designed to promote connectivity, NOT security. One close observer noted: "I think we have a mismatch between our perceived level of [cyber] threat and our level of preparation. In other words, we have high concerns about cyber-attacks, but our preparation, frankly, is not what it should be."[1]

---

1 James Stavridis, "'A Difference Between Knowledge and Wisdom,'" *Proceedings*, August 2013, p. 52; "Defending the digital frontier," *The Economist*, July 12, 2014, p. 3.

Critical infrastructure encompasses the full spectrum of our approach to national security. While the public sector is tasked to ensure a high level of oversight and protection, the fact remains that to fully assure effective cyber-security for our military, supply chain networks, and power-water-fuel grids requires a full and transparent public-private interaction. Traditional lines between war and peace are being blurred by cyberspace. Routine physical facilities' security, communications networks, and information security and assurance for protecting against both outsider and insider threats no longer apply. Private sector liability relating to shared information and investigation of cyber-crimes, for example do IT vendor assume any liability for faulty or compromised products. "Comprehensive cyber security needs to insure that this critical infrastructure is sufficiently hardened and resilient," noted NSA Director Keith Alexander, "*as it is the storehouse of much of our economic prosperity.*"[5]

Cyber Trends and Challenges

There is little doubt that cyber threats will continue and intensify. What has been created by humans can be broken or penetrated by humans. These systems are manmade and thus their use for good or bad will face the same challenge of all new inventions over the millennium. The creation of new malware and creative exploits knows no bounds, as the vector for intrusion into the Internet and communications only compounds with the increased usage of mobile devices and social networks. Physical locations and barbwire mean nothing to cyber adversaries who remotely attack. As computer security continues to improve with new fire walls and the requirement for encryption, as well as robust security/access policies and protocols, secure mobile access, patch management, and malware protection, so too will cyber hackers and criminals reach to develop and enhance new means and focused specific configurations to bypass any and all cyber defenses. One cyber forensic and intrusion detection

---

[5] Farwell, "Industry's Vital Role in National Cyber Security," pp.19-23; Tomer Teller, "The Biggest Cybersecurity Threats of 2013," www.forber.com/site/ciocentral/2012/12/05; The White House, "Improving Critical Infrastructure Cybersecurity," Exec. Order 13636, Washington, D.C.: February 12, 2013; General Keith Alexander to Senator Harry Reid, Washington, D.C., July 31, 2012.

company estimated that in their annual caseload, only 6% of advanced intrusions were detected by 'internal processes.'[6]

Daily real time innovation is functionality outpacing the norms in cyber security, thus success in the cyber world demands a strategy that couples agile, adaptive national security policies, with market incentives to defeat an increasingly savvy, tech-driven enemy. An example would be to limit the multiple access points on the electric grid or supply chain and mandatory required authentication for any and all access. Traditionally, cybersecurity was based on "perimeter defense." Data was in a "physical box" secured by guards and fences. No longer. Data, and the rise of 'big data,' has been moved by virtualized systems into cyber space and the cloud. As connectivity and technology progress, so too does the void in the legal approach to cyber, with no straightforward means for government agencies to share classified data with US companies, a continued lag in the forensic abilities to positively determine attribution and motive, and the progressive collapse of individual privacy due in large part to social media. The concern by the Pentagon is such, DARPA has announced the "Cyber Grand Challenge," to award $2 million in competitive prize money to university and business teams that design security systems to protect online networks and stop the wave of cyber-attacks on military systems.[7]

Notwithstanding, there are a number of trends and challenges that will shape the future of cyber security:[8]

---

6   Ronald Deibert and Rafal Rohozinski, "Risking Security: Policies and Paradoxes of Cyberspace Security," *International Political Sociology*, 2010, pp. 15-32; www.mandiant.com/reserves/trends/

7   www.darpa.mil/cybergrandchallenge/ ; "How to save the net," *Wired*, September 2014, pp. 96-9.

8   Note: There are a number of sources that regularly do threat assessments and trends, to include: McAfee Labs, "2013 Threats Predictions," Santa Clara, 2012; Georgia Institute of Technology, "Emerging Cyber Threat Report 2013," 2013, www.gtisc.gatech.edu; Symantec, "Internet Security Threat Report 2013," April 2013; James M Stewart, Global Knowledge, "Top Ten Cybersecurity Risks: How Prepared Are You for 2013?" www.globalknowlegde.com; Rueters Cybersecurity Summit 2013, "US grapples with cyber threats," May 13, 2013; US Department of Justice, FY 2014 Budget Request: Cyber Security, Washington, D.C.: 2013; Monica Giovachino and Sarah Tidman, "A Roadmap for Improving Cyber Preparedness," July 10, 2013, www.domesticpreparedness.com/Cyber; Harry D. Raduege, Jr., "The Public/Private Cooperation We Need on Cyber Security," http://blogs.hbr.

Preparedness:

Communities across the United States have the best trained and dedicated first responders in the world — to respond to situations they have been trained for. They are trained to attack any situation. The hallmark of responders and the command and control to foster the robust network across the nation is a unified effort to coordinate activities, share information, constantly plan and maintain an appropriate level of readiness in advance of the call respond and mitigate the emergency situation. Manpower, equipment, and resources are brought to response on an emergency based on the geographic size and impact of the incident. Such responses can range from a localized fire in a small urban community to the regional impact of hurricane. Such events are often short in duration, from a few hours to a week. Of course, the lingering recovery from a massive hurricane can have multiple weeks of disruption and displacement of the population and infrastructure. The later scenario borders on the initial impact during first days of the cascading multi-layered cyber-attack. Furthermore, a cyber-attack could be launched against critical civilian infrastructure in a manner that completely bypasses military defenses! Local communities and states are not ready or prepared for a cyber-attack.[9]

The recent 'National Preparedness Report' from DHS noted, "States continue to have low overall awareness of risks to their information systems and low confidence in their ability to protect them against cyber threats." A number of reasons account for the dearth of preparation for a cyber-incident: first, a void of active training and awareness; second, a local feeling that someone else will handle the cyber problem if it accrues; third the total disregard of awareness for the rapid cascading impact a cyber-attack can have on a community or region following a massive attack on the power grid. Such an attack would in rapid order shut down communications, water supplies, and fuel pumps. It would hamper emergency services due to panic and crowding at hospitals, and isolate people from the Internet, TV, and radio transmissions. Basic food

---

org/2013/06; Tom Larkins, "Threats and Opportunities Growing in Cybersecurity," June 2013, www.nationaldefensemagazine.org/archive/2013/June; Richard A. McFeely, Exec. Asst. Dir., Criminal Cyber Response, FBI, Statement before the Senate Appropriations Committee, June 12, 2013, www.fbi.gov/news/testimony/cyber-security

9   Adam P. Liff, "Cyberwar: A New 'Absolute Weapon'? The Proliferation of Cyberwarfare Capabilities and Interstate War," *Journal of Strategic Studies*, June 2012, p. 410.

supplies would be exhausting within as short a time as a week. Auxiliary power supplies to maintain operations at health facilities, recue shelters, cell towers, and first responders would be expended. Within a short time, local command and control could be called into question, resulting in the Federalization of the incident. For example, the governor would call out the National Guard for protection of both citizens and property while officials work to repair equipment and systems, for which there are very few spare parts, possibly taking months to replace such items as power transformers. Cell communications and Internet could be out for weeks as the system recovers.[10]

Infrastructure: the grid

The greatest threat in a cyber-attack would be the damage that could be done to the electric power grid across the nation. See Chart 6-1. This critical infrastructure system is very fragile and exposed on an hourly basis to multiple attacks and disruption. Electric power is the key component and life-blood of our nation's security and serviceability, given the degree to which we have tied out industrial base, national security, and daily lives to the use of electricity. The electric grid is further connected with downstream infrastructure to include potable water, fuel distribution, transportation systems, communications, health care facilities, and food distribution.[11]

A recent headline in the *Wall Street Journal* reads, "Meltdowns Hobble NSA Data Center." While not a cyber-attack, it clearly drives home the critical nature of reliable electricity, especially for the very agency that monitors and tracks cyber events:

> *Chronic electrical surges at the massive new data-storage facility central to the National Security Agency's spying operation have*

---

10   DHS, National Preparedness Report, March 30, 2011, p. 25. Note: DHS continues to claim shortfall of preparedness is due to "lack of funding and skilled staff as top barriers to improving cybersecurity capabilities."

11   Bipartisan policy Center, "Cybersecurity and the North American Electric Grid: New Policy Approaches to Address an Evolving Threat," February 2014.

destroyed hundreds of thousands of dollars-worth of machines and delayed the center's opening…..[12]

A disruption of as few as nine power substations could result in a nationwide cascading blackout. Damage to the massive transformers, which regulate both voltage and distribution across power lines, could be further hampering due to the fact it can take a year or more to build and install new transformers. Currently, we do not fully know, nor has it been disclosed, how vulnerable the grid is and how many disruptive incidents go unreported, or more concerning … undetected. Foreign espionage agents as well as rogue hackers have penetrated our electrical grid, and who knows what malware they have implanted to create future chaos.[13]

Cyber-notes: An off the shelf desktop computer can test anywhere between one and fifteen million passwords per second, and crack a password from a dictionary in less than 1 minute[14]

Insider threats: the black market

Long before Army Private Manning dumped volumes of top secret military and US State Department documents on WikiLeaks and analyst Edward Snowden divulged NSA secrets, the threat of insider espionage and rogue actions have been common. Common, not just in the military and government agencies, but also in critical industry, non-profits, R&D facilities, and at US universities. Up

---

12 Siobhan Gorman, "Meltdowns Hobble NSA Data Center," *Wall Street Journal*, October 8, 2013.

13 S. Gorman, "NSA Chief Warns of 'Dramatic' Cyberattack," *Wall Street Journal,* November 21, 2014, p. 2; National Academy of Sciences, "Terrorism and the Electric Power Delivery System," Washington, D.C.: National Research Council, 2012; Rebecca Smith, "Power Station's Security is Breached, Again," *Wall Street Journal*, August 29, 2014; James Wooley, "The Growing Threat from EMP Attack," *Wall Street Journal*, August 13, 2014. Note: New transformers can weigh in excess of 500,000 pounds posing a logistical challenge to ship and install in a timely situation.

14 John Adams, "The Government of Canada and Cyber Security: Security Begins at Home," *Journal of Military and Strategic Studies*, Vol. 14, 2012, p. 9.

until 2013, much of the concern has been with outside rogue hackers and terrorist groups as well as Chinese, Russian, and Iranian efforts to penetrate our IT systems. This is a real and ongoing threat, yet the more perplexing is the insider, a privileged user who has access to key data. Given the vast expansion of data and the numerous points of access, an insider either as a foreign agent, a vendor, or a disgruntled employee can do massive long term damage. For example, a study funded by the US Secret Service and DHS found that insiders within the financial industry are able to foment fraud and theft for nearly 32 months before detection. A number of items have made it more difficult to track and identify the insider. Such rogues have numerous options to record data on disc or thumb drives, and second, the increased number of private contractor and outsourcing of jobs create multiple levels of vulnerability.[15]

Once they are inside "the wire," unless care is taken with passwords, authorization levels, and double human confirmation, the problems will persist. Motives for the actions of the insider can vary greatly. In the private sector, the cause can be as simple as being passed over for a promotion or an argument with a fellow employee. In the case of a government agency, these reasons can also apply. In the case of Private Manning and NSA employee Snowden, they claim their breaching top secret data was a "protest of government overreach" and obligation to expose what they felt was wrong doing that needed to be made public. No one knows the depth to which we have disgruntled employees or spies embedded across the United States, in critical sectors of the private economy and government. And by the time the secret data is hacked and gone, it's too late![16]

The insider threat does not have to be a spy, but a trusted employee who unintended opens a cleverly-worded email. This means of inadvertently breaching and penetrating a web site or company security include the massive spread of social media networks and social engineering profiles to hack into an unsuspecting site. The random opening of an email is a cause for pause, with many companies automatically adding a warning to each employee incoming email:

---

15 John F. Gantz, "The Link between Pirated Software and Cybersecurity Breaches," Singapore: National University of Singapore and IDC, March 2014.

16 James Bamford, "The most wanted man in the world," *Wired*, September 2014, pp. 86-95.

> This is an EXTERNAL email. STOP. Think before you CLICK links or OPEN attachments.

The process of social engineering, taking advantage of human vulnerabilities, is most often used by phishing to fool the recipient, yet can be followed by APTs. Gaining access to the weakest link of security is usually a slow process, the results of tremendous planning, repeated targeting, and reconnaissance by the attacker, which makes such intrusions difficult to detect.[17]

> **Cyber-notes:** Globally, over 150 billion emails, 400 million tweets, and 1 million blog posts are sent each day. Some 52 trillion words are composed via email and social media — the equivalent of 520 million books.[18]

Encryption: closing the barn door

With the greater access to data comes a greater chance to breach of systems, exfiltration of IP, and fraud. Currently, few protocols call for mandatory encryption, viewed by many as too complicated and expensive for the average user.

Encryption should and will soon be standard protocol for all operation on the Internet. The US military and government security agencies are well along to making encryption the backbone for their security measures. Any system anywhere can be penetrated, thus encryption is a near fool proof means to slow down hackers and protect sensitive data. The advent of 'big data' and the 'cloud' demands the expedited use of encrypted data.

Employees can further complicate access by not installing unauthorized hardware, using remote access tools, and tethering to unsecure mobile devices, all of which can expose the organization to malware and remote access attacks. Concern by the federal government was echoed by Secretary of Treasury Jacob

---

17 Lena H. Sun, "Cybersecurity issues hurting health care," *San Antonio Express-News*, June 14, 2014.

18 Clive Thompson, "Thinking Out Loud," *Wired*, October 2013, p. 164. See also Viktor Mayer-Schonberger and Kenneth Cukier, *Big Data*, New York: Eamon Dolan Book, 2014.

Lew, "A malicious cyber actor can cause catastrophic damage to our financial system without directly attacking a bank. One back door is all a malicious actor needs to transmit large scale damage."[19]

Few cyber-attacks have been as publicly vetted as the massive attack on the retailer Target in December 2013 that breached accounts and personal credentials of over 100 million credit card accounts. Even with the FireEye malware detection software, used by intelligence agencies worldwide, in place, the Target security staff failed to detect the breach in real-time. And even after the Feds notified Target on December 12, it took the company days to confirm the attack and fully realize the extent of the hacking. The loss in sales was in the hundreds of millions of dollars over the holiday season, and the long term damage to Target's reputation that is hard to quantify.[20]

The Cloud: "smoke and mirrors"

The speed of the transition and advancements driven by innovation of the cyber world and the Internet is no better displayed than by the rapid rush to embrace the cloud. The rise of the cloud is no surprise given the mountains of information and data that has been aggregated with big-data analytics to both store and manage the volume of captured records. The primary issue and concern with the cloud is that collectively we are putting all the eggs in one or two huge baskets! During 2014, business spent some $100billion on cloud computer services, a fraction of the global $2 trillion outlay on IT. Firms are wary to give up total control of their data due to two primarily concerns: security in the cloud, and

---

19 Sec. Jacob Lew, "Remarks," New York: Alpha Conference, July 16, 2104. Note: For proof of Sec. Lew's comments see Emily Glazer, et al, "Citi, E*Trade, 3 Others Saw Signs of Hackers," *Wall Street Journal*, October 9, 2014.

20 Michael Riley, et al, "The Epic Hack: Target," *Bloomberg*, March 17, 2014, pp. 41-47. See also Matt Kodama and Bill Ladd, "Mapping the Cyberwar Battlefield," *Harvard Business Review*, September 2013, pp. 32-3; Brett Molina, "Hackers Hit EBay; Millions Warned," *USA Today*, May 22, 2014; Shelly Banjo and Danny Yadron, "Home Depot Admits Breach of Card System," *Wall Street Journal*, September 9, 2014, and Jordon Robertson and Michael Riley, "JP Morgan Hack Said to Span Months via Multiple Flaws," August 29, 2014 seen at www.bloomberg.com/news/print/2014-08-29

government regulations on handling and storing sensitive data, such as banking and healthcare records. Big brother is watching.[21]

On the surface the cloud is intended to give the user a broader access to more and more data in real time, which clearly establishes the cloud, due to remote connections, applications, operating systems, and the co-mingling of data on shared resources, as a target-rich environment for espionage, fraud, and hackers. A term for such a massive breach of cloud data has already been coined — 'hyper jacking!' Industry, universities, and even the government are being sold on the cloud based on savings, not security. Authorization, enhanced credentialing, and 'need-to-know' protocols are the key weaknesses in cloud services and security.[22]

The criminal element, while looking for access to the cloud, will continue to advance and perfect their attacks by botnets. These methods have been tested and found advantageous in spite of massive industry and government efforts to take them down as soon as discovered, which means they will continue to enhance the capabilities of botnets. Plausible deniability is a tremendous limitation to the development of an international cyber monitoring and agreement. And thus, there is no reduction of risk using the cloud.[23]

The Symantec "Internet Security Threat Report 2013" captures the prime concern with the cyber security challenge:

> The most ominous example of malware authors knowing all about us is in targeted attacks. Creating successful targeted attacks requires attackers to learn about us. They will research our emails addresses, our job, our professional interests, and even the conferences we attend and the websites we frequent. All this information is compiled to launch a successful targeted attack. Once on our devices, the attacker's tools are designed to pull as much data as

---

21 "Cloud computing: Silver lining," *Economist*, August 30, 2014.

22 Nathan Jurgenson, "Hiding in Public: How Privacy Thrives Online," *Wired*, April 2014, 21-22; Rachel Duran, "Answers to Data Questions in the Cloud," *Business Expansion Journal*, July 2914, pp. 11-4.

23 DOD, CIO, "Cloud Computing Strategy," Washington, D.C., July 2012.

>possible. Undiscovered targeted attacks can collect years of our emails, files, and contact information. These tools also contain the ability to log our keystrokes, view our computer screens, and turn on our computers' microphones and cameras. Targeted attackers truly act as an Orwellian incarnation of Big Brother.[24]

Mobile devices: mini-super processors

As communications, the mobility of data, grows more compact and mobile and accessible from anywhere, threats both to systems and the cloud will compound opening new potential gateways to attack. Mobile devices by early 2013 outnumbered PCs and desktop computers: for example, Apple selling over 9 million iPhones during the last weekend of September 2013. The trend to embrace the bring-your-on-device (BYOD) further enhances the complex need for security, as users use their hand-held devices as if they were their PCs, thus making them open to web-based attacks. Most mobile devices have little native security.

Furthermore, securing sensitive data on smart devices by IT departments that have very little control over the user is problematic and an ongoing challenge. Given the fact that phones with near-field communications (NFC) enabled are becoming the norm, these new "digital-wallets" will be a boon to the hackers and thieves planting mobile worms to steal data, and will able to compromise the system at will. The larger and denser a population area (center-city metro areas, airports, football crowds), the more damage a hacker can do.

In 2012, there were more than 35,000 malicious Android programs, six times the previous year. Often, the boundaries between private and business use are blurred — further confused by who owns and uses the device. Only a single device needs to escape detection to compromise an entire network. Thus, IT and systems security is rapidly shifting from a device-centric function to a roving user-centric mode. Wireless applications and entry points need to be

---

24   Symantec, "Internet Security Threat Report 2013, " April 2013, p. 4.

encrypted and hardened, with a corresponding ability to have remote diagnostics to monitor threats.[25]

> **Cyber-notes:** FY 2014 US Department of Justice view of cyber:
>
> Cybercrimes are becoming more common, more sophisticated, and more dangerous. Our adversaries increasingly use computers and the Internet to further their illicit activities. Terrorists seek to sabotage critical infrastructure; organized crime syndicates seek to defraud banks and corporations; and spies seek to steal defense and intelligence secrets and intellectual property. Each threatens our Nation's economy and security.

From a community and local perspective during emergency situations, a key factor is the secure interoperability of communications. This is a multi-dimensional challenge. Emergency responders and local leaders must have secure operable means of communications. A cyber-attack combined with an electromagnetic pulse (EMP) event could silence all networks, including sat-phones and all hand-held devices for a long period of time. Of prime concern at all echelons of response is the level of verifiable command and control.

Rise of non-state threats

Non-state and nation-state threats, particularly China, Russia, and Iran, will be an ongoing threat and frequent source of cyber intrusion. Deniability is the hallmark of rogue and nation-state attackers. Without attribution, there is little or no risk to the hacker. This trend is further fueled by the growing emergence of the online black market that enables low skill attackers to pay for services and access. Online resources further allow hackers to improve skills at a very low cost. This growing segment of non-state actors, many with no affiliation or loyalties, is a serious threat vector. [26]

---

25   Lauren LaCapra, "Wall Street banks learn how to survive in staged cyber attack," October 21, 2013 Note: The financial backbone was tested by SIFMA designed "Quantum Dawn 2" exercise on July 18, 2013.

26   Thomas Holt and Max Kilger, "Know Your Enemy: The Social Dynamics of Hacking," Honeynet Project, May 28, 2012, www.honeynet.org

The Arab Spring and the cascading turmoil and revolution across the Middle East is a clear sign of the power and ubiquity of the Internet and 'cyber revolution.' Never before has unrest been so orchestrated than what we have seen in recent months. With access and capabilities to perpetrate large-scale violence, governments are being over thrown, only to be replaced by more radical anti-American elements. A patchwork of ethnic minorities and religious zealots have found voice and power in stirring up the grass roots of their groups to foment crisis and violence.

Loss of Privacy:

The more connectivity, the more our daily privacy is at risk — communications, travel habits, buying profile, and health records. Most do not know the magnitude of loss of privacy that occurs, and the intent to do harm that propagates it. Sites and services, most particularly social media that share data and sell data profiles to marketers, daily reduce any notion of privacy. Thus, your private data isn't truly private — nor will it ever be private again. Connectivity has proven to yearly be less secure. The rise of global markets and business travel has greatly raised the risk factors for both the prepared and unprepared. Being prepared for theft of data is an imperative. Within hours of landing in many countries, to include China, Russia, Egypt, or India, there will be malware planted on your phone. The threat is equally bad in hot spots in both the United States and France. No place is considered safe. Confirming the magnitude of aggressive external cyber threats, James Comey, Director of the FBI, candidly concluded, "There are those who've been hacked by the Chinese, and those who don't know they've been hacked by the Chinese."[27]

The more devices you travel with, the more vulnerable you are to hacking. Furthermore, never use public access computers, or computers in-room iPads. The odds are high that crooks have installed 'key logging' malware, and thus there is no privacy. A prime example is the FBI investigation in the fall of 2014 of what appeared to be a breach of celebrity iCloud accounts, exposing hundreds of nude images of Hollywood actresses. Always password protect a laptop and,

---

27 CBS Sixty Minutes, "The Director," aired October 5, 2104.

if possible, encrypt all data. However, in many countries it is illegal to encrypt data, particularly Russia and China.[28]

> **Cyber-notes**: most common mis-used passwords:
>
> 123456   password   abc123   111111   iloveyou   adobe123

Tips for Foreign Travel Computer Protection

- Allow no one to use any of your electronic devices.
- Be highly suspicious of 'generically' named hotspots.
- Carry computer with only minimal data.
- Disable Blue-tooth protocols.
- Limit phone and computer use to necessary items.
- Do not use public access computers.
- Turn off phone in business meeting and remove the battery for security.
- Low connection speeds could hint that you are being hacked.
- If at all possible, do not go to any Web site that needs a username/password.
- Change password often.
- Don't assume anything.
- Avoid social media.

While these seem very small items to be concerned with, note they are a hacker's means to penetrate any of our best computer systems. It's the ease of entry that creates the vast amount of cyber threats. These threats will only continue to grow.

---

28   Louis Sahagun, "FBI joins hunt for hacker who leaked nude photos of actresses," September 1, 2014 seen at www.latimes.com/local

Conclusion

The wired world we live in becomes more connected and more vulnerable to cyber-attack every day. The explosion of mobile devices, social media, and applications alone has exponentially increased security vulnerabilities. The prospects for significant cyber disruptions should be of concern for both the public and private actors — from the smallest local entity (securing SCADA controls for municipal owned power company) to national organizations and agencies (protecting mission-critical data and systems). The cyber threat is further complicated by the fact that there are both nation-state actors as well as hacktivists that can cause massive interruptions for low or no cost. The low end threat is a driven by two sets of threats, social-political activists and organized crime syndicates worldwide. And such cyber breaches can be carried out with little or no attribution.

Structural-political aspects of how the internet was developed, and who owns the various elements of the cyber-world system and access, pose tremendous challenges. Over 90 percent of the critical cyber infrastructure in the United States alone is owned by the private sector — i.e. communication, SCADA systems, and supply chain infrastructure. Our government has oversight and security concerns at all levels, yet not necessarily control over the Internet and cyber space. The government's needs for security and the private sector's demands for autonomy and unfettered access to the internet are in conflict and on a head on collision unless resolved..

Thus, one of the primary keys of the cyber-space is a fully functioning public-private partnership to vet protocols and craft a framework for a "proactive, layered defense" for cyber. Fast-evolving technology and cyber threats are challenging the strategic implications of a potentially crippling cyber-attack. An end-to-end approach to insure the best means to limit threats and protect critical infrastructure (and the ability to respond in a timely-coordinated manor to address breaches) is critical to the future integrity of the internet and cyber space.

FIGURE 6-2

Sample List of Cyber Attacks

Date	Attacker	Named Event	Target	
June 1982	US/CIA	Gas Pipelines	Russia	1st Logic Bomb
Spring 1991	Netherlands	Rouge Hackers	US DoD	34 Sites Penetrated
March 1994	British Hacker	Datastream Cowboy	USAF Rome Lab.	'Sniffer'
Feb 1998	3 Teenagers	Solar Sunrise	Pentagon	500 Sites Hit
Sept 1999	China	Op. Allied Force	NATO	Network Hackers
May 2000	Unknown	Love Bug	U.S. Govt	Virus Outbreak
April 2001	China	Honker Union	U.S. Targets	Post-Recon Crash
2001	Russia	Moonlight Maze	U.S. Govt	
July 2001	Unknown	Code Red	White House	DoD DDoS
Jan 2003	Unknown	Slammer Worm	Power Grid	DDos/banks/airlines
2003-2005	China	Titan Rain	U.S. & EU	Computer Networks
2006	China PLA	Byzantine Hades	U.S.	U.S. State Dept
Feb 2006	United States	Cyber Strom I ##	Govt Exercise	Targets; IT, Commo
June 2006	Lebanon	Team Evil	Israel	Defaced 8K Websites
Spring 2006	China PLA	Byzantine Hades	U.S.	U.S. State De
March 2007	Russia	Bronze Night	Estonia	Entire Nation
May 2007	China	Chan. A. Merkel	Germany*	Used Trojan Horse
2007	Unknown	US SecDef Email	Robert Gates	Unclassified System
Aug 2008	Palestinian	Cold Zero	Israel	Lukid Party Website
2008-09	Russian ***	W32 Conficker	US, UK, France	Military Units
2009	Russia***	N/A	Georgia	.ge Domain Down
2009	China	F-35 designs	Night Dragon	Espionage
July 2009	North Korea#	4th of July	U.S. Govt	Damage Contained
Jan 2010	China	Trojan Horse	Google	DDoS/Sabotage
July 2010	US/Isreal	Stuxnet	Iran	Weaponised Virus
Nov 2010	Rogue	Wiki-leaks	U.S.	Massive Data Breach
2011	Chinese	^GhostNet	103 Countries	1,300 Infected Sites
March 2011	China	N/A	N/A	Pentagon 24,000 files/theft
Oct 2011	Unknown	W32.Duqu	Espionage	Malware
Dec 2011	Unknown	N/A	N.A,. Pipelines ICS-Cert	Amber Alert
March 2012	Unknown	System Shutdown	USDOC	EDA Down 8 Weeks
May 2012	US Cyber Team ###	N/A	Yemen	al-Qa'ida Websites
May 2012	Unknown^^	Flame	Middle East	Extensive DDoS
Aug 2012	Iran	Shamoon	Aramco	Oil/Gas 30K Computers
Oct 2012	China?	N/A	South Carolina	Million Tax Records
Nov 2012	Unknown	N/A	New York Times	Hacked for 3 Months
Feb 2013	China ****	Unit 61398	Global 141 Companies	Mandian Report
March 2013	Netherlands	CyberBunker	Blacklisting	Spamhaus Crashed
April 2014	Unknown	Heartbleed	SSL Protocol Attack	Data Mining Malware
Dec 2013	Unknown	Target	Credit Card Accountsextent	Unknown
Sep 2014	Unknown	Home Depot	Credit Card Accountsextent	Unknown
Nov 2014	North Korea	Sony Corp.	New Movies	FBI Investigating

NOTE: The above list is only a random sample to allow the reader to gauge the scope and vastness of cyber-attacks. All date was obtained from open source data; thus, dates, attacker, and targets are the best evidence available to date.

Sources: Archive of hacker exploits at www.zone-h.org ; Robin Gandhi et al, "Dimensions of Cyber-Attacks," IEEE Magazine, Spring 2011, pp. 28-38; GAO, "Cybersecurity: Threats Impacting the Nation," Washington, D.C.: April 24, 2012; "APT1," February 2012, www.mandiant.com

*German security officials, in 2008, estimate 40 percent of all German companies have been victims of nation-state-sponsored industrial espionage; see CSO Online, April 21, 2008.

***blamed on 'hacktivists' and criminal botnets which jammed websites, crippling Georgia's ability to connect abroad; followed by a coordinated military attack

**suspected origin developed by Chinese hackers in September 2008 and first sold as a 'commercial' package for $37.80 to replace classic command and control functions, then passed to Ukrainian and Russian agents; see SRI, "Analysis of Conficker's Logic," March 19, 2009.

#this cyber-attack included targets in South Korea and caused an internal political up evil as factions within South Korea questioned the ability of the SK National Intelligence Service (NIS) to properly identify the origin of a cyber-attack and a response, partly brought on by Seoul's participation in a U.S.-led cyber exercise; NIS later reported that the attacks were traced to 86 internet protocols addresses in 16 countries. See Confidential cable, U.S. Embassy, Seoul, July 10, 2009, 0720Z, seen at WikiLeaks.com.; with copies sent to U.S. Embassies in Moscow, Tokyo, and Beijing, as well as the US Pacific Command in Honolulu

Cyber Storm is an exercise of the U.S. government, that has increased with complexity, every other year (2008, 2010, with Cyber Storm IV scheduled for fall 2012) with the addition a dozen nations, eleven states, cabinet level departments, and critical infrastructure; Cyber Storm II tested the National Cyber Incident response Plan (NCIRP); see www.dhs.gov

^ uncovered by Canadian researchers, it is estimated that 30% of the infected host included numerous NGOs, the malware, via a Trojan horse of RAT "ramsts aseses tool;" known first as 'ghOstRAT,' the attackers gained control to web cams and audio, exfiltrated massive data, and captured scores of passwords and usernames; see Carr, Cyber Warfare, pp. 146-7.

very rare public admission of covert U.S. cyber response by the U.S. State Department – Center for Strategic Counterterrorism Communications, in this case to neutralize al-Qa'ida extremists and terrorist in an effort to stabilize the new Yemeni government

^^ existence of Flame was known since 2010 and considered 20X more destructive than Stuxnet; a worm tool to do sabotage and system disruption

**** Extensive private sector report by Mandiant reviews how one Chinese military cyber unit, 61398, in Shanghai has conducted an extensive global cyber-attacks systematically stealing hundreds of terabytes from at least 141 companies in 13 countries, www.mandiant.com

Cyber Lexicon, Jargon, and Acronyms

Note: the following list is by no means complete as new acronym and terms are added daily

AAA — authentication, authorization, and accountability

ACL — access control list

ACT — advanced cyber threat

Air gap — type of security where network is kept separate from local networks and the internet, a lack of an electronic connection between the system and the rest of the world.

AMI — advanced metering infrastructure

AoA — analysis of alternatives

AoR — area of responsibility

API — application programming interface

APT — advanced persistent threat

'Assassin's mace' — translation of ancient Chinese strategy, *shashou-jiang*, the enemies ability to take advantage of the weaknesses of an combatants seemingly superior capabilities — ignoring conventional wisdom and taking the fight to the enemy at a level that fits the lesser aggressors abilities

Assurance — establishment of the grounds of confidence that set security controls in an IT and ICS

Asymmetric warfare — combat and conflict between two or more state or non-state actors whose relative military power, strategies, tactic, resources, and goals differ significantly

AT&L — acquisition, technology, and logistics

Authentication — verifying the identity of user, process, or device

Backdoor — gaining remote control of a victims computer by reconfiguring installed legitimate software and/or installation of a specialized program

BARDA –Biomedical Advanced research and Development Authority

BBS — bulletin board system

BCP — business continuity plan

BDA — battle damage assessment

Beacon — computer code inserted in computer system to map or monitor operations and behavior to determine how they are controlled; also called web bug, pixel tag, or a clear GIF

Border Gateway Protocol — a standardized exterior gateway protocol designed to exchange routing and reachability information between autonomous systems on the Internet.

Botnet — (robot-networks) a collection of compromised computer systems, referred to 'zombies', each of which is referred to as a 'bot', connected to the Internet and forced to operate on unauthorized remote commands, usually without the owners knowledge

Black Hat — jargon for a hacking villain who works to gain illicit entry

Blacklisting — the action of too many e-mails arriving from the same domain too quickly, with the receiving server denying entry

Blowback — shorthand for unintended consequences of covert operations

Buffer overflow — specified application that allows a remote attacker to execute arbitrary code and gain full control of ICS host it runs on

BYOD — bring-your-own-device

C2 – command and control

C4ISR — Command, Control Computers, Communications, Intelligence, Surveillance, Reconnaissance

CAGR — compound annual growth rate

Cyber Blackout

CAPEC — Common Attack Pattern Enumeration and Classification

CAT — crisis action team

Cat 5 or 6 – twisted pair of cables that connect computer networks

CBRNE — Chemical, biological, radiological, nuclear and high yield explosives

CCI — cyber counterintelligence

CCMD — combatant command

CCMT — cyber combat mission team

CCSMM — Community Cyber Security Maturity Model

CDC — Centers for Disease Control and Prevention

cDc — Cult of Dead Cow; a group that is believed to first used the term 'hacktivism' in 1996

CDCs — cleared defense contractors CENTCOM — US Central Command

CERT — computer (community) emergency response team

CFCOE — Cyber Force Concept of Operations and Employment

CIAO — Critical Infrastructure Assurance Office; est. 1998 by presidential directive PDD-63

CICPA — Critical Infrastructure Cyber Protection and Awareness, defeated in 2012

CI — critical infrastructure; or counterintelligence

CIKR — critical infrastructure and key resources

CIO — chief information officer

CIP — Critical Infrastructure Protection

Cipher — an algorithm for converting text to an unreadable form and then converting back to readable text

CISPA — Cyber Intelligence Sharing and Protection Act of 2011

Clicktivism — use of social digital media and online methods to promote a cause, facilitate social change, and activism; used by NGOs to promote their cause

Cloud computing — internet based computing whereby data and software applications are stored on the Internet, via a browser, rather than running standalone software on a personal computer or server — open to a host of security threats

Coder — programmer who writes software language code

Compromise — (verb) to gain unauthorized access to a computing system

Cookie — a small piece of data from a website and stored in a user's web browser while the user is 'browsing' that site

COOP — Continuity of Operations Plan

COTS — commercial-off-the-self

CPGS — conventional prompt global strike

CPU — central processing unit

CNA — computer network attack or CNE — computer network espionage

CNCI — Comprehensive National Cyber Security Initiative

CND — computer network defense; (non-kinetic cyberwar)

CNE — computer network exploration…..espionage and spying!

CNI — critical national infrastructure

CNO — computer network operations

COM — communications

CRA — coordinated response architecture

Crackers — cyber hackers who target credit card data

Cross-site scripting — third party web resources to run script within the victim's web browser or scriptable application

CSTARC — Cyber Security Tracking, Analysis and Response Center

CTO — Chief Technology Officer

CUI — controlled unclassified information

CWE — common weaknesses enumeration

Cyber — derived from the word 'cybernetics' which has the general meaning, through use of a computer or other digital systems or units

Cyber actors — any person or entity that communicates or operates in cyberspace

Cyber architecture — an embedded, integral part of the system-IT architecture that describes the structure and behavior for security processes, and alignment with risk and strategic plans.

Cyber security controls — operational, management, and technical controls to protect the integrity and confidentiality if an IT system

Cyber deterrence — reducing the risk of cyber-attacks to an acceptable level at an acceptable cost

Cyber domain — see cyberspace below

Cyber espionage — systematic penetration of networks for covert means

Cyber forensics — use of electronic tools to reconstruct media data to retrieve digital evidence after attempts to breach, hide, disguise, or destroy data following cyber-attack or intrusion

Cyber integrity — risk measures to guard against improper information modification or destruction, to include ensuring information authenticity and security

Cyber Infrastructure — includes all electronic, IT, and communications systems and services composed of both hardware and software that process, store and communicate information

Cybernauts — slang for those engaged in cyber tactics and execution

Cyber threats — natural or man-made incidents, intentional or unintentional, that areis detrimental to the cyber domain/ cyber space

Cyber ShockWave — simulated cyberattack on the US on February 16, 2010, to determine governmental response, highlighted nation is unprepared cyber threats

Cyber manipulation — an attack that results in the compromise of the operations or corruption of data, delays in deliveries, sabotage

Cyber Power — the ability to use cyberspace to create advantages and influence events in the other operational environments and across the instruments of power

Cyber security — ability to protect or defend the use of cyberspace from cyber attacks

Cyber strategy — the development and employment of capabilities to operate in cyberspace, integrated and coordinated with the other operational domains

Cyber terrorism — unlawful attacks and threats against computers, networks, and info systems

OCO — offensive cyberspace operations

OCC — offensive counter-cyber

DCC — defensive counter-cyber

Cyberspace — a global domain within the information environment consisting of the interdependent network of information technology infrastructures, including the Internet, telecommunications networks, computer systems, and embedded processors and controllers. (DOD defined, 2008)

Cyberwarfare — actions by a nation-state to penetrate another nation's computers for the purpose of doing damage

Joint cyber-kinetic attack — blended or "cyber-plus" attack

Operational cyberwar — cyberwar to support the warfighting

Strategic cyberwar — cyber-attacks to affect state policy

Cryptography — discipline for the transformation of data in order to hide their semantic content, prevent their unauthorized use, or prevent undetected modification

DC3 – Department of Defense Cyber Crime Center

D5 – disrupt, deny, degrade, deceive, and destroy

DAC — discretionary access controls

Cyber Blackout

DEFCON — Defense Readiness Condition

Defense-in-Breadth — systematic set of multidisciplinary activities to identify, manage, and reduce risk of exploitable vulnerabilities throughout the IT system, network, or subcomponent of the life-cycle, from production design to supply chain, maintenance, and retirement

Defense-in-Depth — Information security strategy integrating people, technology, and operations capabilities across multiple layers and missions of the organization

DARPA — Defense Advanced Research Project Agency

DDoS — distributed denial of service

DHCP — Dynamic Host Configuration Protocol

DHS — Department of Homeland Security: principal federal agency for domestic incident response management

DIA — Defense Intelligence Agency

DIB CS/IA — Defense Industrial Base Cyber Security/Information Assurance

DISA — Defense Information Systems Agency

Domain — routing suffix, for example: .mil — military, .gov –government, .com — corporate

DMCA — Digital Millennium Copyright Act

DMEA — Defense Microelectronics Activity

DMS — distribution management system

DNSA — domain name service

DNI — Director of National Intelligence

DOE — US Department of Energy

Dos — denial of service

DPRK — Democratic [?] People's Republic of Korea, i.e. North Korea

DRP — Disaster Recovery Plan

DSB — Defense Science Board at DOD

DSCA — Defense Support of Civil Authorities

Dumpster Diving — obtaining sensitive information, such as passwords, by searching through discarded media in the 'trash'

ECM — electronic countermeasures

ECPA — Electronic Communications privacy Act (1986)

EEA — Economic Espionage Act of 1996 (18 USC 1831-1839)

EMP –electromagnetic pulse (also Emergency Management Plan)

EMS — emergency management system or electromagnetic spectrum

EOP — emergency ops plan

EINSTEIN I — automated process for collecting computer network security information from federal executive agencies

EINSTEIN 2 – like E-1, and adds an intrusion detection system (IDS) and alerts when specific malicious network activity is detected

EOC — Emergency Operations Center

EW — electronic warfare

Existential Cyber Attack — event of sufficient wide scale and damage, capable to lose control of the country, to include significant portions of the military and critical infrastructure

Exploit — a piece of software, data, or sequence of commands that take advantage of a bug, glitch or vulnerability in order to alter the behavior of a computer software or hardware

Exploit kits — prepackaged malware programs (that first began to appear in 2006) that provides a turnkey solution for installation of malware on end-user systems

FAR — flexible, adaptable, robust

FedRAMP — Federal Risk and Authorization Management Program

FEMA — Federal Emergency Management Agency

FERC — Federal Energy Regulatory Commission

FISMA — Federal Information Security Management Act of 2002

FIS — foreign intelligence service

FISC — Foreign Intelligence Surveillance Court

FISA — Foreign Intelligence Surveillance Act (1978)

Firewall — a gateway that limits access between networks in response to local installed security

Five Eyes Club — US, Britain, Canada, Australia, New Zealand

Flash Drive — a data storage device that includes memory with an integrated UBS interface

Flood — a user assesses a target repeatedly in order to overload the target's capacity

F/OSS — free and open-source software

Flow records — records of connections made to a federal executive agency's IT system

FOCI — foreign ownership control and influence

FOIA — Freedom of Information Act (1966)

FQDNs — fully qualified domain names

FSE — full scale exercise

FTP — file transfer protocol

FUD — fear, uncertainty, and doubt (disinformation)

Future-proof — process of anticipating the future and developing methods to minimize shocks or stress of future events; ability of something to be of value into the distant future

Fuzzing — technique to inject unexpected or random data into inputs of a computer program

Fuzzy scanner — automated tools to test a target with a barrage of input constructions to discover a specific input set that triggers an abnormal response

Gbps — gigabits per second — one billion or 2/30th bits per second

GCHQ — Government Communication Headquarters (UK)

GCSM — Global Cyber Security Management

GHDB — Google Hacking Database (OSINT tool)

GIG — global information grid

GMD — geomagnetic disturbance

GOTS — government off-the-shelf

GPS — global positioning system

Green Dam — Chinese government censorship program, started July 1, 2009, to monitor Internet URL connections, banned Web sites, and selected text typed on the computer

GSA — Government Services Administration

Hack-backs — breaking into the intruders computer (illegal in the U.S.)

Hacktivists — those hackers involved in computer attacks (hacktivism) driven by social, religious, or political agenda, purposes or motivation; with the intent of disrupting normal computer operations

HPM — high-powered microwave

Hazmat — hazardous material

Honey pot — a computer made openly vulnerable to attract an attacking software

Hongke — Chinese term for cyberwarriors

Hot site — off-site data processing facility used in the event of a disaster situation

Hot wash — incident-exercise debrief

HSPD — Homeland Security Presidential Directive

HTML — Hypertext Markup Language

HTTP — Hypertext Transfer protocol

HUMINT — human intelligence collection

Hypervisor — or virtual machine monitor (VMM) is a piece of computer software, firmware or hardware that creates and runs virtual machines.

IAEA — International Atomic Energy Agency

ICANN — Internet Corporation for Assigned Names and Numbers

ICS — Incident command system

ICS-Cert — Industrial Control Systems Cyber Emergency Response Team (DHS)

ICT — information and communication technology

IC — intelligence community

ICS — industrial control system

IDA — institutional analysis and development

IEEE — Institute of Electrical & Electronics Engineers, developed 802.11 protocols for wireless networks

IMT — Incident Management Team

INL — Idaho National laboratory

Intrusion — unauthorized bypass of security mechanisms

IO — information operations; also I/O Input/output

IOU's — investor owned utilities

IP — Internet protocol — data sent from one computer to another via internet (IPv4 and IPv6)

IPOE — intelligence preparation of the operational environment

IRC — Internet Relay Chat

INEW — integrated network electronic warfare

InfraGard — partnership between FBI and private sector for sharing to protect U. S CIKR against physical and cyber threats

Informationalization — common word used in East Asia to denote interface with computerization of business, industry, and military systems

IPS — Intrusion Prevention System

ISAC — Information Sharing and Analysis Center

ISACA — Information Systems Audit and Control Association

ISPs — internet service providers

IUID — item unique identification

IW — information warfare

JCCC — Joint Cyber Component Command

JIE — Joint Information Environment

JTTF — Joint Terrorism Task Force

JWICS — Joint Worldwide Intelligence Communications System

Key logger — surveillance software or spyware capable to recording keystrokes

Kill-chain — a systematic process to target and engage as adversary to create desired effects: phases include recon, weaponization, delivery, exploitation, installation, C2, action

'Kinetic military action' — euphemism for war

Klinger-Cohen Act — Information Technology Management Reform Act of 1996 (ITMRA)

KPO — Knowledge Process Outsourcing

LAN — local area network

LEAP –Lightweight Extensible Authentication Protocol

LVC– live-virtual-constructive simulations

LOA — level of assurance

LOAC — Law of Armed Conflict

Login bombs — malicious programming code intentionally inserted into software system that will target and configure an attack

LPI — low-probability-of-intercept

Malware — (malicious software) any program that infects a computer and operates without the user's consent to include viruses, worms, Trojan horses, logic bombs, backdoors or trapdoors

MAD — mutually assured destruction

MANET — Mobile, Ad hoc Network

MBVA — model-based vulnerability analysis

MDM — mobile device management

MEECES — money, ego, entrance (to social group), cause, entertainment, and status (based on counterintel acronym MICE)

MEF — mission essential functions

Mega tag — special HTML tag to store information about a Web page or site, yet not displayed in a Web browser

MEMS — micro-electro-mechanical systems

MITM — man-in-the middle attack by intercepts of communication between two systems

MLS — multilevel security

MO — modus operandi

MOE — Mission Operating Environment

MoEs — measures of effectiveness

MoMs — measures of merit

MOOTW — military operations other than war

Moore's Law — postulates that the number of transistors per square inch on integrated circuit boards will double approximately every 18 months, meaning computing power rises exponentially over time

MMOGs — massively multiplayer online games

MS-DOS — Microsoft-Disc Operating System

MSCA — Military Support to Civil Authorities

MUCD — military unit cover designator (five digit numerical sequence for Chinese military units)

Maushup — a web page or application that uses content from more than one source to create a single new service or API

NCCIC — National Cybersecurity and Communications Integration Center (DHS)

NCFTA — Nnational Cyber Forensics Training AllianceInstitute

NCIC — National Crime Information Center

NCIJTF — National Cyber Investigation Joint Task Force

NCIRP — National Cyber Incident Response Plan

NCPS — National Cybersecurity Protection System

NCRAL — National Cyber Risk Alert Level

NCSD — National Cyber Security Division

NDAA – 2013 National Defense Authorization Act

NDPTC — National Domestic Preparedness Consortium

Networkization — word coined by Chinese military, *wangluohua*, to implement technologies to deal with and neutralize and paralyze battlefield computers capabilities

NERC — North American Electric Reliability Corporation

NERRTC — National Emergency Response and Rescue Training Center

NFC — near-field communications

NGO — non-governmental organization

NIDS — network based intrusion detection system

NIMS — National Incident Management System

NIPP — National Infrastructure Protection Plan

NIOPRNet — Non-securedclassified Internet Protocol Router Network

NIST — National Institute of Standards and Technology

NOC — network operations center

NPCIS — National Partnership for Critical Infrastructure Security

NRC — Nuclear Regulatory Commission

NRF — National Response Framework

NSA — National Security Agency

NSTB — National Supervisory Control and Data Acquisition Test Bed

NSTIC — National Strategy for Trusted Identities in Cyberspace

Obfuscation — technique to hide or to mask the sources and methods of a security relevant event

OEM — original equipment manufacture

ODNI — Office of the Director of Nnational Intelligence

OFAC — Office of Foreign Asset Control

OT — operational technology

OSINT — open source intelligence

OSTP — Office of Science and Technology Policy

P2P — peer-to-peer

PaaS — platform as a service

Password pilfering — attacks that violate system confidentiality, via password sniffing

Patch — updated release of software to fix a 'bug' in existing programs

Patch Tuesday — second Tuesday of each month when Microsoft issues routine security updates

Passive wiretapping — The monitoring or recording of data, such as password, while they are being transmitted over communications link

PCA — Posse Comitatus Act, passed June 18, 1878

PCII — Protected Critical In Infrastructure Information

PCCIP — President's Commission on Critical Infrastructure Protection

P/DIME — political/diplomatic, informational, military, and economic

PDD — Presidential Decision Directive

Pharming — method used by phishers to deceive user into believing that they are communicating with a legitimate web site Phishing — cyber-attack that deceive recipients into giving out passwords, bank data, account numbers by masquerading as a legitimate inquirer

Phone phreaking — cracking telephone systems for free call access and manipulate systems

PII — Personally identifiable information

PIV — personal identity verification

PLA — People's Liberation Army (China)

Plausible deniability — the ability of Actor A (the attacker) to launch a cyber-attack against Actor B (9the target) in a manner such that it is difficult for B to prove A's responsibility

Port — An integer that uniquely identifies an endpoint of a communication stream

POTS — plain old telephone service

PPD — Presidential Policy Directive

'PRISM' — covert cyber security program started in 2007 by NSA and FBI to monitor Internet data of "foreigners" using US Web site and telecommunications services (leaked May 2013)

PRC — People's Republic of China

Proofing — a pre-authentication step in which the user and the identity provider exchange each other's authenticators

Psyops — psychological warfare operations

PT — persistent threat

Pwned — hackerspeak for having a system or password breached

QDR — Quadrennial Defense Review

RAM — random access memory

Ransomnware — malicious code that encrypts drive contents of a victim's computer, then extorts money for the release of hostage data

RAT — remote access control (i.e. Trojan) or Routing Activity Theory

Reciprocity — Mutual agreement among participating organizations to accept each other's security assessments to share information and resources

RFID — radio frequency identification

RMA — revolution in military affairs

RPMP — risk management process

ROE — rules of engagement

ROM — read-only memory

RRM — Risk ReductionManagement Process

RS — remote sensing

RTO — recovery time objective

SaaS — software as a service

SALUTE — size, activity, location, unit, time, equipment (to summarize foreign force activity)

Sandboxes — a security program mechanism for separating running programs, to verify untested code or program

SBU — sensitive but unclassified

SCADA –supervisory control and data acquisition; software that control networks and electric power, water, oil and gas grids

SCC — Service Cryptologic Component

SCIF — sensitive compartmented information facility

SCLC — Supply chaindevelopment life cycle

SCM — supply chain management

SCRM — supply chain risk management

Script — a computer script is a list of commands that are executed by a program or scripting engine

Script Kiddie — generally unsophisticated hacker that uses off the shelf programs to exploit weaknesses

SECURE IT — Strengthening and Enhancing Cybersecurity by Using Research, Education, Information and Technology

SEO –

SHODAN — Sentient Hyper Optimized Data Access Network

SIPRNet — Secret Internet Protocol Router Network

SLE — single loss expectancy

Spear-phishing — targeted personalized e-mail crafted to be open by computer to gain access to systemScript Kiddies — low level hackers, that down load readily available code vs. writing their own

SLTPS — state, local, tribal, and private sector

SMADA — Strategic Measurement of Advanced Disruptive [cyber] Attacks

Smurf — spoofing the target address and sending a ping to the broadcast address for a remote network, to disrupt a target computer or system

Sniffer — software that observes and records network traffic

SNS — social networking sites

SNRA — Strategic National Risk Assessment

SOC — Security Operation Center; also state ops center

SOP — standard operating procedures

Spam — spamming or spammers — those that widely distribute unsolicited e-mail which may haveith hidden or false information or data; with the possible intent of conducting phishing schemes, distribution of spyware/malware, and DOS

Spoof/spoofing — term used for falsification of data by man-in-the-middle attacks or message replays; such as altering e-mail header to appear as though the e-mail originated from a different source

SQL — structured query language

Spyware — malware installed on a computer without the explicit knowledge or consent of the user, monitoring system actions and/or taking control of the computer

SROE — standing rules of engagement

SSA — sector-specific agencies

SSDLC — Secure Software Development Life Cycle

SSL — secure socket layer (used for encryption)

Steganography — the science and art of writing and *hiding* information and messages in such a means that no one can read them or detect them, apart from the sender and the intended recipient

Sturgeon's Law – 90 percent of everything is crap

Supply chain hacking — embedded backdoor and malware by foreign computer manufacturer to cripple systems

Swatting — calling 911 with false caller ID to disrupt incident response by first responders

TAO — Tailored Access Operations

T&E — test and evaluation

TCP/IP — Transmission Control Protocol/Internet Protocol

TEWG — Terrorist Early Warning Group

Title 10 – outlines the role of the armed forces in the United States Code

Title 50 – National Security Act of 1947: outlines the role of War and Defense in the United States Code

TOR — The Onion Router; or, terms of reference

Trapdoor or 'Trojan Horse' — a brief number of computer code lines that resemble other gibberish in order to disrupt a computers operating system

Triage — processes to categorize, correlate, and prioritize information

Trojan Horse — a non-self-replicating computer program that conceals a harmful code, by masquerading as a normal or useful program

TTL — 'time to live'

TS SCI — top secret sensitive compartmentalized information

Tweet — jargon for sending short 140 character or less message over Twitter

UAV — unmanned aerial vehicle

UPS — uninterruptable power supply

URL — universal resource locator

USA Patriot Act – 2001 – Uniting and Strengthening America by Providing Appropriate Tools Required to Intercept and Obstruct Terrorism Act

USB — Universal Serial Bus

US-CCU — US Cyber Consequences Unit

US-CERT — United States Computer Emergency Readiness Team

USCYBERCOM — US Cyber Command

UTC — universal time clock (GMT or Zulu time)

V & V — verification and validation

VDI — Virtual Desktop Infrastructure

Virus — a program that 'infects' computer files and memory and spreads through system relying on human help (usually unwittingly) to access a computer to implement infection

VMM — virtual machine monitor

VPN — virtual private network

VOIP — Voice over IP

Wan — wide area network

WAP — wireless application protocol

Water ISAC — water information sharing and analysis center

WEP — Wired Equivalent privacy

War driving — method of driving through cities with a wireless-equipped computer search for unsecured wireless networks

Water holing — hacking strategy in which attacker guesses where to plant malware

Watermarking — a pattern of bits inserted into a digital image, audio, or video file that identifies the file's copyright and/or ownership; unlike printed watermarks, digital imprints are designed to be invisible; also called data embedding or information hiding

Wiki — a space that's highly public and where the audience can respond by deleting or changing your words

WLAN — wireless area network

WM — web money

WMD — weapon of mass destruction

WoG — Whole of government

Worm — an independent computer program that reproduces by copying itself as a state of the art malware that can spread from one system to another across a network; unlike viruses, worms do not require human involvement to propagate

XSS — cross-site scripting

Y2K — Year 2000 bug

Zero-day — or 'O-day'... attack that exploits undisclosed computer applications, extremely dangerous

Zombies — slang for botnet or bot

Selected Bibliography

Government Documents:

Central Intelligence Agency. "Cyber Threats and the U.S. Economy." Statement to the U. S. Congress, Joint Committee on Cyber Threats, Washington, D.C.: February 23, 2001, www.cis.gov/news

———. "CIA Red Cell Special Memorandum," Washington, D.C.: February 8, 2010.

Department of Defense. Joint Chiefs of Staff. *Joint Doctrine for Information Operations, Joint Publication 3-13*, Washington, D.C.: October 1998.

———. "Information Operationns." Joint Publication 3-13, Washington, D.C.: November 27, 2012.

———. JCS. "Homeland Security." Joint Publication 3-26, Washington, D.C : August 2005.

———. "Strategy for Homeland Defense and Civil Support." Washington, D.C. June 2005.

———. "2010 Quadrennial Defense Review." Washington, D.C.: 2010.

———. "Department of Defense Strategy for Operating in Cyberspace." Washington, D.C.: July 2011.

———. "Department of Defense Cyberspace Policy Report: A Report to Congress, Sec. 934, Washington, D.C., November 2011.

———. "Before Disaster Strikes: Imperatives for Enhancing Defense Support of Civil Authorities." Washington, D.C.: Advisory Panel to SecDef/DOD, September 15, 2010.

———. "Remarks on the Department of Defense Cyber Strategy." Deputy Secretary William J. Lynn, National Defense University, Washington, D.C.: July 14, 2011.

———. "Strategy for Operating in Cyberspace." Washington, D.C.: July 2011.

———. Secretary of Defense. *Annual Report to Congress: Military and Security Developments Involving the People's Republic of China 2011*. Washington, D.C., 2011.

———. *Annual Report to Congress: Military and Security developments involving the People's Republic of China 2012*. Washington, D.C. May 2012.

_____. HQ, U.S. Air Force. Mark T. Maubury, "Air Force Cyber Vision 2025." 2013.

_____. HQ, U.S. Air Force. Maj. Gen. Earl Matthews, "Cyberspace Operations" HAF Cyber Matrix and Force Deployment." June 27, 2012.

_____. U. S. Air Force. "Cyberspace Operations." Doctrine Document (AFDD) 3-12, July 15, 2010; Incorporating Change 1, November 30, 2011.

_____. Defense Science Board. Task Force Report. "Resilient Military Systems and the Advanced Cyber Threat." Washington, D.C.: DOD, January 2013.

_____. Chief Information Officer. "Cloud Computing Strategy." Washington, D.C.: July 2012.

Department of Energy. Idaho National Laboratory. "Vulnerability Analysis of Energy Delivery Control Systems." Idaho Falls: INL, September 2011.

Department of Homeland Security (DHS). "National Cyber Incident Response Plan." Washington, D.C.: September 2010.

_____. "Cyber Storm III: Final Report." Washington, D.C.: July 2011.

_____. "Cyber Storm IV: Report." Washington, D.C.: 2012.

_____. "Roadmap to Secure Control Systems in the Energy Sector." Washington, D.C.: 2006.

_____. "Energy: Critical Infrastructure and Key Resources Sector-Specific Plan." Washington, D.C.: May 2007.

_____. "National Response Plan." Washington, D.C.: December 2004.

_____. "Homeland Security Presidential Directive/ HSPD-5" Washington, D.C.: February 28, 2003.

_____. "National Cyber security and Communications Integration Center." December 6, 2011. xxx

_____. "National Response Framework." Washington, D.C.: May 2012.

_____. "National Preparedness Report." Washington, D.C.: March 30, 2012.

_____. "National Preparedness Report." Washington, D.C.: March 30, 2013.

_____. "Fact Sheet: National Level Exercise 2012." Washington, D.C.: June 5, 2012.

_____. "A Roadmap for Cybersecurity Research." Washington, D.C., November 2009.

_____. "Transportation Systems: Critical Infrastructure and key Resources Sector-Specific Plan as input to National Infrastructure Protection Plan, 2010

_____. "Critical Infrastructure." Washington, D.C.: May 4, 2012.

_____. "Leftwing Extremist Likely to Increase Use of Cyber Attacks over the Coming Decade." (U//FOUO) Washington, D.C.: January 26, 2009.

_____. "Daily Open Source Infrastructure Report." Washington, D.C.: May 4, 2012.

_____. "A Guide to Critical Infrastructure and Key Resources Protection at the State, Regional, Local, Tribal, and Territorial Level." Washington, D.C.: September 2008.

_____. "Interoperability Continuum." Washington, D.C.: n.d.

_____. U. S. Coast Guard. "Incident Management Handbook." USCG, P3120.17A, August 2006.

Director of National Intelligence, James R. Clapper, "Worldwide Threat Assessment of the US Intelligence Community for the Select Committee on Intelligence, Washington, D.C, January 31, 2012.

Department of Transportation. "America's Container Ports: Linking Markets at Home and Abroad." *Bureau of Transportation Statistics*. Washington, D.C.: January 2012.

Federal Communications Commission (FCC). "Cyber Security Planning Guide." Washington, D.C.: 2011.

Federal Emergency Management Agency (FEMA). "Strategic National Risk Assessment." Washington, D.C.: December 2011.

_____. "Comprehensive Preparedness Guide 101." Washington, D.C.: 2103.

_____. "National level Exercise 2012: Fact Sheet." Washington, D.C.: 2012, NEP@dhs.gov

_____. "Presidential Policy Directive ppd8: National Preparedness." Washington, D.C.: May 2, 212, www.fema.gov/ppd8

France. Ministere des Affairs etrangeres. " France and Cyber Security." Paris: January 2013, www.diplomatie.gouv.fr/en/frech-foreign-policy-1

_____. French Network and Information Security Agency (ANSSI). "France's strategy." Paris: February 2011. www.ssi.gouv.fr

_____. Decree No. 2009-834, Paris: July 7, 2009 [to establish ANSSI]

_____. French White Paper on Defense and National Security. Paris: April 13, 2013.

Germany. Federal Ministry of Interior. "Cyber Security Strategy for Germany." Berlin: February 2011. www.bmi.bund.de

Government Accounting Office. (GAO) *Information Security: Computer Attacks at Department of Defense Pose Increasing Risks*. U.S. GAO: Washington, D.C., May 22, 1996. [AIMD 96-84}

_____. "Cybersecurity: Challenges in Securing the Modernized Electricity Grid." Washington, D.C.: February 28, 2012. [GAO 12-50TT]

_____. "Cybersecurity: Challenges in Securing the Electricity Grid." Washington, D.C.: July 17, 2012. [GAO 12-926T]

_____. "Cybersecurity: Threats Impacting the Nation," Washington, D.C., April 24, 2012. [Gao 12-666T]

_____. "Information Security: Cyber Threats facilitate Ability to Commit Economic Espionage," Washington, D.C.: June 28, 2012. [GAO 12-876T]

_____. "Critical Infrastructure Protection: Update to National Infrastructure Protection Plan Includes Increased Emphasis on Risk Management and Resilience." March 2010. [GAO 10-296]

_____. "Critical Infrastructure Protection: Cybersecurity Guidance I Available, but More Can Be Done to Promote Its Use." December 2011. [GAO 12-92]

_____. "Defense Department Cyber Efforts: More Detailed Guidance Needed to Ensure Military Services Develop Appropriate Cyber Capabilities." May 2011. [GAO 11-695R]

_____. "Defense Department Cyber Efforts: DOD Faces Challenges in its Cyber Activities." July 2011. [GAO 11-75]

_____. *"DOD Information Security: Serious Weaknesses Continue to Place Defense Operations at Risk."* Washington, D.C., August 1999. [AIMD 99-107]

_____. "Freight Rail Security." Washington, D.C.: April 2009. [GAO 09-263]

_____. "Iinformation Security: Cyber Threats and Vulnerabilities Place Federal Systems at Risk." Washington, D.C.: May 5, 2009 [GAO-09-661T]

_____. "CYBERCRIME: Public and Private Entities Face Challengers in Addressing Cyber Threats." July 2007. [GAO-07-705]

_____. "IT Supply Chain: National Security Related Agencies Need to Better Address Risks." Washington, D.C.: March 2012. [GAO-12-361]

_____. "Cybersecurity: National Strategy, Roles, and Responsibilities Need to Be Better Defined and More Effectively Implemented." February 2013. [GAO-13-187]

_____. "Cybersecurity: A Better Defined and Implemented national Strategy Is Needed to Address Persistent Challenges." March 2013. [GAO-13-462T]

_____. "Communications Networks: Outcome-Based measures Would Assist DHS in Assessing Effectiveness of Cybersecurity Efforts." April 2013. [GAO 13-275]

Krekel, Bryan et al, Northrop Grumman Corp, Prepared for the U.S.-China Economic and Security Review Commission, *Occupying the Information High Ground: Chinese Capabilities for Computer Network Operations and Cyber Espionage.* Washington, D.C.: March 7, 2012.

Library of Congress. Federal Research Division. "Military Support to Civil Authorities: The Role of Department of Defense in Support of Homeland Defense." Washington, D.C.: February 2007.

National Intelligence Council (NIC). "Global Trends 2025." GPO: Washington, D.C., November 2008.

_____. "Global Trends 2030: Alternative Worlds." GPO: Washington, D.C., December 2012.

National Institute of Standards and Technology (NIST). "Managing Information Security Risk." Gaithersburg: March 2011.

_____. "Guide to Industrial Control Systems (ICS) Security." Pub. 800-82, Gaitherburg: June 2011.

_____. "Notional Supply Chain Risk Management Practices for Federal Information Systems." Draft NISTIR 7622, Washington, D.C.: USDOC, March 2012.

_____. "US Government Cloud Computing Technology Roadmap." Draft. Washington, D.C.: SP 500-293, November 2011.

_____. "Challenging Security Requirements for US Government Cloud Computing Adoption." Draft. Washington, D.C.: SP 500-296, May 2012.

NATO. "Defending the Network: The NATO Policy on Cyber Defense." Brussels: 2011, www.hq.nato.int

National Security Agency (NSA). "(U) Learning from the Enemy: The GUNMAN Project." Sharon Maneki: Center for Cryptologic History, Series VI, Vol. 13, 9 January 2007. Declassified May 2013.

Office of the National Counterintelligence Executive. "Foreign Spies Stealing US Economic Secrets in Cyberspace: Report to Congress on Foreign Economic Collection and Industrial Espionage, 2009-2011." Washington, D.C.: October 2011, www.ncix.gov

Public Utility Commission of Texas. Alan Rivaldo, ed. "Project 40128: Report on the Electric Grid Cybersecurity in Texas." Austin: November 2012.

State of Nevada. "Cyber Security Training and Exercise Program." n.d., http://cias.utsa.edu

State of Texas. Public Utilities Commission of Texas. "Report on Electric Grid Cybersecurity in Texas." Project 40128, Austin: November 2012.

_____. Texas A&M University TEEX. "Cyber Security Awareness." PST604 College Station: TEEX, 2013

United Kingdom. Intelligence and Security Committee. "Foreign involvement in the Critical National Infrastructure: The implications for national security." London: Parliament, June 2013.

_____. GCHQ. "Countering the cyber threat to business." Spring 2013. www.cpni.gov.uk/advice/cyber

U.S. China Economic and Security Review Commission. "2011 Report to Congress." 112th Cong., 1st sess., Washington, D.C., GPO, November 2011.

_____. "Indigenous Weapons Development in China's Military Modernization." Washington, D.C.: April 5, 2012.

_____. "China's Evolving Space Capabilities: Implications for U.S. Interests." Washington, D.C.: April 2012.

_____. "An Analysis of Chinese Investments in the U.S. Economy." Washington, D.C.: October 2012.

_____. "2012 Report to Congress of the U.S.-China Economic and Security Review Commission." 112th Cong., 2nd sess., Washington, D.C.: GPO, November 2012.

U.S. House of Representatives. Select Committee on Intelligence. "Investigative Report on the U.S. National Security Issues Posed by Chinese Telecommunications Companies Huawei and ZTE." 112th Cong, October 8, 2012.

_____. Subcommittee on Emerging Threat, Cybersecurity, and Science and Technology of the Committee on Homeland Security. "The Cyber Threat to Control Systems: Stronger Regulations are Necessary to Secure the Electric Grid." 110th Cong., 1st sess., No. 110-78, October 17, 2007.

_____. "SCADA Systems and the Terrorist Threat: Protecting the Nation's Critical Control Systems." 109th Cong., 1st sess., No. 109-45, October 18, 2005.

_____. "Security Protect Yourself Against Cyber Trespass Act." 108th Cong., 2nd sess., July 20, 2004.

_____. Republican Cybersecurity Task Force, "Recommendations of the House Republican Cybersecurity Task Force." October, 5, 2011, http://thronberry.house.gov

_____. "National Defense Authorization Act for Fiscal Year 2013," (NDAA) 112th Cong., 2nd sess., H.R.4310, January 3, 2012.

_____. "National Defense Authorization Act for Fiscal Year 2013." 112th Cong., 2nd sess., Report 112-705, December 18, 2012., Subtitle D — Cyberspace-Related Matters, pp. 829-838.

_____. "Cybersecurity: Threat to the Financial Sector." 112th Cong., 1st sess., Hearing of the Subcommittee on Financial Institutions and Consumer Credit, September 14, 2011.

_____. Cong Edward J. Markey and Cong. Henry A. Waxman, "Electric Grid Vulnerability: Industry Responses Reveal Security Gaps." Report to the U. S. House, May 21, 2013.

U.S. Senate. Committee of Homeland Security and Governmental Affairs. "Cyber Security: Recovery and Reconstruction of Critical Networks." 109th Cong., 2nd sess., S. Hrg. 109-893, July 28, 2006.

_____. Senator Dianne Feinstein (D), Chairman Intelligence Committee, Presentation, Senate Floor, Cyber Security Bill, 84-11, July 26, 2012, 6:00 EST, Live.

_____. Senate Select Committee on Intelligence. James R. Clapper, "Worldwide Threat Assessment of the U.S. Intelligence Community." Washington, D.C.: Mmarch 12, 2013.

_____. Committee on Armed Services. "Inquiry into Cyber Intrusions Affecting U.S. Transportation Command Contractors." 113th Cong., 2nd sess., Report, 2014.

White House. Jay Carney, Press briefing: Aboard Air Force One, March 23, 2011. www.whitehouse.gov

_____. Executive Order 13010, "Critical Infrastructure Protection." Washington, D.C.: July 16, 1996.

_____. Presidential Decision Directive/NSC—PDD-63, "Critical Infrastructure protection." May 22, 1998.

_____. Executive Order 12333, "U.S. Intelligence Activities." Washington, D.C.: December 4, 1981. CIA only US Agency authorized to conduct covert action, unless waved by the President

_____. "The National Strategy to Secure Cyberspace." Washington, D.C.: February 2003.

_____. Executive Order 13434, . "Development of Security Professional." Washington, D.C.: 2007.

_____. "Cyberspace Policy Review." Washington, D.C.: May 2009

_____. "National Security Strategy of the United States." Washington, D.C.: May 2010.

_____. "2010 Joint Strategic Plan on Intellectual Property Enforcement." Washington, D.C.: June 2010.

_____. Executive Order 13549. "Classified National Security Information Program for State, Local, Tribal, and private Entities." Washington, D.C.: August 18, 2010.

_____. "Cyberspace Policy Review." Washington, D.C.: May 2011.

_____. "National Strategy for Trusted Identities in Cyberspace." Washington, D.C.: April 2011.

_____. "International Strategy for Cyberspace." Washington, D.C.: May 2011.

_____. "The Comprehensive National Cybersecurity Ininatiative." Washington, D.C.: March 5, 2010.

_____. "National Strategy for Global Supply Chain Security." Washington, D.C.: January 2012.

_____. Presidential Policy Directive/ PPD-8: "National Preparedness." Washington, D.C.: March 20, 2011.

_____. Statement of James R. Clapper, Director of National Intelligence, "Worldwide Treaty Assessment of the US Intelligence Community for the Select Committee on Intelligence." Washington, D.C.: January 31, 2012.

_____. Presidential Policy Directive / PPD 20, "Cyber Security," Washington, D.C.: October 2012.

_____. Executive Order 13636. "Improving Critical Infrastructure Cybersecurity." Washington, D.C.: February 12, 2013.

ARTICLES and Reports

Adams, John. "The Government of Canada and Cyber Security: Security Begins at Home." *Journal of Military and Strategic Studies*, Vol. 14, No. 2, 2012, pp. 1-27.

Adams, John A. "When the Llights Go Out." *Economic Development Journal*, Summer 2013, pp. 49-56.

Allen, P. O. "The Palestinian-Israel Cyber War." *Military Review*, March 2003, p. 52-9.

Ancker, Clinton J. and Michael D. Burke. "Doctrine for Asymmetric Warfare." *Military Review*, July 2003, pp. 18-25.

Baker, Stewart et al. "In the Dark: Crucial Industries Confront Cyberattacks." McAfee and CSIS, April 21, 2011, www.mcafee.com/us

Ball, Desmond. "China's Cyber Warfare Capabilities." *Security Challenges*, Winter 2011, pp. 81-103.

Bamford, James. "The Most Wanted Man in the World." *Wired*, September 2014, pp. 86-95.

Banks, William C. "The Role of Counterterrorism Law in Shaping Ad Bellum Norms for Cyber Warfare." Syracuse: Institute for National Security and Counterterrorism (INSCT), September 27, 2012.

_____. "The Legal Landscape for Emergency Management in the United States." Washington, D.C.: New America Foundation, 2010.

Black & Veatch. "2012 Strategic Directions in the U.S. Electric Utility Industry." Overland Park: 2012.

Bosman, Ruud. "The New Supply Chain Challenge: Risk Management in a Global Economy." Windsor: FM Global, 2006.

Bowden, Mark. "The Enemy Within." *The Atlantic*, June 2010 at www.theatlantic.com

Boyson, Sandy. "The ICT SCRM Community Framework Development Project." College Park: University of Maryland, 2012

Brackney, R. and R. Anderson. "Understanding the Insider Threat." CF-196, Santa Monica: Rand Corporation, March 2004.

Breen, Michael and Joshua A. Gettzer. "Asymmetric Strategies as Strategies of the Strong." *Parameters*, Spring 2011, pp. 41-55.

Bronk, Christopher, Cody Monk and John Villasenor, "The Dark Side of Cyber Finance," *Survival*, April 2012, pp. 129-142.

_____. "Blown to Bits: China's War in Cyberspace, August-September 2020." *Strategic Studies Quarterly*, Spring 2011, pp. 1-20.

Butler, Sean C. "Refocusing Cyber Warfare Thought." *Air & Space Power Journal*, January 2013, pp. 44-57.

Cantu, Ana. "The History of Cloud Computing." *Forbes.com*, December 20, 2011.

Cardenas, Alvaro A. "Attacks Against Process Systems: Risk Assessment, Detection, and Response." Hong Kong: ASIACCSS '11, March 22, 2011, pp. 355-366.

Cavelty, Myriam D. "Cyber- Terror — Looming Threat or Phantom Menace? The Framing of the US Cyber-Threat Debate." *Journal of Information Technologies and Politics*, 2007, pp.19-36.

Chee-Wooi Ten et al. "Vulnerability Assessment of Cybersecurity for SCADA System." *Proceedings IEEE, 2008, pp. 1836-1846.*

Collins, Sean and Stephen McCombie. "Stuxnet: The emergence of a new cyber weapon and its implications." *Journal of Policing, Intelligence and Counter Terrorism*, April 2012, pp. 80-91.

"Cyberwar." *The Economist*, July 3, 2010, pp. 10-11, 25-28.

Davis, Joshua. "Hackers Take Down the Most Wired Country in Europe." *Wired Magazine*, August 21, 2007. www.wired.com/politics/security

De Borchgrave, Arnaud et al "Cyber Threats and Information Security." Washington, D.C.: CSIS, May 2001.

"Defining the digital frontier: cyber-security." *The Economist*, July 12, 2014, pp. 1-16.

Diebert, Ronald J. "Black Code: Censorship, Surveillance, and the Militarization of Cyberspace." International Studies Association Conference: Portland, February 9, 2003.

_____ and Rafal Rohozinski. "Risking Security: Policies and Paradoxes of Cyberspace Security," *International Political Sociology*, March 2010, pp. 15-32.

Davis, Joshua. "Hackers Take Down the Most Wired Country in Europe." *Wired Magazine*, Issue 15.09, 08.21.07 at www.WIRED.com

The Economist, "War in the fifth domain." July 1, 2010 seen at www.economist.com/node/1648792

Enoch, Yusuf S. et al "Mitigating Cyber Identity Fraud using Advanced Multi Anti-Phishing Technique." *Journal of Advanced Science and Application*, Vol. 4, No. 3, 2013, pp. 156-164.

Ellis, Evan, "Chinese-Latin America Military Engagement: Goodwill, Good Business and Strategic Position," Carrisle Barracks: SSI, August 2011.

European Union. "EU Focus: Thwarting Cybercrime." *Foreign Policy*, November 2012, pp. 1-4.

Farwell, James P. "Industry's Vital Role in National Cyber Security," *Strategic Studies Quarterly*, Winter 2012, pp. 10- 41.

Fidler, David. "Tinker, Tailor, Soldier, Duqu: Why cyberespionage is more dangerous than you think." *International Journal of Critical Infrastructure*, 2012, pp. 28-9.

Fischer, Eric A. "Federal Laws Relating to Cybersecurity: Discussion of Proposed Revisions." CRS Report R 42114, November 9, 2012, www.crs.gov

Fritz, Jason. "How China Will Use Cyber to leapfrog in Military Competitiveness," *Culture Mandala*, October 2008, pp. 49-50.

Gandhi, Robin et al. "Dimensions of Cyber-Attacks: Social, Political, Economic, and Cultural." *IEE Technology and Society Magazine*, Spring 2011, pp. 28-38.

Geer, Kenneth. "The Cyber Threat to National Infrastructure: Beyond Theory." *Information Security Journal*, 2009, pp. 1-7.

Grant, Rebecca. "Old Lessons, 'New Domain.'" *Air Force Magazine*, September 2013, pp. 86-91.

Hathaway, Melissa E. "Cyber Security: An Economic and National Security Crisis," *The Intelligencer: Journal of the U.S. Intelligence Studies*, Fall 2008, pp. 31-6.

Healey, Jason. "Claiming the Lost Cyber Heritage." *Strategic Studies Quarterly*, Fall 2012, pp. 11-19.

Hearn, Kay et al. "International Relations and Cyber Attacks: Official and Unofficial Discourse." Perth: Australian Information Warfare and Security, December 2010, pp. 7-12.

Herzog, Stephen. "Revisiting the Estonian Cyber Attacks: Digital Threats and Multinational Responses." *Journal of Strategic Security*, Vol. IV, 2011, pp. 49-60.

Hintsa, Juda et al. "Supply Chain Security Management: An Overview." *International Journal of Logistics Systems and Management*. January 2009, pp. 344-355.

Hoyle, Jonathan. "Setting the cyber standard." *Defense Management Journal,* Spring 2013, pp. 29-30.

Hurley, Matthew M. "For and From Cyberspace." *Air & Space Power Journal*, November 2012, pp. 12-32.

Hutchins, E.M., M.J. Cloppert and R.M. Amin. "Intelligence-Driven Computer Network Defense Informed by Analysis of Adversary Campaigns and Intrusion Kill Chains." Proceedings 6th Int'l Conf on Information Warfare and Security, 2010, pp.113-125.

Inkster, Nigel. "China in Cyberspace." *Survival*, August 2010, pp. 55-66.

Iasiello, Emilio. "Getting Ahead of the Threat: Aviation and Cyber Security." *Aerospace America*, July-August 3013, pp. 22-25.

Jabbour, Kamal. "The Science and technology of cyber Operations," *Air Force Space Command Journal High Frontier*, May 2009, pp. 11-15.

Johnson, Kevin, "Power grid concerns mount in Congress," *USA Today*, March 5, 2014.

Jones, Jason B. "The Necessity of Federal Intelligence Sharing with Sub-federal Agencies." *Texas Review of Law & Politics*, Vol. 16, no. 1, pp. 175-210.

Jones, Peter. "The Long Road to Nuclear Zero." *Global Brief*, summer 2008, pp. 28-33.

Joubert, Vincent. "Five years after Estonia's cyber attacks: Lessons learned for NATO?" Rome: NATO Defense College, May 2012, pp. 1-8.

Kahn, R.E. et al. "America's Cyber Future: Security and prosperity in the Information age." Center for New American Security, May 31, 2011, www.cnas.org/files .xxxxxx

Kallberg, Jan. "Designer Satellite Collisions from Covert Cyber War." *Strategic Studies Quarterly*, Sprin 2012, pp. 124-136.

Kallberg, Jan and B. Thuraisingham. "State Actor's Offensive Cyber Operations." IEEE, 2013.

_____. "Cyber Operations: Bridging from Concept to Cyber Superiority." *JFQ*, issue 68, 1st quarter, 2013, pp. 53-8.

Kan, Paul R. "Anonymous vs. Los Zetas: The Revenge of the Hacktivist." *Small War Journal*, June 27, 2013, http://smallwarjournal.com/jrnl/anonymous-vs-los-zetas

Kanwal, Gurmeet. "China's Emerging Cyber War Doctrine." *Journal of Defense Studies*, July 2009, pp. 14-22.

Kelly, Jason. "A Chinese Revolution in Military Affairs?" *Yale Journal of International Affairs*, Winter 2006, pp. 58-71.

Kleindorfer, Paul and Germaine Saad. "Managing Disruption Risks in Supply Chains." *Production and Operations Management*, 2005, pp. 1-16.

Korn, Stephen W. and Joshua E. Kastenberg, "Georgia's Cyber Left Hook." *Parameters*, Winter 2008, pp. 60-76.

Kosut, Oliver et al. "Malicious Data Attacks on Smart Grid State Estimation: Attack Strategies and Countermeasures." *IEEE Proceedings*, 2010, pp. 220-225.

Le, Xie. "False Data Injection Attacks in Electricity Markets." IEEE *Proceeding*, 2010, pp. 226-231.

Liff, Adam P. "Cyberwar: A New 'Absolute Weapon'? The Proliferation of Cyberwarfare Capabilities and Interstate War." *The Journal of Strategic Studies*, Vol. 35, no.3, June 2012, pp. 401-428.

Liles, Samuel. "Cyber Warfare: As a Form of Low-Intensity Conflict and Insurgency: Conference of Cyber Conflict," *Proceedings*, 2010.

Lindsay, James M. and Ray Takeyb. "When Iran Gets the Bomb." *Foreign Affairs*, March 2010, pp. 33-49.

London, J. P. "Made in China." *Proceedings Magazine*, April 2011, www.usni.org .

Lord, William. "USAF Cyberspace Command: To Fly and Fight in Cyberspace." *Strategic Studies Quarterly*, Fall 2008.

Kraska, James. "How the United States Lost the naval War of 2015." *Orbis*, Winter 2010, pp. 35-45.

Mazanec, Brian M. "The Art of (Cyber) War." *Journal of International Security Affairs*, Spring 2009.

McCullough, Amy. "At a Cyber Crossroads." *Air Force Magazine*, June 2012 at www.airforcemag.com

Media Source Reports. "Espionage: Spies, Codes, Ciphers & Secret Weapons." New York: Media Works, Inc., 2014.

Melzer, Nils. "Cyberwarfare and International law." Zurich: UNIDIR, 2011.

Marks, Paul. "How to leak a secret and not get caught." *New Science Magazine*, January 12, 2007, p. 26.

Mohr, Neil. "The Hacker's Manuel 2014." Bath: Future Publishing, 2013.

Moteff, John D. "Critical Infrastructures: Background, policy, and implementation." CRS Report RL 30153, February 21, 2014.

Mulrine, Anna, "Welcome to CYBERCITY," *Air Force Magazine*, June 2013, pp. 42-9.

Muniz, Jorge. "Declawing the Dragon: Why the U.S. Must Counter Chinese Cyber-Warriors." Fort Leavenworth: U.S. Army Command and General Staff College, 2009.

Nash, Kim S. "The Weakest Links." *CIO*, March 2012, pp. 24-6.

North American Electric Reliability Corporation (NERC). "2011 NERC Grid Security Exercise: After Action Report." Washington, D.C.: March 2012.

O'Conner, T.J. "The Jester Dynamic: A Lesson in Asymmetric Unmanaged Cyber Warfare." Sans Institute: 2012.

Odierno, Raymond T. "The U.S. Army in a Time of Transition: Building a Flexible Force." *Foreign Affairs*, May 2012, pp. 7-11.

O'Hara, Timothy. "Cyber Warfare / Cyber Terrorism." USAWC Strategy Research Project, Carlisle Barracks: Army War College, 2004.

Qioa Liang and Wang Xiangsui. "Unrestricted Warfare." February 1999 at www.terrorism.com

Piore, Adam. "Digital Spies: The Alarming Rise of Electronic Espionage." www.popularmechanics.com

Platsis, George. "The Real Vulnerability of the Cyberworld: You and I." February 29, 2012, www.usa.nationaldefensefoundation.org

"Protect yourself online." *Consumer Reports*, June 2012, pp. 22-33.

Randazzo, Marisa R. et al, U.S. Secret Service and CERT Coordination Center, "Insider Threat Study: Illicit Cyber Activity in the Banking and Financial Sector." Carnegie Mellon: August 2004.

Riley, Michael, et al. "The Epic Hack: Target." *Bloomberg Business*, pp. 42-47.

Rogin, Josh. "The Top 10 Chinese Cyber Attacks (that we know of)," *Foreign Policy*, January 22, 2010, pp.

Roscini, Marco. "World Wide Warfare — *Jus ad bellum* and the Use of Cyber Force." in A. von Bogdandy and R. Wolfrum, eds, *Max Planck Yearbook of United Nations Law, Vol. 14, 2010*, pp. 85-130.

Rosenbaum, Ron. "Richard Clarke on Who Was Behind the Stuxnet Attack." *Smithsonian Magazine*, April 2012.

Sanger, David E. "Obama Order Sped Up Wave of Cyberattacks Against Iran," *New York Times*, June 1, 2012.

Schmidt, Eric and Jared Cohen. "The Digital Disruption: Connectivity and the Diffusion of Power." *Foreign Affairs*, 2010, pp. 75-85.

Shackelford, Scott J. "State Responsibilities for Cyber Attacks: Competing Standards for a Growing Problem," Tillinn: Proceedings — Conference on Cyber Conflict, 2010, pp. 197-208.

Smith, Josh. "GOP Senators Assail White House for Pushing Executive Order on Cybersecurity." *Nextgov*, September 14, 2012, www.nextgov.com/cybersecurity/2012

Sridhar, Siddharth et al. "Cyber-Physical System Security for the Electric Power Grid." *Proceeding of IEEE*, January 2012, pp. 210-223.

_____. "From Nuclear War to Net War: Analogizing Cyber Attacks in International Law." http://works.bepress.com/scott.

Shimeall, Timothy et al. "Countering cyber war." *NATO Review*, Winter 2001/2, pp. 16-18.

Smith, G.E. et al. "A critical balance: collaboration and security in IT-enabled supply chain." *International Journal of Production Research*, June 2007, pp. 2595-2613.

Stavridis, James Adm. and Evelyn N. Farkas. "The 21st Century Force Multiplier: Public-Private Collaboration." *The Washington Quarterly*, Spring 2012, pp. 7-20.

Tabansky, Lior. "Critical Infrastructure Protection against Cyber Threats." *Military and Strategic Affairs*, November 2011, pp. 61-78.

Thomas, Timothy. "China's Electronic Long Range Reconnaissance," *Military Review*, November 2008, pp. 47-54.

Thompson, Mark. "Onward Cyber Soldiers." *Time*, August 21, 1995.

Thompson, Ken. "Reflections on Trusting Trust," *Communications of the ACM*, August 1984, pp. 761-3.

Vatis, Michael. "The Next Battlefield: The Reality of Virtual Threats." *Harvard International Review*, Fall 2006, pp.

Volkman, Ernest. "Top 10 Spy Operations," *George*, October 1997, pp. 17-9

White, Gregory and Natalie Granado. "Developing a Community Cyber Security Incident Response Capability," *IEEE Proceeding*, 2009, pp. 1-9.

Wilson, Clay. "High Altitude Electromagnetic Pulse (HEMP) and High Power Microwave (HPM) Devices: Threat Assessments." Washington, D.C.: Congressional Research Service, July 21, 2008.

Watts, Barry D. "The Maturing Revolution in Military Affairs." CSBA: 2011.

Yan Xuetong. "How China Can Defeat America." *New York Times*, November 20, 2011.

Yang, Y. et al. "Impact of Cyber-Security on Smart Grid." Belfast: 2011, pp. 1-7.

Zager, Robert and John Zager. "Combat Identification in Cyberspace." *Small War Journal*, August 25, 2013. http://smallwarjournal.com/jrnl/art/combat

BOOKS

Acohido, Byron and Jon Swartz. *Zero Day Threat*. New York: Sterling Publishing Co., 2008.

Aid, Matthew M. *Intel Wars: The Secret History of the Fight Against Terror*. New York: Bloomsbury Press, 2012.

Allen, Michael. *Blinking Red*. Washington, D.C: Potomac Books, 2013.

Amoroso, Edward. *Cyber Attacks: Protecting National Infrastructure*. New York: Elsevier, 2013.

Anderson, R. *Security Engineering: A Guide to Building Dependable Distribution Systems*. Indianapolis: Wiley, 2008.

Andress, Jason. *Cyber Warfare: Techniques, Tactics and Tools for Security Practitioners*. New York: Elsevier, *2011*

Assange, Julian et al. *Cyberpunks: Freedom and the Future of the Internet*. London: OR, 2012. Xxxx

Barnet, Richard J. *Roots of War*. New York: Penguin, 1973.

Beebe, Shannon and Mary Kaldor. *The Ultimate Weapon is No Weapon: Human Security and the New Rules of War and Peace*. New York: Public Affairs, 2010.

Bernstein, Richard and Ross H. Munro. *The Coming Conflict with China*. New York: Vintage Books, 1998.

Blum, H. Steven and Kerry McIntyre. *Enabling Unity of Effort in Homeland Response Operations*. Carlisle Barracks: SSI, April 2012.

Blank, Stephen J. *Russian Nuclear Weapons: Past, Present, and Future*. Carlisle Barracks: Army War College, SSI, November 2011.

Bodner, Sean, Max Kilger et al. *Reverse Deception: Organized Cyber Threat Counter Exploitation.* New York: McGraw Hill: 2012.

Bowden, Mark. *Worm: The First Digital World War*. New York: Atlantic Monthly Press, 2011.

Bracken, Paul. *The Second Nuclear Age.* New York: Times Books, 2012.

Brenner, Joel. *America the Vulnerable: Inside the New Threat Matrix of Digital Espionage, Crime, and Warfare.* New York: Penguin Press, 2011.

Burnett, Thom and Alex Games. *Who Really Runs the World?* New York: The Disinformation Company, 2007.

Carafano, James J. *Wiki at War: Conflict in a Socially Networked World.* College Station: Texas A&M University Press, 2012.

Carr, *Inside Cyber Warfare*. Sebastopol: O'Reilly Media, 2012.

Cassidy, John. *Dot.con: The Greatest Story Ever Sold.* New York: Harper Collins, 2002.

Cavazos, Edward and Gavino Morin. *Cyberspace and the Law.* Cambridge: MIT Press, 1994.

Cavelty, Myriam D. *Cyber-Security and Treat Politics*. New York: Routledge, 2008.

Center for Strategic and International Studies. *Securing Cyberspace for the 44th Presidency.* Washington, D.C.: December 2008.

Choucri, Nazli. *Cyberpolitics In International Relations.* Cambridge: MIT Press, 2012.

Cimbola, Stephen. *Coercive Military Strategy*. College Station: Texas A&M University Press, 1998.

Clarke, Richard A. *Cyber War: The Next Threat to National Security.* New York: Harper Collins, 2010.

Clausewitz, Carl von. *On War*. Michael Howard and Peter Paret, eds. and trans., Princeton University Press, 1976.

Coleman, E. Gabriella. Coding Freedom: The Ethics and Aesthetics of Hacking. Princeton: Princeton University Press, 2012.

Collins, Sean and Stephen McCombie. "Stuxnet: the Emergence of a new cyber weapon and its implications." *Journal of policing, Intelligence and Counter Terrorism, April 21012, pp. 80-91.*

_____. Hacker, Hoaxer, Whistleblower, Spy: The Many Faces of Anonymous. London: Verso, 2014.

Conway, M. Cyberterrorism: Hype and Reality. In L. Armistead *Information Warfare: Separating Hype from Reality*, Washington, D.C : Potomac Books, 2007.

Crumpton, Henry A. *The Art of Intelligence*. New York: Penguin, 2012.

Das, Sajal K. *Handbook on Security Cyber-Physical Critical Infrastructure*. New York: Elsevier, 2012.

Diebert, Ronald J. *Black Code: Inside the Battle for Cyberspace*. New York: Signal, 2013.

Dinniss, Heather H. *Cyberwarfare and the Laws of War*. Cambridge: Cambridge University Press, 2012.

Dr. K. *The Real Hacking Handbook*. London: Carlton, 2011.

Dorgan, Byron L. and David Hagberg. *Gridlock*. New York: Forge Book, 2013.

Erbschloe, Michael and John R. Vacca. *Information Warfare: How to Survive a Cyber Attack*. New York: McGraw-Hill, 2001.

_____. *Trojans, Worms, and Spyware*. Oxford: Elsevier, 2005.

Falkenrath, Richanrd A., Robert D. Newman, and Bradley A. Thayer. *America's Achilles' Heel: Nuclear, Biological, and Chemical Terrorism and Covert Attacks*. Cambridge: MIT Press, 1998.

Franke, Volker C. and Robert H. Dorff, eds. *Conflict management and :Whole of Government": Useful Tools for U.S. National Security Strategy?*. Carlisle Barracks: SSI, April 2012.

Freedman, Lawrence. *The Transformation of Strategic Affairs*. New York: IISS, 2006.

Friedberg, Aaron I. *A Contest for Supremacy: China, America, and the Struggle for mastery in Asia*. New York: W.W. Norton & Company, 2011.

Friedman, George. *The Next Decade: Empire and Republic in a Changing World*. New York: Anchor Books, 2012.

_____. *The Next 100 Years: A Forecast for the 21st Century*. New York: Anchor Books, 2009.

Fowler, Andrew. *The Most Dangerous Man in the World*. New York: Skyhorse Publishing, 2011.

Gertz, Bill. *China Threat: How the People's Republic Targets America*. Washington, D.C.: Regnery Publishing, 2000.

Graves, Kimberly. *CEH: Certified Ethical Hacker*. Indianapolis: Wiley, 2010.

Gray, Colin S. *Making Strategic Sense on Cyber Power: Why the Sky is Not Falling."* Carlisle: SSI, April 2013.

_____. *Perspectives on Strategy*. Oxford: Oxford University Press, 2013.

Greenberg, Andy. *The Machine Kills Secrets*. New York: Dutton, 2012.

Hafner, Katie and John Markoff. *Cyberpunk Outlaws and Hackers on the Computer Frontier*. New York: Touchstone Book, 1992.

Harris, Shane. @ War: The Rise of the Military-Internet Complex. Boston: Houghton Mifflin, 2014.

Hicks, Denver. *Private: Bradley Manning and WikiLeaks*. Chicago: Chicago Review Press, 2012.

Hoffman, David E. *Dead Hand: The Untold Story of the Cold War Arms Race*. New York: Anchor Books, 2009.

Hollis, David M. "USCYBERCOM: The Need for a Combatant Command." *JFQ*, 3rd Qtr. 2010, pp. 48-53.

Honeynet Project. *Know Your Enemy: revealing the Security Tools, Tactics, and Motives of the Blackhat Community*. Boston: Addison-Wesley, 2001.

Hyacinthe, Berg P. *Cyber Warriors at War*. Xlibris: 2009.

Jackson, Gary M. *Predicting Malicious Behavior: Tools and Techniques for Ensuring Global Security*. Indianapolis: John Wiley & Sons, 2012.

Johnson, Chambers. *Dismantling the Empire*. New York: Metropolitan Books, 2010.

Jordon, Tim. *Hacking*. Cambridge: Polity Press, 2008.

Karake-Shalhoub, Zeinab. *Cyber Law and Cyber Security in Developing and Emerging Countries*. London: Edward Elgar Publishing, 2010.

Kagan, Robert. *The World America Made*. New York: Alfred A. Knopf, 2012.

Kahin, Brain and Charles Nesson, eds. *Borders in Cyberspace: Information Policy and the Global Information Infrastructure*. Cambridge: MIT Press, 1997.

Kamphausen, Roy et al. *Learning by Doing: The PLA Trains at Home and Abroad*. Carlisle Barracks: SSI, November 2012.

Kelly, Kevin. *What Technology Wants*. New York: Penguin, 2011.

Kramer, Franklin et al. *Cyberpower and National Security*. Washington, D.C.: National Defense University Press, 2009.

Krepinevich, Andrew F. *7 Deadly Scenarios: A Military Futurist Explores War in the 21st Century*. New York: Bantam Dell, 2009.

_____. *Cyber Warfare A "Nuclear Option?"* Washington, D.C.: Center for Strategic and Budgetary Assessments, 2012.

Leigh, David and Luke Harding. *WikiLeaks*. London: Guardian Books, 2011.

Lewis, Ted G. *Critical Infrastructure Protection in Homeland Security*. Hobeken: John Wiley & Sons, 2006.

Libicki, Martin C. *Cyberdeterrence and Cyberwar*. Rand Corporation, 2009.

_____. *Conquest in Cyberspace: National Security and Information Warfare*. New York: Cambridge University Press, 2007.

Lucus, Edward. *The New Cold War*. New York: Palgrave, 2009.

_____. *Deception: The Untold Story of East-West Espionage Today*. New York: Walter, 2012.

Lusasik, Stephen et al. *Protecting Critical Infrastructure Against Cyber-Attack*. New York: IISS, 2003.

McClure, Stuart, Joel Scambray and George Kurtz.. *Hacking Exposed 7: Network Security Secrets & Solutions*. New York: McGraw-Hill, 2012.

Mengin, Francoise., ed. *Cyber China: Reshaping National Identities in an Age of Information*. New York: Palgrave, 2004.

Mitnick, Kevin D. and William L. Simon. *The Art of Intrusion*. Indianapolis: Wiley, 2006.

Morozov, Evgeny. *The Net Delusion: The Dark Side of Internet Freedom*. New York: Public Affairs, 2011.

Moyo, Dambisa. *Winner Take All: China's Race for Resources*. New York: Basic Books, 2012.

Myers, Lawrence W. *Spycomm: Covert Communication Techniques of the Underground*. Boulder: Paladin Press, 1991.

Nye, Joseph. *Soft Power*

O'Hanlon, Michael E. *Budgeting for Hard Power: Defense and Security Spending Under Barack Obama*. Washington, D.C.: Brookings, 2009.

O'Neill, Jim. *The Growth Map*. New York: Penguin, 2011.

Parker, J, Shaw.et al. *Cyber Adversary Characterization: Auditing the Hacker Mind*. Rockland: Syngress, 2004.

Pearson, Stephen and Richard Watson. *Digital Triage Forensics*. New York: Syngress, 2010.

Peng, Guangqian and Youzhi Yao. *The Science of Military Strategy*. Beijing: Military Science Publishing House, 2005.

Penttila, Risto E. *The Role of the G8 in International Peace and Security*. New York: IISS, 2003.

Pollard, Neal. *Strategic Cyber Security and Conflict: A Primer for Policy Makers in an Age of Anxiety*. Washington, D.C.: Congressional Quarterly Press, 2012.

Pumphrey, Carolyn W. ed. *The Energy and Security Nexus: A Strategic Dilemma.* Carlisle: SSI, November 2012.

Qioa Liang and Wang Xiangsui. *Unrestricted Warfare.* Beijing: PLA Literature and Arts Publishing House, 1999.

Randazzo, Marisa et al, "Insider Threat Study: Illicit Cyber Activity in the Banking and Finance Sector," Carnegie Mellon: Software Engineering Institute, August 2004.

Rattray, Gregory J. *Strategic Warfare in Cyberspace.* Cambridge: MIT Press, 2001.

Rich, Ben R. and Leo Janos. *Skunk Works.* Boston: Little, Brown and Company, 1994.

Rid, Thomas. "Cyber War Will Not Take Place." *Journal for Strategic Studies*, February 2012, pp. 5-32.

Rosenzweig, Paul. *Cyber Warfare: How Conflicts in Cyberspace are Challenging America and Changing the World.* Denver: Praeger, 2013.

Russell, Ryan, Tim Muller, Johnny Long. *Stealing the Network: The Complete Series Collectopr's Edition.* Jordan Hill: Syngress, 2009. B&N

Saadawi, Tarek, et al, eds. *Cyber Infrastructure Protection.* Carlisle Barracks: U.S. Army War College Press, May 2013.

Sanger, David E. *Confront and Conceal: Obama's Secret Wars and Surprising Use of American Power.* New York: Crown Publishing, 2012.

Satter, David. *Darkness at Dawn.* New Haven: Yale University Press, 2004.

Sawyer, Ralph D., trans. & ed. *The Seven Military Classics of Ancient China.* New York: Basic Books, 2007.

_____. *The TAO of Deception: Unorthodox Warfare in Historic and Modern China.* New York: Basic Books, 2007.

Schlosser, Eric. *Command and Control: Nuclear Weapons, the Damascus Accident, and the Illusion of Safety.* New York: Penguin Press, 2013.

Schneier, Bruce. *Secrets and Lies: Digital Security in the Networked World.* Indianapolis: Wiley, 2004.

_____. *Schneier on Security.* Indianapolis: Wiley, 2008.

Sebesta, Robert N. *The World Wide Web.* 3rd ed., Boston: Pearson, 2006.

Sheffi, Yossi. *The Resilient Enterprise: Overcoming Vulnerability for Competitive Advantage.* Cambridge: MIT Press, 2007.

Spade, Jayson M. "Information as Power: China's Cyber Power and America's National Security," Carlisle Barracks: Army War College, May 2012.

Stiennon, Richard. *Surviving Cyber War*. New York: Government Institutes, 2010.

Stokes, Mark A. *China's Strategic Modernization: Implications for the United States*. Carlisle Barracks: SSI, 1999.

Sun Tzu. *The Art of War*. C. 500B.C, translated from Chinese by Lionel Giles, 1910.

Sung-woo Cho and Myong-sop Pak. "An Integrative View on Cyber Threat of Global Supply Chain Management Systems." Seoul: 2010.

Taleb, Nassim. *Black Swan: The Impact of the Highly Improbable*. New York: Random House, 2007.

Thomas, Timothy L. *Decoding the Virtual Dragon — Critical Evolution in The Science and Philosophy of China's Information Operations and Military Strategy — The Art of War and IW*. Washington, D.C.: IMSO, 2007

Tibbils, Dale. *Cyber Invasion*. Bloomington: 1st Book Library, 2002.

Vachon, Bob. *CCNA Security*. Indianapolis: Cisco Press, 2012.

Verton, Don. *Black Ice: The Invisible Threat of Cyber-Terrorism*. New York: McGraw-Hill, 2003.

Westby, Jody R., ed. *International Guide to Cyber Security*. Chicago: ABA Publishing, 2004.

Wheeler, Winslow T., ed. *America's Defense Meltdown*. Washington, D.C.: Center for Defense Information, 2008.

William, Phil and Vanda Brown. *Drug Trafficking, Violence, and Instability*. Carlisle Barracks: April 2012.

White, Jonathan R. *Defending the Homeland*. Belmont: Thomson-Wadsworth, 2004.

World Economic Forum. "Global Risks 2012 Seventh Edition." Geneva: WCF, 2012.

Wu, Xu. *Chinese Cyber Nationalism: Evolution, Characteristics and Implications*. Lanham: Lexington Books, 2007.

Zetter, Kim. *Countdown to Zero Day: Stuxnet and the Launch of the World's First Digital Weapon*. New York: Crown Publishers, 2014.

Unpublished Reports, Research, web data, and Documents:

Adams, John A. "Cyber Threats, Fish Nets, and MCM Ops." Draft paper, July 2014.

Billo, Charles and Welton Wang. "Cyber Warfare: An Analysis of the Means and Motivations of Selected Nation States." Institute for Security Technology Studies, Hanover: December 2004.

Bloomberg. Video. "Supply Chain Cybersecurity." New York: April 10, 2012, www.bloomberg.com

Borg, Scott. "How Cyber Attacks Will be Used in International Conflicts." 2010, www.usccu.us

Bumgarner, John and Scott Borg. "The US-CCU Cyber-Security Check List." N.p.: U.S. Cyber Consequences Unit, 2007.

CACI. "Keeping the Nation's Industrial Base Safe from Cyber Threats." Washington, D.C.: September 2011, www.asymmetricthreat.net

Cloud Security Alliance. "Top threats to Cloud Computing." March 2010. www.cloudsecurityalliance.org/topthreats/

Cordes, Joseph J. "An Overview of the Economics of Cybersecurity and Cybersecurity Policy." Cyber Security Policy and Research Institute, June 1, 2011.

CNBC. "Code Wars: American Cyber Threat." New York: May 26, 2011; July 28, 2013.

DeZabala, Ted. "Cyber Crime: a clear and present danger." Deloitte: Center for Security & Privacy Solutions, 2010.

Hathaway, Melissa. "Cyber Policy: A National Imperative." Harvard: Belfer Center, March 1, 2011.

_____. "Five Myths About Cyber Security." Mosaic: 2009.

Gantz, John F. "The Link between Pirated Software and Cybersecurity Breaches," Singapore: National University of Singapore and IDC, March 2014.

Grant, Rebecca. "Old Lessons '"New Domain'" *Air Force* Magazine, September 2013, pp. 87-91.

IBM. "IBM X-Force 2012 Mid-year Trend and Risk Report." Somers: IBM, September 2012.

_____. "IBM X-Force 2013 Trend and Risk Report." Somers: IBM, March 2013.

Jurgenson, Nathan. "Hiding in Public: How Privacy Thrives Online." *Wired* pp. 21-2.

Kallberg. "State Actor's Offensive Cyber Operations.' IEEE: May 2013.

Kroft, Steve and Graham Messick. "Huawei." *60 Minutes*. New York: CBS, October 7, 2012.

Lockhart, Bob and Bob Gohn. "Utility Cyber Security: Seven Key Smart Grid Security Trends to Watch in 2012 and Beyond." Pike Research: 2011.

London, J. P. "Surprise, Deception, Denial, Warning and Decision: learning the lessons of History." White Paper, March 2012, www.asymmetricthreat.net

Martin, David. "Cyber Computer Wars." New York: CBS Evening News, May 29, 2012.

_____. "Cyber Pearl Harbor." New York: CBS Evening News, October 12, 2012.

Microsoft. "Elevation of Privilege: A Threat Modeling Card Game for Developers," 2010.

Mandiant. "APT1: Exposing One of China's Cyber Espionage Units," February 2013, pp. 1-60, www.mandiant.com

Marlatt, Greta E. et al "Information Warfare and Information Operations (IW/IO): A Bibliography." January 2008. www.nps.edu/Libary/Research

National Academy of Sciences, "Terrorism and the Electric power Delivery System," Washington, D.C.: National Academy Press, 2012.

National Bureau of Asian Research. "The IP Commission Report on the Theft of American Intellectual Property." Washington, D.C.: NBAR, 2013.

Reuters. "Scores of U.S. firms keep quiet about cyber attacks." June 13, 2012. www.cnbc.com

_____. "U.S. blames China, Russia for cyber espionage." November 3, 2011. www.reuters.com

"Significant Cyber Incidents Since 2006." Modified May 4, 2012. http://csis.org/files/publication/110103_significant%20Cyber%20Incidents

SMI-PWC. "Transportation & Logistics 2030: Securing the supply chain." 2011, www.pwc.com/tl2030

Sommer, Peter and Ian Brown. "Reducing Systemic Cybersecurity Risk." OECD/IFP Project, January 2011.

"Stuxnet: Computer Worm Opens New Era of Warfare." *60 Minutes*. New York: CBS, March 4, 2012 www.60minutesovertime.com

Transportation Sector Working Group. "Roadmap to Secure Control Systems in the Transportation Sector." August 2012.

Index

Alexander, Keith, 5, 41
Anonymous, 60
ATP (advance persistent threat), 15, 48, 98-100, 144, 156
ARAMCO, 41
Assassin's mace, 34
asymmetric tactics, 22, 28
Berners-Lee, Tim, 18
Black Swan, 70
Boeing, 47, 68-9
bring your on device (BYOD), 159
Bronze Statue, 38
Bush, George H. W., 7
Carafano, James, 147
Carr, Jeffery, 2
Cartwright, James, 25, 41
Chemical Facilities Anti-Terrorism Standards (CFATS), 112-6
Chengdu J-20, 16-17
China (PRC), x, 14-17, 19-20, 25-30, 33, 36, 44-45, 52-5, 74-5, 82-6, 88, 99, 113, 155, 160;
    suspected cyber-attacks, 42;
    China National Defense Policy, 53
CIA, 55, 58, 61, 74, 134-5
Clarke, Richard, 6, 59
cleared defense contractors (CDC), 78-9
Clinton, William, 8, 10
Cold War, 14, 20-22, 26, 35, 43, 74
Community Cyber Security Maturity Model, 120
computer network exploitation (CNE), 17, 28
cloud computing, 89, 136-9, 157-8
critical infrastructure, 5-6, 8;
    CIKR, 94, 102, 150, 153
Cushman (oil and gas), 82
cyber domain, 10, 34, 60, 92, 132

Cyber Intelligence Sharing and Protection Act (CISPA), 79
cyber kill chain, 144
cyber security policy, ix, 22
cyber warfare capabilities, 31
DARPA, 151
Dead Hand, 43
Defense Science Board, 15, 119
Department of Energy, 138
Department of Homeland Security (DHS), 6, 12-13, 55, 79, 90, 111, 116-7, 125, 145
Desert Storm, 8, 25
Deutch, John, 10
Disaster Relief Act of 1974, 125
Economic Development Administration (EDA), 128
Economic Espionage Act, 48
EMP (electromagnetic pulse), 4, 160
encryption, 156-7
Estonia, 6, 37-40
Fang, Fenghui, 20
FBI, 17, 57, 111, 130, 135, 161
Federal Trade Commission, 14
fifth domain, 2
first logic bomb, 74
Florida, 5, 81
food security, 80-2
Gates, Robert, 3, 16-17
Gray, Colin, 10
Gulf War, 27-28
Hanover Hackers, 7
Hamilton, Alexander, 119
Hess, Markus, 7
HUMINT (human intelligence), 12, 44
Hussein, Saddam, 28
IBM X-Force 2012, 19, 54

211

informationization, 16, 30-32
International Telecommunication Union, 65
Iran, 14, 53, 126, 155, 160
Lewis, Ted, 94
Lockheed Martin, 17, 69, 118
Los Alamos National Laboratory, 138
Los Zetas, 60
Mandiant, 99, 126
manufacturing, 84-8;
    off shore, 85
McCain, John, 62
McConnell, Mike, 50
mutually assured destruction (MAD), 34
Microsoft, 13
National Academy of Science, 7
National Defense Authorization Act, 78-9
National Domestic Preparedness Consortium, 146
National Infrastructure Protection Plan (NIPP), 95-6
NATO, 13, 37
Netanyahu, Benjamin, 59
North Korea, 14, 33, 53
NSA, 9, 32, 51, 55, 61, 98, 143
Nye, Joseph, 53
Olympic Games, 62
OSINT (open source intelligence), 11, 133-4, 137
Panetta, Leon, 93-4
Patriot Act, 6
Pentagon, 3, 9
Poison Ivy, 115-6
Project Gunman, 43
Putin, Vladimir, 26
rare earth metals, 70, 88
Reagan, Ronald, 74
recovery time objective (RTO), 104-6
revolution in military affairs (RMA), 27-29
Russia, 13-15, 19, 25-26, 33, 36-39 ,55, 57, 74, 94, 126, 155, 160-1;
    Dead Hand, 43;
    Project Gunman, 43
SCADA (supervisory control and data acquisition), 61, 96-7, 108-111, 113, 115, 130, 148, 163

Slammer Worm, 13
SMADA, Strategic Measurement of Advanced Disruptive Attacks, 35-40
Soft Power, 53
Solar Sunrise, 36, 58-9
South Carolina, 82, 89, 126-131, 138
Stafford Act, 123-5
Star Trek, 56
Stuxnet, 6, 61-63, 98, 113-4
Sun Tzu, 29
Super Bowl XLVII, 145
supply chain, 67-92;
    lead times, 69;
    risk matrix, 72, 80;
    supply chain risk management (SCRM), 73, 87;
    weakest link, 76-78;
    information security risk, 90
supply chain mapping, 83
Symantec, 158
Syrian Electronic Army, 56
Tibbils, Dale, 13
Thompson, Ken, 56
Toffler, Alan, 30
US Cyber Command, 5, 41, 51
US Export Control Laws, 47
US Secret Service, 129
Van Meter, Kenneth, 118
Verton, Dale, 13
Walker, John A., 46
Wang, Pufeng, 29, 32
War of the Worlds, 7
WarGames, 7
White House, ix, 3, 7-10, 13, 23, 44, 46, 59, 64, 74, 94, 117, 124, 132;
    Presidential Directive 20, 64-5
WikiLeaks, 45, 47, 59, 135
Woolsey, James, 15
World Trade Center, 12-13
Y2K, ix, 12

About the Author

John A. Adams, Jr. was formerly president and CEO of Enterprise Florida and served on the Executive Committee of Space Florida. He received the 1986 National Exporter of the Year Award from President Ronald Reagan in the White House Rose Garden. As a past chairman of the Industry Sector Advisory Council he provided Congressional testimony on GATT, NAFTA, CAFTA, and on U.S.-Mexico cross-border infrastructure and trade issues.

Adams holds a Ph.D. from Texas A&M University and served as a captain in the United States Air Force and speaks nationwide on economic and industrial development, competitiveness, risk management, and cyber security trends.

Dr. Adams lives deep in the heart of Texas, where he has written a dozen books.

CPSIA information can be obtained
at www.ICGtesting.com
Printed in the USA
LVHW090527261118
598259LV00001B/175/P